Henry Havard

The Heart of Holland

Henry Havard

The Heart of Holland

ISBN/EAN: 9783743321731

Manufactured in Europe, USA, Canada, Australia, Japa

Cover: Foto ©ninafisch / pixelio.de

Manufactured and distributed by brebook publishing software (www.brebook.com)

Henry Havard

The Heart of Holland

THE

HEART OF HOLLAND

BY

HENRY HAVARD

AUTHOR OF
'DEAD CITIES OF THE ZUYDER ZEE' AND 'PICTURESQUE HOLLAND'

TRANSLATED BY MRS CASHEL HOEY

With Eight Illustrations

LONDON
RICHARD BENTLEY & SON, NEW BURLINGTON STREET
Publishers in Ordinary to Her Majesty the Queen
1880

CONTENTS.

CHAPTER I.

Dordrecht, the 'Hospitable'—The Court of Holland—John and Cornelius de Witt—Ancient and Modern Painters—Old Streets and Old Houses 1

CHAPTER II.

On the Maas—Gravendeel's and Puttershoek—The Hollandsch Diep—An Accident—An Heroic Passage—The Sound . 32

CHAPTER III.

Zierikzee—Its History—Battles and Sieges—Greatness and Decay—The 'Beggars of the Sea'—A Stone Giant—Gates and Ramparts—The Fisheries and the Fish Market . . 49

CHAPTER IV.

The Island of Schouwen—The Ravages of the Sea—The Val—Blaas-poepen, and Brown Seals—A Daughter of the Fields—Tholen—War and Fire—A Sleeping City . . . 68

CHAPTER V.

Bergen-op-Zoom—A Military Reception—The Schutterij—The Camp—The History of a Warlike City—Marshal von Lowendahl—The Great Siege of Bergen-op-Zoom . . . 88

CHAPTER VI.

An Old Commercial City—Streets and Buildings—The Land of Saint Gertrude—Epitaphs and Tombs—'Jan mette Lippen'—The Porter of the Stadhuis. 111

CHAPTER VII.

Bad Weather and a Dull Voyage—The Village of Wormeldingen—Politeness in Zealand—Goes—The Susceptible Jacqueline and the Seigneur of Borselen 128

CHAPTER VIII.

The Zand Kreek—A Storm on a Sandbank—Kats—The Schipper Krijn—Kortgene—The Appearance of Veer . . . 147

CHAPTER IX.

Veer—A Huge Church—The Birth of a Town—Commercial Wealth and Splendour: their sudden melting away—A Reverie 160

CHAPTER X.

A Dispute on Board—An Antique Fountain—A Walk through Ruins—The Stadhuis—The Cup of Veer—An Heroic Woman—An Excursion in Noordbeveland—A 'Zinkstuk' . . 174

CHAPTER XI.

The Country—The 'Dime'—Country Morals and Manners—The 'Tol'—Westhoven and Duinbeek 193

CHAPTER XII.

Overduyn—The 'Bibliotheca Catsiana'—Domburg—Nehalennia—Westkapelle—A Famous Battle—The Dam—The Polderjongens—The Spanish Type 206

CHAPTER XIII.

Middelburg—Its Origin—Its First 'Keure'—Its High Commercial Fortunes — Foreigners at Middelburg — Its Relations with France—The 'Abbey of Good Will'—The Wijnheeren—Arnemuiden and Veer—A Long Siege—Revival and Decline 232

CHAPTER XIV.

A Breakfast on Board—The Abdy Hotel—The Abbey and the Stadhuis—'Lange Jan' and 'Gekke Betje'—The Treasure-house of the town—The Zealand Society—The Tapestries—The Kermesse 265

CHAPTER XV.

Arnemuiden—The Country—The Zealand 'Polders'—Souburg and the Emperor Charles V. 292

CHAPTER XVI.

Flushing—Mutiny on Board—In Search of a Dinner—The Beginnings of a Great Port—Philip II. and William the Silent—Spaniards and Zealanders—'The Beggars of the Sea'—The Bombardment—Good Wishes 307

CHAPTER XVII.

The Rage of the Scheldt—Breskens—Fort Napoleon—Groede—The Flemish Nose—Axel—Sieges and Pitched Battles—'Dura Lex'—Hulst—The Virtues of a People—Flemish Fidelity . 329

CHAPTER XVIII.

Rosendaal, the Vestibule of Zealand—Breda—Its Castle, Walls, and Bastions—The History of a Peat-boat—The Museum of Arms—A Marvellous Print—The 'Compromise' and the Peace of Breda—Tombs in the Church . . . 352

CHAPTER XIX.

Tilburg—The Monument to William II.—A Capital—Hertogenbosch's—The Ducal Forest—The Budding of a Town—Two Memorable Sieges—Industry and Courage—An Architectural Pearl—The Stadhuis and its Treasure—'Adieu, baskets! the grapes are all gathered.' 371

APPENDIX . . . 385

ILLUSTRATIONS.

THE HOUSE OF THE SCOTTISH MERCHANTS AT
VEER . . . *Frontispiece*

THE FUNERAL OF A CHILD AT GRAVENDEEL'S . *To face page* 38

THE ZUIDHAVEN POORT AT ZIERIKZEE ,. 56

OUR LADY'S GATE AT BERGEN-OP-ZOOM ,, 114

THE STADHUIS OF VEER ,, 178

THE DIJKGRAAF VAN LEEUWEN. (From a Photograph) . . . . . ,, 192

MIDDELBURG, DURING THE KERMESSE . . ,, 290

THE EXCHANGE AT FLUSHING . . ,, 328

THE
HEART OF HOLLAND.

CHAPTER I.

DORDRECHT, THE 'HOSPITABLE'—THE COURT OF HOLLAND—JOHN AND CORNELIUS DE WITT—ANCIENT AND MODERN PAINTERS—OLD STREETS AND OLD HOUSES.

EVEN yet, in this day of universal facilities, it is no easy matter to travel through the whole of the province of Zealand. Although Middelburg, its capital, and Flushing, its great seaport, have been of late years united to the mainland, and certain of its principal towns are connected with each other by railroad, communications between the islands of which the province is composed are infrequent, and there is no regular system of transport between their more distant points.

The traveller who wants to see everything, and to see all thoroughly, must provide himself with a means of locomotion which shall be always fit for use: in these countries, where water chiefly abounds, the only vehicle that fulfils these conditions is a boat.

Besides, how is one to paint, to write, or to study, unless things are comfortable about one? Imagine a man travelling in this region of rivers and canals with an easel, colour boxes, canvases, wraps, books, and all the rest, unless he has his own boat, and can do as he likes with it! Again; it is not by staying at an inn that one can enjoy the grand spectacles of Nature, the rising of the sun over vast sheets of empurpled water, the straying of the silvery moon-rays over boundless plains, or the unchained tempest as it growls and roars in the fiery sky. So I and my travelling companions, Van Heemskerk and Baron Constant de Rebecque, both painters, resolved on fitting up a boat for ourselves; and we again engaged the same commodious *tjalk* in which we had formerly explored the sandbanks of the Zuider Zee.

The *tjalk* was sent up to Delft, and there it was scraped, and pumiced, and varnished, and bedecked, until the old craft was turned out in all the virginal freshness of a brand-new boat just off the stocks. In roomy lockers, cunningly fitted to her curved sides, was laid up a good store of provisions,—coffee, sugar, tea, preserves of every kind, *foie gras*, and biscuits, not to speak of bottles and jars 'galore.' Then came the upholsterer upon the scene, and the saloon was hung with cotton stuff, pale grey in colour; *portières* divided the little space into its allotted portions, and the sleeping-room was furnished with three beds and the indispensable cupboards. The kitchen assumed quite a martial air; its *batterie* glittered like an arsenal; the shining stove was ready to rumble at its task, the glasses and dishes were gleaming in their pigeon-hole press, and the plate lay in its chest, handy for transfer to the saloon table. We prided ourselves particularly upon the saloon. In each corner was a flower-stand; and brackets adorned the walls, on which our arsenal of weapons was displayed, amid maps and sketches. There was a sofa which made one lazy to look at it, easy-chairs extending their arms in most enticing fashion, and a table with a beautiful cover, worthy of the lofty gastronomic destiny that awaited it. So alluring and hospitable was the general aspect that Heemskerk succumbed to its temptations. After her fitting was complete, he declined to leave the *tjalk*, and on the pretext of testing her behaviour he set out for a trial trip on the Zuider Zee.

In a fortnight he returned, slightly discomfited. He had come in for almost continuous bad weather, and the *tjalk* had not behaved altogether to his satisfaction. She had sustained serious damage in shipping a heavy sea, and he had been barely able to make Zwartsluis, where he left her and her crew. The latter had not conducted themselves particularly well either; for they lacked energy and 'go' when in difficulties, and were neither well disciplined, nor pleasant in their manners. These were items of information which might have sobered the spirits of travellers less undaunted than ourselves, but the die was cast. We decided on starting, and telegraphed orders to the crew to bring the boat to Dordrecht, whither we proceeded, to wait for her, and embark from thence.

Are you acquainted with Dordrecht? It is one of the most interesting towns I have ever been in. If I had to give it a surname, I should not be at a loss for a moment. I would call it the 'Hospitable,' for there is not a town in Europe more cheerful, pleasant, and cordial of aspect. From whatever side it may be approached, its aspect is the same, smiling, kindly, with an air of welcome, and no sooner does one get into the midst of it than one feels at home. Even at first sight there is nothing foreign, nothing strange about it. The traveller wonders where he has previously seen that graceful, picturesque outline; the black windmills, with their ochre-tinted sails, the outer ring of leafy trees, the red quays, the top-heavy houses, and, towering above them all, the lofty steeple with its four-faced clock-dial. Ah, he remembers! It was in the paintings of Cuyp, Van Goyen, and Ruysdael, those masters who were all three in love with that delicious landscape, with that magic river, and with the brightly-tinted city which looks into its waters as into a silver mirror.

A boat used to be the only means of approach to the town, for the water surrounds it on all sides, and, as Dordrecht boasted, it took no less than four rivers to form a vestal zone for her.[1]

Formerly the only approach to the town was by the river. What an animated scene was that! the great barges with their brown sails were gently rocked by the passage of the 'stoomboot'; a forest of masts crowded the roadstead; and dainty boats cut rapidly-effaced furrows in the water on every side. The quay was always crowded; groups of people loitered about under the majestic trees, or stood amid the heaped-up barrels and huge bales of merchandise; and they all seemed to be assembled there for the express purpose of greeting the newly-arrived traveller.

Add to this picture the stately city-gate, built of red brick and white stone, reared upon antique pilasters, and adorned with busts of emperors, lordly escutcheons, and grim lions; beyond it a medley of houses, streets, canals, and boats, all bathed in warm, harmonious, scintillating light, while the countless voices of busy life aid the effect of the many-tinted picture. Surely, nothing more picturesque and charming could be seen, no spectacle more complete of aspect, more lively of expression, more cordial and cheery. Now that steam plays its pranks everywhere with everything, the traveller does not always

---

[1] These four rivers are the Maas, the Waal, the Linge, and the Merwede. On the occasion of the visit of Philip II. in 1549, the city adopted the following lines as its device:—

    Me Mosa, me Vahalis, me Linga Mervaque cingunt
    Æternam Batavæ virginis ecco fidem.

come to the town by sea; but Dort is ever hospitable, let it turn which side of its face it may to the new arrival; and it is by avenues bordered with those gardens which won for the Dutchmen of old the reputation of being 'the first florists of the world,' that the town is connected with the handsomest railway station in Holland.

It is also worthy of note that the characteristic of cordial hospitality is not confined to the streets, the canals, the quays, and the houses of Dort; the inhabitants are likewise largely endowed with that virtue; they have an established reputation for it some centuries old.

Two hundred and forty years ago, the Sieur de la Serre, historiographer of France, who was appointed to accompany Marie de Medicis on her travels in Holland, wrote as follows: 'I must not fail to give the praise that is due to them to the magistrates of Dordrecht, on the occasion of the reception of her Majesty. They acquitted themselves so worthily of the duties of their station, to the honour of the country and of their city, and to the special contentment of her Majesty, that, if some others have imitated, none have surpassed them.'[1]

Such a tribute from such a pen is equivalent to a title of nobility for a town; and the Sieur de la Serre in nowise exaggerated the splendour and heartiness of the reception given by Dordrecht to the queen.

---

[1] *Histoire de l'entrée de la Reyne, mère du Roi très-Chrétien, dans les Provinces-Unies des Pays Bas.* Londres, 1639.

'For,' he adds, 'right pleasant, of a surety, was it to see all the citizens of the town richly armed and ranged in a long line, and yet more so to contemplate the infinite number of fair dames, all in sumptuous attire, who crowded the windows of the houses, while an agreeable noise of musketry, mingled with a thousand shouts of joy, charmed all hearts through all ears.'

The queen was delighted with this tumultuous welcome, but a further surprise was in store for her, and it was not until supper-time that the festival was complete. 'A great number of tables were set out in different places for the entertainment of all the Court. The tables of her Majesty and his Highness, which were separate, were laid with incomparable splendour and every kind of abundance. All these banquet-halls were lighted up, and in the streets were so many bonfires that the whole town looked from a distance like a huge pile of wood in flames; and the splendour of these feasts was all the more agreeable that they could be seen and heard on all sides, so that the merry-making was general.'

The Sieur de la Serre was in the right when he dealt out such hearty praise to the magistrates and the people of Dordrecht. But, it may be objected, Marie de Medicis was a queen, and it is not every day a town gets the chance of entertaining a royal guest. That is quite true, and I could not venture to assert that in such a matter the rank of the individual does not count; but I fearlessly add that the hospitality of Dordrecht is—it cannot be too loudly proclaimed—a princely hospitality, though its objects be only unpretending strangers. To prove this I will relate a personal experience, already of old date, which enabled me to estimate Dort and its inhabitants aright.

Four years ago I was at Dort, with the same two friends, and we three were keeping house together in this same *tjalk*. Madame de Stolopine, the wife of the Russian Minister at the Hague, a charming woman, very clever and highly informed, of artistic tastes, and consequently largely endowed with curiosity, had expressed a desire to inspect our river-house. On our arrival at Dordrecht we telegraphed to Madame de Stolopine that we were at her service, quite ready to receive her, and hoped she would breakfast on board our boat on the following day. Two hours after the despatch of our message her answer arrived. It was as follows: 'I accept your invitation; I shall arrive to-morrow, at eleven. May I bring some one with me?' We had never thought of such a thing as her coming all by herself, and we answered, 'Bring anyone you please.' As, however, I was cook and butler on board, I added, as a measure of precaution, 'Please say how many guests we may expect.' Having sent off this pertinent question, I began to make out the bill of fare for the morrow, and to consider seriously how we should manage so as not to run short of china, glass, and silver on the great occasion.

The problem was a difficult one; we had just eight covers. But I was flattering myself that I had hit upon a clever combination, and that all would go well, when a second telegram arrived, 'We shall be ten in all!'

Ten! Good heavens, what was to be done? Heemskerk and Constant were in a boat in the middle of the river, absorbed in sketching! To apply to them for aid or comfort was impossible; so I put a bold face on the matter, and went off to confide my perplexity to M. Blussé, who was then director of the Museum, and has since become a member of the States General. M. Blussé listened to me with malign curiosity, under which I detected a strong inclination to laugh 'consumedly.' This inclination I did not share in the least, for my reputation was at stake.

'I understand your difficulty,' said he, at length; 'but we can easily set things right. In the first place, what do you want? Provisions? You can get everything in the town, and very good.'

'But I don't know the town. Where are the purveyors to be found?'

'That will be all right. I will send you the *Kastelein* from our club, and he will take you to all the best places.'

'And the silver, the glasses, the plates and dishes?'

'I will take care you have everything of that kind. The *Kastelein* shall see to those also. And as for fruit, you must let me send you some. I have more than I know what to do with.'

'Many thanks; I accept most gratefully. Oh, the carriages! Is there a good livery-stable in the town? We shall have to send to the station to fetch our guests.'

'I'll manage that; the carriages also shall be my affair. You shall have four, up to time, to-morrow, and I hope you will find everything all right.'

These comforting assurances relieved my anxiety, and seemed to lift at least a hundredweight from off my breast. We went at once to the club; the *Kastelein* placed himself at my disposal, and he and I sallied forth to lay in the requisite provisions. In the evening I drew up the programme of our breakfast, which was to consist of eight *plats*, in three courses. Heemskerk and Constant set to work with a will, and designed some lovely *menus*, and I sent Slurnik, our *schipper*, with a modest handbasket, to bring back the fruit that the admirable M. Blussé had promised me. Slurnik returned in an hour, staggering under the weight of a huge hamper, loaded with a rich treasure of melons, pears, peaches, and grapes; which, to judge by their size, might have been grown in the land of Canaan.

'What in the world do you mean by bringing such a basket as that?' Thus had M. Blussé addressed the *schipper*. 'You might as well have brought a plate!' And, regardless of the apologies of Slurnik, he helped him to hoist on his shoulders a hamper which weighed as much as a humane man would like to put on the back of a middle-sized donkey.

This, however, was not the only surprise in store for us. The next morning, at eight o'clock, just as I was warming to my cooking, a messenger arrived in charge of a superb service of plate. The handles of the knives and forks bore splendid heraldic shields; and there were eighty-eight covers. At nine came a dinner-service of exquisite china, a quantity of richly-cut glass, and table linen of the finest damask. We were somewhat like Marguerite; 'we did not know what to say.' Finally, at half-past ten o'clock, four faultless equipages—princely landaus—each drawn by two superb horses, and with a coachman and groom in full-dress liveries and gold lace—drew up, and we were informed that they awaited our orders. The admirable M. Blussé had simply requisitioned the four handsomest carriages in the town, and their owners had sent them to us with the greatest pleasure. Five minutes later the four carriages started at a brisk trot which shook the windows, and in a very short time we brought back our guests, greatly amazed at such a display of magnificence, and enchanted with the cheers and acclamations that greeted them as we drove along; for the cordial and friendly inhabitants associated themselves with our little festival, and got up a reception of the distinguished strangers on their own account.

Permit me to pass, with fitting reserve, over the breakfast, prepared by your humble servant, set out, presented, and served by Heemskerk and Constant de Rebecque, who were correctly arrayed in black clothes and white gloves. The little feast was a merry one; everyone laughed and talked a great deal, and ate and drank even more; and nothing could be more enthusiastic than the admiration lavished upon our queer quarters and their 'get-up.' The splendour of our table appointments was extolled, and we received the tribute of praise in modest silence, carrying it all the while to the account of the good town of Dordrecht, and its dear good people in general, and our inestimable friend the admirable M. Blussé in particular.

Four years have elapsed since then, and those things are yet held in wondering memory. (I am borne out by the reminiscences of two fascinating countesses, and those of the charming friend who brought them to Dort.) That princely reception, and the fame of those superb carriages and magnificent horses, are still celebrated in a small aristocratic circle, and indeed it is but just, for they are not to be beaten in the Low Countries. At Dordrecht fine equipages are highly esteemed, and nowhere are they more numerous; for no town in Holland is richer than old Dort, that joyous, gracious, smart, brightly-tinted city of millionnaires, so inexplicably neglected by artists in general. There are few great enterprises in the country but the capitalists of Dordrecht have a hand in them, and if ever you travel into Sweden and Norway, you will do well to get letters of introduction and recommendation from Dordrecht, for the money which the people there have placed out to fructify in the cold countries is almost incalculable.

This great wealth is easily explicable. Dordrecht used formerly to enjoy an exceptional privilege—a sort of lion's share, in fact, of a very lucrative kind—which gave the town a leading place in the commerce of Holland. This privilege, known as 'The Staple of Dordrecht,' is referred to by Guicciardini, in the sixteenth century, in his 'Descrittione di tutti i Paesi Bassi, altrimente detti Germania Inferiore,' as follows: 'The privileges of the Staple of Dordrecht are so substantial that all carriers, by way of the Rhine and the Maas, of wine, grain, wood, and other merchandise passing by that town, are under obligation to unload their barges or barks in that port, and there to pay all the duties imposed, and to unload and land their goods solely by means of the boats or the citizens of that place, or else to agree with them, and with the keepers of the customs and the toll-houses.'

It is easy to perceive the great advantage of so important a privilege, especially when it is borne in mind that wine, grain, wood, etc., had all to be imported into Holland, and that almost the whole of these goods came by way of the Rhine. Guicciardini is quite justified in saying that Dordrecht was highly favoured by 'this great commodity and benefit,' which formed 'a rich revenue and large profit' for the inhabitants.

It is to be remembered too that Dort possessed this privilege for centuries. It was, in fact, a 'gift of happy accession' granted by the Counts of Holland, who were invested with their authority within the walls, and habitually dwelt in the city. After their time the Burgundian princes recognised the right of Dort; the princes of the house of Austria, and Charles V. in particular, confirmed it by successive edicts; and, in the seventeenth century, after the liberation of the United Provinces, Dort still asserted that right, and demanded observance of it from her rivals and her neighbours.

The following curious and little known fact is deserving of record. On the 19th March, 1618, Sir Dudley Carleton (afterwards Lord Dorchester), who was then Ambassador to the States General of Holland, wrote to Secretary Naunton :—

'Here is a troublesome dispute betwixt two towns, Dort and Rotterdam, touching the Staple of wines, which Dort doth challenge by ancient privilege of the Emperor Charles V., and Rotterdam disputes the same, in regard of the French wines, which come now more frequently into those provinces than when that privilege was granted. Hereupon those of Rotterdam some weeks since took an armed boat from those of Dort, which lay upon the river to guard the passages. Those of Dort, in revenge hereof, have within these two days shot a passage-boat of Rotterdam, which refused to strike sail to one of their ships, with a piece charged with musket-bullets, and therein killed one and hurt five or six. Betwixt unruly multitudes (as the people of these towns are), of small beginnings many times follow greater consequences, which makes me give your honour so particular an account of this accident.'[1]

Thus, in the seventeenth century, at the moment when the union of the provinces was accomplished, when the murder of Olden-Barneveldt had given Prince Maurice of Nassau authority which was almost that of a dictator, two neighbouring mercantile cities belonging to the same nation were falling foul of each other, and exchanging shots upon the Maas on account of this enviable privilege.

Unhappily for Dordrecht, not all its angry and urgent vindication of its right availed for its retention. Only at the cost of keeping up a fleet, and being perpetually at war with all the seaport towns of Holland, could the Staple have been maintained. That fertile source of great revenues had to be renounced, and the city was destined simultaneously to experience a rapid decline in power and influence.

Until then Dordrecht had, in fact, held the first rank in the councils of the province. Not only did that city take precedence of Rotterdam, Delft, and Gouda, but also of Haarlem, Leyden, and even Amsterdam. Adriaan Boens, the poet, an ardent

---

[1] *Letters to and from Sir Dudley Carleton, Knight, during his Embassy in Holland, from January* $161\frac{6}{6}$ *to December 1620.* London: Printed in the year MDCCLVII.

admirer of the prosperous city, might write, unchallenged :—

> De la Hollande, ainsi, Dort a le premier rang ;
> Et prudente a produict le plus illustre sang,
> Qui gouverne avec heur sa sage République.[1]

This foremost place was, in truth, Dordrecht's due. The city could claim it, not only as 'rich and vast, fair and puissant, well built and stately,' but because of its ancientness ; for it was acknowledged to be the oldest in all the land. According to its own inhabitants, the origin of their beloved Dort might be traced to the earliest Christian times. Legendary personages, St. Dorothea, Doretus, a wealthy Roman, and the god Thor, or Thur, so popular in all the Batavian country,[2] were invoked in explanation of the name—which has been written in so many ways, as Dort, Dordracum, Dorrechstsdrecht, and even Turdrecht. The rapid advance of its fortunes, and the abundance of precious metals in the city, led to the establishment of the Mint of the Counts of Holland at Dort, in 1064. The charter (No. 89) is preserved among the archives of Middelburg. In the fourteenth century the coins struck at Dort were circulated in the Low Countries, and even in the province of Zealand payments were made in 'Dordrecht florins.' This important privilege, which was afterwards confirmed by the sovereign houses of

---

[1] See the *Beschryvinge der Stad Dordrecht*.

[2] Jans Rutgers says the name was simply derived from the river Dort, which gave its name to the village of Dortmunde, and disappeared in the 15th century.

Bavaria, Burgundy, and Austria, had been renewed by Charles V. with much state and ceremony. It was under that great monarch that the Mint, which had been rebuilt on an enlarged scale, suitable to the requirements of the time, was adorned with the handsome Renaissance façade, with attic and pilasters, hat still bears the dedicatory inscription : 'Moneta . Divo . Carolo . V . Cæs.'

As early as 1048, Dordrecht was sufficiently flourishing to excite the cupidity of the Archbishop of Cologne and the Bishop of Liège, and those worthy prelates sent an army, commanded by the Marquis of Brandenburg, to take it.

Floris IV. and the succeeding Counts of Holland held their 'court' at Dordrecht, and their residence, which is still to be seen, and continues to bear the name of Het Hoff van Holland, enables us to discern the primitive signification of the word 'court,' which seems hardly to be defined. This Het Hoff consisted, in fact, of a real court of almost circular form, surrounded by lofty buildings, most of them connected with the neighbouring houses, and which could be reached only by narrow and winding streets leading to strongly-fortified gates. In the primitive times when firearms were unknown, this 'court' in the middle of the city formed an impregnable retreat. There troops could be concentrated, and the evil designs of adversaries defeated, because ingress and egress through the various gates opening into different quarters was always practicable without the possibility of prevention.

In short, every circumstance and condition contributed to render Dordrecht an exceptionally flourishing city. The seat of the Mint and of Government, and of the court of the Counts of Holland, it was enriched, embellished, and favoured beyond all others by its sovereign princes. In addition to all this, the most terrible visitations did but aggrandise its destinies and minister to its greatness.

On the south side of its bell tower the following inscription, cut in stone, and terrible in its laconism, may be read :—

ANNO CHRISTI 1421—NOVEMBRIS 18—
SUBMERSÆ MANSERUNT 72 VILLÆ CONTINUÆ DORDRACO.

'In the year of Christ 1421, on November 18, seventy-two villages in the environs of Dordrecht remained in the water.' Says a chronicler of the Low Countries, 'Seventy-two good and fair villages, and more than one hundred thousand persons, perished miserably with all their goods and substance.' On that fatal night, the Maas and the Waas, swollen by the influx of an extraordinarily high tide, overflowed their banks and spread over the country, carrying ruin with their onward rush, and in a few hours transforming rich and fertile fields into lakes and rivers.

And Dordrecht? Dordrecht, which, the day before, belonged to the mainland, which was 'joined to the Duchy of Brabant,' awoke on the following morning, intact indeed, and unhurt, but forming an island, surrounded by deep running water, with four rivers encircling its old ramparts. For a city like Dordrecht, rich, industrious, trading largely, and possessing the privilege of the Staple, this meant the doubling of its prosperity, an unlooked-for and unequalled stroke of fortune.

In vain did a terrible fire destroy one half of the houses in the town, in 1457. Like the phœnix, it arose from its ashes more vigorous, more full of life, wealthier, fairer than ever, so that when some years afterwards the *Sieur de la Serre* visited Dordrecht he recorded that, 'there are to be seen a vast number of fine houses, builded upon great vaulted cellars, wherein are stored wines, timber, marbles, slates, lime, iron, and coals, which come down the Rhine and the Maas.'[1]

A sonnet, by Isaac le Ducq, which was published in 1677 by Matthys Balen, extols the grandeur, the valour, and the wealth of Dordrecht, the wisdom of its magistracy, the beauty of its aspect, the fertility of its soil, and the sweetness of its lavish waters.

> Qui bien contemplera Dordrecht encor Pucelle,
> Ses bâtiments, ses ports et ses temples si beaux,
> L'ordre de ses bourgeois sous ses onze drapeaux,
> En suivant du vieux Mars le martial modelle,
> Et considérera ce qu'est comprins en elle :
> Son terroir fructueux, ses claires douces eaux,
> Riches tant en poissons qu'en nombres de basteaux,
> Qui sur mille Citéz la rendent la plus belle ;

---

[1] *Histoire de l'entrée de la Reyne, mère du Roi très-Chrétien, dans les Provinces-Unies des Pays Bas.* Par Le Sieur de la Serre.

> Qui plus est, ses statutz, de tant de droicts ornéz,
> Qui lui sont tant d'un roy que d'un Cæsar donnéz,
> Qui plus est, ses pasteurs, dont la pióté grande
> Instruict ses citoiens sans négliger un jour,
> Pour les conjoindre à Dieu, et à son sainct Amour,
> Confessera que c'est la PERLE DE HOLLANDE.

In vain did the dukes and the kings who came after the Counts of Holland, slight this 'pearl,' as the poet calls the fair city, forget the 'court' where their predecessors had loved to dwell, and make but rare and brief sojourn within its walls. Dordrecht consoled itself readily, preferring solid wealth to sovereign grandeur, independence, and government 'by its own born citizens,' to the gilded chains of a direct vassalage, and holding the welfare of its people above barren honours.

A breezy breath of republicanism and independence has always been abroad in the streets and the market-places of Dort. To this day its inhabitants point, with a kind of pride, to the place where Count Henry II. was killed by an archer, and it should be borne in mind that Dordrecht was the first town in Holland to cast off the yoke of the foreigner, that at Dordrecht the deputies from the cities assembled for the first time, and resistance to the Spaniards was organised, on the 16th of July, 1572.

The patriotic, generous, and liberal past of the city bears two stains; the Synod of Dort, which led to such disastrous consequences, and the arrest of the illustrious Cornelius de Witt. I have no intention of discussing the Synod of Dort: that great act of intolerance would need to be studied at leisure, contemplated from every point of view, and considered under all its aspects, before one could venture to pass final sentence upon it. But is it not strange to find these emancipated pastors, on the morrow of their victory, on the morrow of their escape from a yoke which they denounced as all that was cruel, abusing the authority they had arrogated to themselves, and calling in the sword of the civil authority to sanction their conduct? Is it not especially strange to find the followers of Arminius using the same arguments against their adversaries with which the Reformers opposed the Council of Trent, and the Gomarists putting forward their monstrous claim to be at once judges and suitors, refusing their adversaries not only the right of suffrage, but also the deliberative vote, and thus constituting themselves infallible, just after they had denied the infallibility of the Pope?

In vain did the Arminians protest against the doctrinal judgment of so novel a tribunal, one which claimed to impose a religion by force, while it denied that God had endowed anyone on earth with the gift of infallibly defining the dogmas of faith. The Arminians were regarded as heretics, and the self-same ministers who had risen against censures and excommunications pronounced by the Councils, treated them as excommunicated.

The Gomarists, having won a cheap victory over antagonists whom they had put to silence, drew up ninety-three canons, which were ratified on the 2nd of July by the States General, and then was seen a political party availing itself of religious subtleties to crush its adversaries. The remonstrants were, in fact, pursued on all sides, hunted like outlaws, and expelled from the country, and the ' secular arm ' was employed in the extermination of their tolerant sect. One hundred ministers and professors who refused to subscribe to the decree of the Synod were banished without appeal. Grotius, one of the most learned men of the age, and Hogerbets, Pensionary of Leyden, were both condemned to perpetual imprisonment, and confined in the castle of Lowvestein. Gilles of Leydenberg was found dead in his prison, but his body was hung upon the gibbet at Voorburg, and the aged servant of his country, Olden-Barnveldt, the companion of William the Silent, laid his head upon the block when seventy-two years old! What a hideous ending to all those fiery and eloquent orations!

The other dark, grievous, and terrible event that troubles the patriotic history of Dordrecht like a bad dream, also found its close at the Hague. It was in 1672, in the course of that terrible year in which Holland, half conquered, seemed to be on the brink of destruction. The armies of the States were melting away, so to speak, before the troops of the ' Roi-Soleil,' and the people, in their alarm, distress, almost despair, threw the responsibility of these successive disasters on the brothers de Witt.

Cornelius, the elder brother, who had been obliged

to relinquish the command of the fleet, had returned, ill and exhausted, to his house at Dordrecht, that he might recruit his rapidly failing strength by quiet and rest. He who had formerly been the idol of the city of his birth was received with imprecations, and day after day a fierce, threatening, cursing crowd gathered under his windows, ready for an outbreak. In vain did all the cooler heads strive to appease those turbulent spirits; and yet there was one moment when they seemed to have succeeded. With loud cries, and under threats of death, the people had constrained the magistrate to summon the Prince of Orange to the city, and the rioters hoisted two flags on the church tower. That which streamed from the summit of the flagstaff was orange; the other, lower down, was white, and carried as its device the following halting verse :—

> Oranje boven, de Witte onder,
> Die 't anders meend die flaet den donder![1]

The Dutch have always been partial to that kind of wit which consists of a play upon words. 'De Witte' is Dutch for 'the white,' and in the present instance stands for the brothers de Witt. The meaning of the punning motto was pointed by the white flag hung below the orange standard. Ever since that time 'Oranje boven' has become a sort of national cry, and the countersign of the Orange party.

The Prince of Orange came to Dort, was released

---

[1] Orange above, de Witt under,
Who says nay, strike him, thunder!

from his oath, and proclaimed Stadtholder. Cornelius de Witt himself, lying on his bed of pain, was constrained to sign the act of nomination. The tragedy appeared to be concluded; in truth it was but begun.

On the 10th of July, between ten and eleven o'clock in the morning, Willem Tichelaer, a surgeon from Piershil, came to the house of Cornelius de Witt, and requested a private interview with him. As de Witt was in his bed, and suffering from a severe attack of fever, Tichelaer was refused admittance. He persisted, using the names of several friends, and at length he was let in; but Madame de Witt, who suspected some evil design, posted first a servant, and afterwards her own son, on guard in a corner of the room. Nothing unusual occurred during the interview. Tichelaer remained for a quarter of an hour with the invalid, then took his leave quietly, immediately left the city, repaired to the army, and informed the house steward of the Prince of Orange that Cornelius de Witt had planned the murder of his Highness, and endeavoured to suborn him, Tichelaer, to execute the heinous design.

Ten days passed. The Court of Holland ' took informations.' At length, on the 24th of July, Ruysch, the procurator-fiscal, with the provost-marshal and his archers, arrived at Dordrecht, and seized the unfortunate invalid. Then the former Burgomaster of Dort, the ' Ruart,' of Plotten, the Curator of the University of Leyden, one of the greatest personages of his country, and one of the most noble characters of his time, was dragged from his bed, and carried as a prisoner to the castle-ward at the Hague, upon the deposition of a witness who had neither character nor importance of any kind.[1]

The end is well known: the trial, the imprisonment, the snare laid for a brother, the horrible assassination under the Gevangenpoort, the hideous mutilation of the two corpses, and the exposure upon the gibbet of the illustrious victims to the foul insults of the inhuman crowd.

Let us turn away our eyes from this terrible picture, and look upon the fairer aspects of old Dort, while we turn over some brighter pages of its history. Well might it claim to be famous, were it only as the native place of several illustrious artists. Few cities, not only in Holland, but in the world, have been so highly favoured in that respect as Dordrecht. From 1575, in which year Jacob Gerritse Cuyp was born within its walls, a whole series of great painters adorned the city so justly proud of them, with the tribute of their deathless fame. Here, in 1605, was born Aalbert Cuyp, one of the greatest masters of Dutch art, one of the most finished artists of that golden age. In 1611, Ferdinand Bol, and in 1632, Nicolaes Maas, were born at Dort. These painters borrowed from Rembrandt their marvellous spirit, and their surpassing skill in putting light into their work. In 1643, Schalken, also a 'luminarist,' but of another

---

[1] *Histoire de la vie et de la mort des illustres frères Corneille et Jean de Witt.* Utrecht, 1709. See also *Histoire des Provinces-Unies.* Leclerc.

school, was added to the number. After these came Arend de Gelder, Arnold Houbraken, the Vasari of the Dutch school,[1] Dirk Stoop, and a dozen others; and, to come down to a later time, almost to our own days, the world owes to Dordrecht that great and sombre painter, Ary Scheffer.

What a group of names—Cuyp, Bol, Maas, and Scheffer! What a contrast! The first three were all fire, all sun, all life; they either took their subjects from the street, or the fields, or they shut them up in a room through which a warm ray of light filtered. They did wonders with the brush, which interpreted the vehemence of their feeling, seizing upon truth and facts, and, as it were, incrusting them in a marvellous impasto. The last of the four was still, wan, chilly, deliberate, without animation and without strength; he sought his subjects in an ideal world, a vague world, more German than anything else, and he personified in a fine, thin, transparent, emaciated style the fantastic creations of Goethe's hazy genius, or the Platonic idealism of Dante.

Like his predecessors, Scheffer might have been an artist of the robust type, but, while Cuyp, Bol, and Maas dwelt in their own country, in vivid, brightly-tinted Holland, and sunned themselves in its scintillating light, Scheffer went to another country, to see other sights, to become the interpreter of other inspirations. An unfinished portrait, which belongs to the

---

[1] See his work entitled: *De Groote Schouburg der Nederlandsch Kunstschilders.* Amsterdam, 1718.

Museum at Dordrecht, shows us what he might have been. Never was there a head more boldly drawn, more finely modelled, more purely coloured, painted with more masterly breadth and freedom. Only Frans Hals could have equalled it in vigour, life, and expression. It is because that head is all made of impressions and sensations, that it is so powerful and so beautiful; it is because the painter had not time to finish it, to substitute a sickly interpretation for his first fresh and vivid inspiration, to efface its pristine vigour by touches which should make it haggard, pale, and meagre, more poetical in short, according to his notions of poetry. He had not leisure, for this once, to produce idealism, and so he simply produced a true and fine painting.

This beautiful and exceptional work is the most interesting picture in the Dort Museum, which, although it contains some good modern paintings, cannot compete with the collections at Amsterdam, the Hague, and Rotterdam, or with the Van der Hoop Museum. The Dordrecht Museum might, however, have possessed a number of great works by old masters, if a certain inhabitant of the city, who preferred to augment the artistic wealth of Amsterdam, had endowed his birthplace with the treasures he possessed. This collector, whose name was Dupper, and who died in 1870, was a person of sound taste and unerring judgment, and he had by degrees become possessed of one of the most valuable picture galleries in the Netherlands. It included sixty-four old pictures, three-fourths of them masterpieces. Among these was the finest Jan Steen in existence, a superb Jacob van Ruysdael, a wonderful Maas, one of the best Ostades, an admirable Gerhard Douw, the finest Solomon van Ruysdael I have ever seen, a Hobbema, and some Lingelbachs, Wouvermans, and Van Goyens, of exquisite quality. Mynheer Dupper had also some excellent modern pictures. He divided his collection into two parts, of which the Maas, the Steens, the Ruysdaels, the Van Goyens, and the Hobbema were sent off to be swallowed up in the great galleries of the Trippenhuis. Dordrecht had the remainder.

Although the 'Pearl of Holland' has been scurvily treated by fate, insomuch as it has had to part with so many art treasures, and has been unable to preserve any of the works of those great painters whose birth within its walls sheds a lustre upon its history, it has been happier as regards its sculptors. Fine samples of their art still challenge the admiration of the visitor. Beautiful carvings in wood, panelling, and stalls, undoubted masterpieces of Flemish sculpture, decorate that great church, whose spire is visible from so far, and whose nave is the widest and most elegantly designed in all Holland.

These carvings are the works of a great, but hardly known artist, Jan Terven. He was born at Dordrecht in 1511, and died in 1589. His works date from 1538-9, and to name their epoch is to indicate their style. They belong, both in conception and execution, to the best period of the Renaissance. Two

THE HOUSE OF THE SCOTTISH MERCHANTS AT VEER.

friezes, in particular, are worthy of close attention. One of these represents the glorification of the Catholic Faith, the other that of the Emperor Charles V.; the triumph of the spiritual and temporal power respectively. Both are represented by long processions which resemble in the pomp of their ordering and the magnificence of their adjustment those grand and stately pageants which Albert Dürer has immortalised. These wood carvings, of exquisite workmanship, are not the only treasures of sculpture which we find at Dordrecht. They abound on the façades of the houses; on all sides sculptured keystones, consoles, and elegant bas-reliefs are to be seen. I could enumerate at least ten of the latter, but I will be content with a word of praise for the striking design over the gate of the Orphanage.

At Dordrecht, as elsewhere, the number of 'fair houses builded in the ancient style' diminishes apace. General indifference, which is essentially iconoclastic, the needs of commerce, the demands of 'comfort,' so differently interpreted in the present day, lead each year to the disappearance of some one or other of those gems of the good old time; but their memory will not be lost for evermore. Ere they disappear before the advance of the demolishing pick and crowbar, Mynheer Van G——, a learned son of Dordrecht, whose feelings are as acute as his tastes are cultivated, makes drawings of them. He has indulged me with the sight of his huge portfolios, in which he has carefully embalmed (if I may be permitted that expression), a hundred venerable, elegant, artistic, or curious façades, which have been destroyed within half a century. I could not but be affected by the collector's reverence for his natal city, and by the filial piety with which he cherishes its ancient memories; nor could I fail to share his regret for those stately houses which in former days adorned old Dordrecht.

It is useless to detain you longer with vain regrets; I shall do better to show you the ancient streets, the antique dwellings, and the picturesque nooks still existing in the city, to take you to the 'old' and the 'new' harbour—they are both old—full of boats, and shaded by great trees, and to introduce you to 'the Street of Wine,' last vestige of 'the Staple,' with its venerable houses, built over the vast vaulted cellars which were storehouses in the palmy days of Dordrecht. I wish I could take you to the neighbourhood of the church, to the great canal without quays, where brown old houses, with rickety staircases and black balustrades, stand in the water, and reflect their red roofs in its silvery flow.

Nothing could be more picturesque, more characteristic, more perfect as an assemblage of lines, curves, and colouring, than those curious corners of the old river-girdled city, especially when a barge, crowded with peasant women wearing long veils, or the gigantic country caps, comes lumbering by. Then, to the fancy of the beholder, the old times return. The warm and decided colours, the sea-green water, in which everything is reflected so distinctly, the buildings in which red predominates, and black is blacker than anywhere else in the world, the blue sky dappled with grey, these sun rays which dart into every corner, produce delicious harmonies which rest the mind while they delight the eyes.

We talk and talk, and time passes. Our boat should have arrived ere this. Let us return to the harbour, and have another look at the quays, at the grand stretch of the two ports, at the basins. From the Bellevue Hotel we can sweep this wonderful panorama with our glasses.

What is this which we descry in the distance? A double flag, a streaming tricolor, and a red sail spread above a shining hull? Who is that mariner bending over the helm? He is our *schipper*; that is our *tjalk*. Quick with the signals! We are seen. Caps are waved, the great sail falls, the *tjalk* comes alongside, and in a twinkling we are on board.

CHAPTER II.

ON THE MAAS—GRAVENDEEL'S AND PUTTERSHOEK—THE HOLLANDSCH DIEP—AN ACCIDENT—AN HEROIC PASSAGE—THE SOUND.

T was on a Friday, at three o'clock, that we set sail. We had told our crew that we wanted to go direct, without a stoppage, to Zierikzee, and they had objected strongly. We had signified our desire to arrive on the Saturday evening, so that we might pass the Sunday at Zierikzee, and they had sternly made answer that such a possibility was not to be entertained for a moment.

No doubt the undertaking was an ambitious one, and we had only to look at the map to understand the protestations of the *schipper* and his men. We should have to descend the old Maas, to bear to the left, to double the point of Gravendeel's, to follow the Nieuwe Waal, to gain the Moerdijk, and cross it, to navigate the Hollandsch Diep to Willemstad, to get into the Volke-Rak, and by way of the Maast Zijpe gain the eastern Scheldt. From thence only could we discern the promised land, and throughout all that great extent we should have to take the wind, the current, and the tide into account.

The objections of the crew derived additional reasonableness from the nature of the Dutch rivers, which renders navigation uncertain, irregular, and to a certain extent dangerous. These rivers are variable in depth, frequently intersected by sand-banks, and full of shallows, so that it is extremely difficult to steer a boat in the midst of the many-coloured buoys, which are laid along the route like watchful sentinels warning the navigator against venturing farther. We felt, however, that it would never do to yield to the remonstrances of the crew on the first day and on the first question raised, so we determined to carry our point, and the event proved that we did well.

The voyage was slow at first, and we proposed to wait patiently for high water at Puttershoek. At six o'clock the tide began to rise, and enabled us to round the point of Gravendeel's. These regions were already familiar to my friends and to me; three years previously we had thoroughly explored them. We greeted them, therefore, like old acquaintances, and I distinctly remembered the interminable dyke at Puttershoek on which stands the village, bordered with great trees, and the inquisitive inhabitants assembling to see the foreigners pass by; the women congregated on the thresholds, in gossiping groups, wearing complicated head-dresses

D

with circlets above the forehead and golden corkscrews on the temples. In my mind's eye I could still see their faces, so fair and rosy, with great blue eyes—in some cases with the bistre mark of fever underneath the lids; and here and there among them a young girl, with hollow cheeks and dead-white diaphanous complexion, one of the victims of that dismal malady, consumption, which levies a terrible tribute on this country. The solemn, plodding men, too, in black clothes, driving long narrow green carts with high wheels, all these came back to me, with the delicious scent of the newly-mown hay in the air.

As we follow the course of the old Maas, on whose bosom we are floating, many vivid memories are awakened within us. By merely letting ourselves go with the current we should come to Brill, the cradle of the liberties of the Low Countries. It is a 'douce' and tranquil city nowadays, whose silent canals and deep-tinted houses, shaded by great trees, in no wise recall the heroic deeds of old. Never did more peaceful aspect contrast with more turbulent renown; for it was here that the terrible 'Beggars of the Sea,' the soldiers of Lumey, Treslong, and Jacques Cabilleau, set up their first bulwark.

On April 1, 1572, they surprised the city. Knowing it to be ill guarded, indeed almost destitute of troops, they disembarked on the island and came on to assail it. One of the gates, to which they set fire, afforded them a convenient mode of entry, and they took possession of it without bloodshed. Their first purpose was to pillage the churches and to take toll of the inhabitants, and they began by doing so; but the eligibility of the city as a station for themselves struck them so strongly that they resolved to keep it, and to 'hold the place to extremity.' They disembarked several guns, enrolled the citizens, and also the peasants of the island, and wrote to the Prince of Orange, asking his assistance. The latter, as Meteren relates, was displeased at the taking of Brill, fearing that his other designs would be discovered, and that the Duke of Alva would be prematurely apprised of them. The signification of Brill is, in Dutch, 'spy-glass,' or 'spectacles,' and the word, together with the date, the 1st of April, tended to the production of dull jokes, and furnished the conquerors with a theme for their lumbering pleasantry.[1]

It needs only a slight knowledge of what are called 'the troubles of the Low Countries' to enable

[1] *Translator's note.*—In Mr. Motley's 'Rise of the Dutch Republic' we find the following :

'Den eersten dag van April
Verloos Duc d'Alva zijnen Brill '—

which may be translated,

'On April Fool's Day
Duke Alva's spectacles were stolen away,'

became a popular couplet. A caricature too was extensively circulated, representing Admiral de la Marck stealing the Duke's spectacles from his nose, while the Governor was supposed to be uttering his habitual expression, whenever any intelligence of importance was brought to him —*No es nada! no es nada!* ' 'Tis nothing! 'tis nothing!'

us to form an idea of the feverish, restless, riotous existence of Brill during half a century. After that long period of storm came calm, but Holland has never ceased to regard the first rampart of her independence with grateful veneration; and it was within the walls of Brill, that, after an interval of three centuries, the country held the solemn commemoration of the hard-won conquest of its liberties.

In 1872 and 1873, high festival was held at Brill. I was in the fair city, when the king, the princes, and the great official personages of the kingdom came thither. The houses were hung with flags, the façades were decorated, the streets, the squares, and the canals were all crowded with brilliant groups in holiday attire, and with countless soldiers and sailors. At intervals the cannon thundered on the Maas, and the roll of the drum alternated with the shouts of the Dutch mariners. It seemed as though the grand old time had come back again; but this was only the illusion of a day, and Brill now wears its habitually solitary and tranquil aspect; its clean, picturesque little streets have again become silent, and over its tree-shaded canals broods the customary calm. The grassy ramparts of Brill are more like dykes than fortifications; they seem to guard the place against the waters rather than against human foes; and—as also at Puttershoek, where the whole village is perched on a height—the chief objects of dread are storm and flood.

At Gravendeel's we had also seen a long steep

dyke, all covered with houses, making one interminable street of the village, and away at the far end of it, behind a great sheet of water, a timeworn, decayed old church in the midst of a green and grassy cemetery, planted with fine far-spreading trees. It was noonday, the street was silent, and God's acre was quite solitary. The impressive stillness was not broken except by the swarming gnats wheeling and humming in the air. After we had made out a few of the inscriptions on the tombs we were returning to the boat, when we descried in the distance two strange forms. They were those of two men, clothed in black, walking gravely, in profound silence, and with fixed expressionless eyes. One was dressed like a peasant, the other wore a three-cornered hat with a hatband and 'weeper' of black crape, and something like a box was slung across his body by a thick leather strap. Never shall I forget that lugubrious pair. They were carrying the corpse of a child to the cemetery after this fashion. No father, no brother, not even a friend of the family was there to follow that small coffin, to testify that at least one tear had fallen on the pallid little corpse. Poor child! all alone, committed to the hands of two hirelings, he passed unregretted from the glimpses of the day, out of a world into which he had certainly not come of his own accord.

This sight made us sad; we returned to our *tjalk* in silence, and we should have gone on our way in a melancholy mood had we not caught sight of three long veils fluttering in the breeze, and of bright and rosy faces on the opposite bank. Cheered by this charming apparition, we waved kisses from our finger-tips in its direction, replying to the gracious salutations which were bestowed upon us. Our aerial kisses were returned, accompanied by a burst of girlish laughter, and then the wearers of the veils jumped lightly down from the ridge of the dyke and vanished. It was only the eternal *fugit ad salices.*

All these old recollections came back to my mind with extraordinary vividness; the same picture seemed to pass before my eyes again, I fancied I could hear the silvery laughter of the three pretty girls; and so we reached the headland of Moerdijk. It was then twilight; the waterway opening before us was dangerous, and almost unknown to our crew; the tide also was against us, so that we had to cast anchor and wait for day.

We settled ourselves comfortably on the deck. Night came on, warm and beautiful, but not as it is in the East—clear, limpid, starry. This was the northern night, with all its mysteries; the sky, covered with dark rolling clouds, mingling at the horizon-line with the greenish-brownish water, divided from it only by a long track of luminous specks, which, reflected by the waves in a quivering ray, seemed to dart into the depths of the river in the far distance.

In aid of the fires on board the ships at anchor

THE FUNERAL OF A CHILD AT GRAVENDEEL'S.

came the lights along the coast, piercing the dark sky, stretching out in one single line, like a procession, two leagues in length, while close to us the large *koffs* with grey sails looked like gigantic phantoms in winding-sheets, skimming the surface of the water. All around was silence, that absolute silence which is so impressive, broken every now and then by the ripple of a wave against the bow of our boat, or by the murmur of the strongly flowing water. All was at rest, except the great river, for ever in movement and for ever murmuring low, as if, before it flowed on to be lost in a nameless sea, it would fain whisper an eternal farewell to those green and grassy shores.

Towards midnight the moon began to emerge from the clouds. Its pale and sickly light first pierced the mists which hung about it with a luminous dart, and then by degrees dispersed them, until all at once Luna appeared in her splendour, proudly reflecting herself in the white water, studding the tops of the masts with her silver spangles, and sprinkling showers of them on the crests of the little waves that went dancing down the river. At this moment a dog barked on the shore, and we heard many voices and the rolling of carriage-wheels. All these sounds came to us from land which we could not see; as the waters bore them to our ears with clearness, limpidness, and precision, they had a strange fantastic effect. The carriage rolled on, the sound of its wheels was lost in the distance, all was again silence, grander, more solemn, more mysterious than before. Then the river resumed for a while its murmur of regret, but at length even that was heard no more.

At dawn we were awakened by the joyous crowing of half a dozen cocks. Their clear and piercing clarion call served as the alarum of a neighbouring farm; presently everybody on land would be up and busy. As for us, we rose on the instant and went on deck. Around us was a complete flotilla at anchor, and everybody afloat seemed also to be astir. Hatchways were opened; and from out them popped rough heads with blinking eyes, while on board some of the *tjalks* which kept earlier hours smoke rose in curling spirals in the morning air, announcing the speedy appearance of coffee, without which no good *schipper* could possibly begin the day.

At seven o'clock the tide was full. Then there was a general hubbub. On every side was lifting of anchors and hoisting of sails, grave and thoughtful masters took the helm, busy *knechts* ran to the staysails or worked the *zwaard*, and fifty boats under sail spread themselves jauntily over the vast basin called the Moerdijk.

No sight could be prettier than the simultaneous start, or, as it were, development of that flotilla, sailing in convoy. The dark-reddish sails, the tricolour flags, the red or blue pennants, the rounded poops all painted green, with their little curtained windows like two curious prying eyes, the rudders with their copper fittings glittering like gold upon the sea-green surface of the water, while the sun, darting oblique rays upon them, added a multitude of quivering and sparkling gleams to the picture. The swelling sails, the hulls bending over to the breeze, described a series of graceful curves and then stood out to sea, leaving behind them the huge bridge over the Moerdijk, a vast sombre mass thrown out against the silvery mist of morning.

What a great problem solved is that gigantic bridge! What a majestic effort of the human mind! Above all, what an indisputable proof of Dutch perseverance; for this colossal viaduct is a truly wonderful work. It is fourteen hundred yards in length, and it serves as a sort of portico to the Pool of Biesbosch, that sullen, rush-grown swamp, where twenty submerged villages sleep beneath the sluggish waters. To be appreciated in the vastness of its proportions, it must be seen from close at hand; at a distance there are no means of comparison, the imposing character of the construction is lost; one sees nothing except fourteen immense cages suspended above the river on fourteen massive pillars. This was the effect it produced upon us at the distance from which we saw it, while with all sails set we floated upon that vast stretch of water which is called the Hollandsch Diep.

I believe it was M. Viardot who called the Moerdijk a rivulet! A strange rivulet, truly, for its two banks are hardly to be seen at the same time, and travellers on it are sea-sick. A strange rivulet, truly, for it is swept by storms so fierce that many Dutch ships and their crews hesitate to encounter them. In 1711, John William, Stadtholder of Friesland, a prince of the house of Nassau, was lost in the Moerdijk, with a colonel of his escort. Many others have perished whose names oblivious history has not preserved. No year passes without some serious accident which spreads dismay throughout these coasts, and twice, during our voyage, we caught sight of broken fragments of masts emerging from the terrible depths to tell of lost vessels beneath the ruthless waters.

We had in our own case a convincing proof of the force of the swell that passes over the inland sea. Hardly had we rounded Strijen point, and sailed in the prescribed curve around the framework of iron on which the new lighthouse is reared, than our flotilla scattered itself over the great grey sheet of water like a flight of migratory birds. Then came a race, in which we competed, each striving to get in advance of the others. We carried no cargo, and the sailing power of our craft was very superior; in less than half an hour we had left all competitors behind, and were at the head of the little fleet. The weather was fine, the river was calm, there was a light breeze, but nothing more, and we were sailing easily before the wind. The boy at the helm, delighted to find himself the winner in this peaceful strife, was bending over the tiller and whistling gaily, while he kept a mocking watch upon the boats which he had outsailed. All at once the master called out, 'Mind yourself, Jan! Take care what you are about, boy! You are taking the swell crosswise.'

He had hardly spoken when we heard a dull thud, followed by a sharp cracking noise; the boat swerved round and began to drift. A mere shock of the wave had sufficed to break an iron bolt thicker than a man's wrist, and to demolish our *zwaard*.

The alarm was given in a moment; everyone was up and lending a hand. The rudder was unshipped, and we let ourselves go with the current, which carried us gently to Willemstad. When we were in safety and shelter we fished up the *zwaard*, and repaired it as well as we could.[1] The crew regarded this as a favourable opportunity for landing at Willemstad, a tempting place, with cheerful cosy houses, and great massive trees stretching their branches to the very edge of the pier. A smith could make us a new bolt, and after such a mischance and this long delay, it would be folly to think of reaching Zierikzee before nightfall. These were sound arguments, but we did not think proper to hearken to such prudent counsel. The *zwaard* was repaired with two iron chains, and the order given to resume our course.

We are off again! We round the point of Willemstad. We enter the Volke Rak, and begin to tack

[1] The *zwaard* is a large brown racquet which the Dutch boats carry on either side. It serves the purpose of the absent keel, and is indispensable in navigating the rivers and inland seas of Holland, in consequence of the round shape of the boats, which is rendered necessary by the shallowness of the water.

about upon that great aquatic plain. In the distance are two flat banks, two lines of greensward, enlivened by an occasional spire, two grassy ribands of earth floating upon the pale green water; these form the horizon. We seem to be on a vast lake, and yet we have to advance with prudence and to move with circumspection. We are limited to a narrow channel, hollowed out by the current between two wide stretches of sand, and on both right and left of us the way is forbidden. Our first mishap has taught the crew prudence; they have learned that lesson a little too well, indeed, for it is six o'clock before we arrive at the entrance of the Zijpe, opposite Bruinisse, where we are obliged to cast anchor again, and once more to wait for the tide.

How calm, tranquil, almost deserted this region is! Above the stockade of the little harbour only a couple of masts are visible. From the distance comes no shouting, no noise of any kind; and when the hours are told to the surrounding country from the little steeple, the warning sound is muffled, half hushed, as though it broke with reluctance upon the general retirement and reverie. A pensive melancholy broods over this picture, which so well fits its frame that we hardly like to disturb such silent restfulness. One would think that no discordant sounds could ever have rung through this peaceful place; and yet it is hard by the scene of one of the most exciting adventures, one of the boldest feats of arms recorded in the history of the Eighty Years' War.

That grassy line which lies to our left is Sankt Philipsland; that belfry which we see beyond, just rising above a cluster of roofs, is Sankt Annaland; and we are close to the spot where, 'the night before the Michaelmas of the year 1575,' the Spaniards accomplished that famous passage which, by striking the Zealanders with terror and dismay, made them deliver up the forts of Bommenede and Vianen, and, a few months later, the town of Zierikzee.

The most daring among the leaders of the Royal army were Mondragon, Sancho d'Avila, and Don Osorio de Ulloa; and their purpose was to cross to Schouwen Island. But the 'Beggars' held the sea. Their vessels watched the coast, and none dared to brave their dauntless crews. Then it was that, on information which he received from certain peasants, the Commander conceived and executed the project of making his troops cross the water on foot at low tide. He then established his camp in 'the country of Saint Anne;' that Sankt Annaland whose picturesque steeple brightens up the horizon; and from thence his troops advanced on 'the country of Philip, which is an inhabited island, and so on to Duivelande, thus avoiding the Zealand ships which were between the two islands, but for the little depth of water could not come into certain places.'

Now that you are acquainted with the locality, you can imagine the scene. Fifteen hundred men, silent and resolute, 'each carrying a little bag of powder hung from his neck, and on his head victuals for three days,'[1] advancing in single file into the water, led by their old chief, the brave Mondragon, and endeavouring to reach the adjacent flat, noiselessly, in the darkness. On a sudden the night itself betrays them; the water, disturbed by this human flood which crosses it, throws out phosphorescent gleams, and, according as the men advance, a luminous streak indicates their path.[2] 'The air was full of shining rays,' says a contemporary, and from afar the watch on board the Zealand ships perceived the dark column which broke the glittering surface of the water. Then arose a clamour on every side; the crews were on foot in an instant; the ships were in motion, the silence of the night was broken by the roar of cannon, and a hail of balls fell upon the marching column. Steadily it advanced, nevertheless, and not a cry, not a groan, revealed the ravages made by the balls and the bullets of the enemy in that long single line. It was impossible for the Spaniards to defend themselves, or to retaliate. The water continued to rise, the Zealand vessels drew near, and it was no longer with firearms alone that the troops were assailed. Mendoza thus describes what followed: 'The Zealanders transfixed some with their fatal harpoons, they dragged others from the path with boat-hooks, they beat out the brains of others with heavy flails.' Nevertheless, the silent terrible column marched on

[1] Meteren.
[2] Mr. Motley, in a note to 'The Rise of the Dutch Republic,' says: 'According to Mendoza, the sky was full of preternatural appearances on that memorable night.'

and attained the shore. Then was a solemn reckoning made, and the loss which had been sustained was computed. One of the bravest of the officers, Hydro Paccieco, was gone; but, on the other hand, the Zealanders had lost their general, Charles Van Boisot, who had been killed in the confusion by his own men at the moment when the royal troops landed.[1]

After such a feat, anything might be expected from such soldiers as these. On the following day they carried Vianen, which was at that time a citadel. Two days later they halted under the walls of Bommenede, then a fortified place, and carried that also, after five terrible assaults. Then they marched on Zierikzee, and occupied all the approaches to the old Zealand city.

Once more the tide serves us, and quitting this ever-famous channel we go on our way, sailing between Tholen and Duiveland, and therefore in Zealand proper. We coast along Stevenisse Point, round that of Ouwerkerk, enter the eastern Scheldt, and descry from afar the massive and gigantic clocktower of the ancient city of Zierikzee.

The glowing purple and gold of the sky makes the horizon look like a vast burning furnace; the last rays of the sun gild Duiveland, 'the country of doves' —a name derived in olden times from the great number of sea birds which frequented its coasts—and in the distance are spires glistening with golden

---

[1] See Translator's note in Appendix.

spangles. On this great tongue of land, which has suffered much from inundation, and was completely covered by the waters in 1530, there are no great towns, no important communities. From end to end of that green and grassy plain the eye discerns only some large villages and domanial dwellings—'abodes of gentlemen,' as Guicciardini calls them.

On our right lies Noord-Beveland Island, rustic, sylvan, thinly peopled, and, like its neighbour, with no busy bustling cities on the flat face of it. An arm of the sea now flows lazily between those two islands, which in former times approached each other so closely 'that the inhabitants talked across to one another where now a wide sheet of water divides them.' It seems to be the destiny of this strange country to be continually re-shaped by the elements.

Night comes on apace; the fires upon the shore are our only guide. A small lighthouse illumines the entrance of the channel of Zierikzee, and for that we steer, having to make long tacks to reach it. It is after eleven o'clock when we come alongside the stockade. The day has been a toilsome one. Quick! a man and a horse—a *jager*, quick! to take us into the port.

CHAPTER III.

ZIERIKZEE — ITS HISTORY—BATTLES AND SIEGES—GREATNESS AND DECAY—THE 'BEGGARS OF THE SEA'—A STONE GIANT—GATES AND RAMPARTS—THE FISHERIES AND THE FISH MARKET.

HAVE not spoken rashly of Zierikzee as an old city. 'It is held,' says Guicciardini, 'to be the most ancient town in the county of Zealand.' You see, therefore, that its reputation is of distant date; and a poem in eight lines, written on parchment, which is to be seen, framed and glazed, in the Gasthuiskerk, sets forth the probable origin of the name of the city, as well as its exact age:—

> 'In 't jaar acht hondert negen en veertich mede,
> Was gefundeert Ziericzee die Stede
> Bij eenen die ZIERINGUS ghenaamt was
> Alsoo men in de ouden Chronyken las.'[1]

One thousand years of existence, especially on such shifty and uncertain soil, is no contemptible record for a city. To that we may add splendid

---

[1] In the year 849 the town of Zierikzee was founded and named by a certain Zieringus, as appears in the old Chronicles.

fortunes, and an honourable rank as the residence of the suzerain princes. 'The Counts of Zealand had also their palace in the said city, of which even to this day the reserves and the enclosure, which are called "the Counts' Court," are visible,' says a chronicler.[1] Nor were these the only gems in the mural crown of Zierikzee, for it can also boast a great military past, and a famous commercial and maritime history. Even though the town had not such reminiscences to offer us, it would still be well worthy of a visit. Its lofty spire, visible from almost everywhere, rises high in massive and majestic pride above a cluster of red gables, which are girt about with a ring of lavish greenery; and then come pointed spires, pepper-box turrets with glittering vanes, and a bulbous belfry, bristling with angles and projections. Picture all these to your fancy, and you will have an idea of this town, which stands out in profile in the distance, a sort of promised land, all the more picturesque for the bareness of the country that lies about it.

So strong is the influence of habit that this bareness—a disfigurement to the country in the eyes of a stranger—passes unperceived by the dwellers in Zierikzee. Indeed, it would seem to possess a certain charm for them, for all along the harbour, which serves as a vestibule to the town, are at least half a dozen hotels, taverns, or cafés, looking out upon the

[1] *Grande Chronique de Hollande et de Zélande.*

boundless green flat, and all called 'Schoon Uitzight,' which means 'Fair View.'

This sonorous general appellation would be intelligible if the fronts of the houses were turned the other way. Ah, then indeed, they might well be so called! Hardly had we passed the first few houses, when we were lost in a labyrinth of nice little streets, very old, very clean, all twisting and turning and doubling back upon themselves, with the cleanest, prettiest, primmest houses, all very low, and seeming to be half underground. The pleased eye follows the fantastic ins and outs of brick gables which the ages have touched with their harmonious hues; there are delightful surprises in those numerous vistas, which end either in a big blustering windmill, tossing its proud sails aloft in the air, or in a rustic 'tapperij,' with its hospitable bench, inviting the customers to sit down, and its screen of little trees, well trained and close cut, offering them shade and privacy.

This is, however, the low quarter of the town, and it needs an artist's eye to find pleasure in these modest nooks. If the patricians of Zierikzee were to meet us wandering about them, they would shrug their shoulders and smile at the facility with which we are pleased; and perhaps they would be right; for the genteel quarters are also picturesque and beautiful, although in a different way. Before we visit them, let me take you to that lofty tower which we have seen from afar; we have but a few steps to go.

This tower is all that remains of the original church, which was one of the finest Gothic monuments of the Low Countries, as Blaeu says: '*cui non aliud usquam in tota Zelandia simile.*' Marvel of size and strength that it was, it held out well until the present century. It had suffered, of course, in the three or four sieges of Zierikzee; its fine vaulted roof had been replaced by a wooden ceiling, but its stout pillars, and its beautiful ogives, six hundred years old, stood firm at their post, and gave good promise of remaining there a long time yet. In 1832 the grand and beautiful church was reduced to a heap of ruins in a few hours. Fire subdued that which time had spared, and man did the rest. The remembrance of this frightful disaster is preserved in an engraving.

Instead of leaving the ruins of the church standing, to bear solemn testimony to the might, the taste, and the artistic genius of their ancestors, the magistrates of the period thought proper to build in its stead, and close by, a big, ugly, pretentious Doric market, a classic construction, which disfigures the poor stone giant; flaunting its commonplace newness in the venerable presence of the grand, noble, worn old tower, the mighty portico of the vanished church, which the Zealanders of olden time dedicated to Saint Lieven. This contrast is very striking; the mock Greek temple looks at once mean and grotesque by the side of the mere ruined remnant of the old tower, and the interior, with its white walls and yellow benches, its common mouldings and its trumpery wooden wings, is bald and vulgar to a degree. One cannot but retrace the past in imagination while contemplating the two, and comparing the modern work with the product of the heroic ages. The latter presents the image of the greatness of Zealand in its glowing morn; the former personifies the fortune of Batavia at its decline.

The two strongly contrasted buildings rise from the centre of a little park, which was formerly a cemetery, and is now a public garden. The old ruin is even more impressive on a near view than when seen from afar. One feels oppressed by the bulk of this stone colossus. Its gigantic arches, its stout buttresses, its sturdy, valiant appearance, somewhat fierce too, with its scars and wounds revealing the solidity and ponderous strength of its masonry, intensify the first effect of its imposing aspect.

Observe, also, this is only a small portion of what the stone giant once was. The tower had four storeys, all of equal size; only two remain. The third must also have been square, but recessed, and flanked by elegant pinnacles; while the fourth was octagon shape and pierced. And then, this majestic and colossal building was surmounted by a tapering and delicate spire, which rose up into the sky from its setting of four graceful bell-turrets.

Some time ago I found, in the profusely furnished portfolios of the *Zelandia Illustrata*, belonging to the Zeeuwsch Genootschap der Wetenschappen at Middelburg, an engraving of the plan and elevation of this fine architectural achievement; and when by an effort of memory I compared the drawing before me with that fragment which no one can look at without wonder, I was astonished at the science and the daring displayed in the marvellous design. It would seem, however, that strangers only are affected by this grand spectacle, and that the natives of the country are insensible to its beauty.

> Quid miserum Thamyram picta tabella juvat?

The men of Zealand are also blind; and not satisfied with having stuck a balustrade, like the calves of prize footmen's legs, on the top of the arches of an antique terrace, they have converted the basement of the most venerable monument of their city into a petroleum store. *Bergplaats von Petroleum* is the only inscription upon the sides of the mutilated giant, predestined to witness the dealings of fate with all this portion of the province of Zealand for five centuries.

Let us escape from these gloomy reflections; the surroundings bid us discard them. Children are playing beneath the shade of the great trees, and a German band, close by, is bestowing treasures of harmony on some dancing groups, who come from the adjacent villages. The present is very pleasant; why then should we think about the past? Let us return to the harbour, where our boat is, keeping to the line of the quay throughout all its length, and so re-enter the town at its other end. On this side we shall find another ancient, picturesque, curious, and venerable building; the Zuidhaven Poort, a construction less vast indeed than the tower that we have just been admiring, but worthy of attention, and especially interesting in a country in which specimens of military architecture are now extremely rare.

The Zuidhaven Poort consists of a lofty rectangular mass of solid masonry, with a pointed gateway. It is flanked up to two-thirds of its height by four slim towers resting on corbels, and capped by lofty pointed roofs, forming hexagonal pyramids. From the centre of the roof rises a pierced bell-tower, which, although it is of a much later period, does no discredit to this noble and warlike edifice.

The Zuidhaven Poort formerly fulfilled a double purpose: it afforded access to the city, and it defended the approaches to the principal basin, or harbour, whose entrance is close by, and which in former times sheltered ships of all sizes. At the present time it extends into the heart of the city, and its tree-shadowed quays form vast and commodious landing-places. On the other side of the harbour, to which we shall return by and by, is the Oosteinde Poort, which is much less bellicose and imposing of aspect. This is a postern rather than a gate: it opens out upon the old rampart, but it has, notwithstanding its more civil aspect, a certain character of its own. It is composed of two massive buildings, surmounted by ornamented turrets, and divided by a little court, about which hangs a strange flavour of the old times. I know few archaic nooks so well preserved as this, so full of the truth and colour of the past.

This gate, and the Nobel Poort—a great square block, with two flanking towers of the elongated pepper-castor order—are the sole remains of the ancient walls; those sturdy ramparts which in the old times were so boldly assailed, so bravely defended, and which for the most part are now converted into spacious and pretty promenades. Fine trees, winding avenues, shady groves, replace curtains, bastions, and palisades, and many-coloured ducks paddle peacefully in the solitary salt-marshes which were formerly the scene of such famous exploits.

I seated myself on the turf, under the shade of an old tree, and amused myself by re-perusing the history of the famous siege of 1303, in an old Chronicle. The defence of Zierikzee on that occasion was the most heroic ever made by the city. I seemed to be living once more in epic times; through the antique forms of the chronicler's phrases I could descry Count Guy of Dampierre and the numerous and powerful army with which he came to lay siege for the third time to the town of Zierikzee. I followed in fancy all his military preparations, the 'trenches, blockhouse, and horsemen,' which must, he thought, terrify the dwellers in the besieged town, and then his breaching of the walls 'with

THE ZUIDHAVEN POORT AT ZIERIKZEE.

heavy blows from battering-rams, with bolts from crossbows, and other engines which discharged stones of great size.'

The citizens were, however, brave, and the magistrates were resolute. All was activity on their side also. 'The besieged, supplied with good soldiers, did no less, having erected three lofty and powerful catapults, which incessantly discharged their bolts upon the enemy.' Such was the artillery of the period. A curious thing happened in this duel of projectiles, and 'one which proves the skill of the Zealand enginers. It so chanced,' continues our old chronicler, 'that the Flemings shot a marvellous great stone into the city, and near the place where it fell there stood a certain mechanic who knew the art of throwing these great stones, which mechanic said, "Give me this stone, I will send it back whither it came," and having set his engine, he shot off the stone so neatly that it fell upon the engine whence it had first been discharged, which it broke in pieces, and tore the hand of the enginer.'

An obstinate and skilfully conducted resistance of this kind did not suit the purpose of Count Guy. He determined to carry the place by assault, and marched his men to the attack upon the walls. The signal for the assault was given, and then all the warlike qualities of the Zealanders revealed themselves. The besieged, quite unmoved, observed closely the advance of the veteran Flemish bands upon them. They swarmed upon the ramparts, and fought bravely with the enemy, 'hand to hand, as well as by discharging stones upon them.' Every man there took a personal part in the struggle. 'The youngest and most active sustained the assault in the breach; the older men were in the towers and turrets keeping up a continual discharge of arrows and stones. The women and girls served out stones in great heaps to the defenders of the town, so that their defence should not fail for want of offensive weapons. . . . In short, this furious assault was so bravely endured, and the enemy were so valorously repulsed, that Guy was constrained to retreat with very great loss of his men, and still more discomfiture.'

This success was so totally unhoped for, and the valour of the citizens of Zierikzee seemed so marvellous, that the credulous and superstitious imagination of that time unhesitatingly assigned it to a supernatural cause. 'At the same time, day, and hour of this victory,' says François Le Petit, 'there appeared in the sky a great cross of purple colour, near to Egmont, which has been held to be a presage of the said victory.' It was the custom of that age to seek and find mystery everywhere. We, being less prone to such notions, would simply say, 'Sons of Zealand, be proud of your ancestors, as you have a right to be!'

The siege by Count Guy of Dampierre was the most important and the most glorious that befel the old Zealand city. It was also the only one of real benefit, for the dwellers in Zierikzee obtained, for having borne themselves so valiantly, a certain number of those enviable privileges which Blaeu describes as '*luculentissimis aliquot privilegiis.*'[1] From that moment the town became an object of special favour with its lawful princes. We learn from a charter in the Archives,[2] that, up to 1830, Middelburg was the only town in Zealand exempted from the Staple of Dordrecht, which was an inestimable advantage. We know, besides, that in 1411 William of Bavaria granted the exceptional privilege 'that no person within its walls declared criminal should forfeit of his goods more than sixty livres of Paris.'[3] Middelburg was also the habitual residence of the Counts of Zealand, and a great number of charters and privileges are dated from thence.

No more was needed, as we may readily conceive, to render Zierikzee an object of covetousness to foreign princes. Thus we find the King of England endeavouring to make the burgomasters and town council 'vote' in his favour. 'He wrote letters full of graciousness that he might attract them,' says a contemporary. 'But they of Zierikzee, having received the said letters without making other answer, save that they would take counsel upon the contents of the same, sent them to the Duke, their lord, who was very ill pleased.'

---

[1] Blaeu. *Theatrum Urbium Belgiæ fœderatæ.*
[2] See *Inventaris van het oud archief der stad Middelburg*, No. 70.
[3] Guicciardini. *Descrittione di tutti i Paesi Bassi, altrimenti detti Germania Inferiore.*.

This was a prudent and loyal mode of action, and it would have been well for the country had its inhabitants been always inspired by a similar sense of duty. In 1472, however, we find them in insurrection against their legitimate sovereign, the Duke of Burgundy. A riot arose in the streets on the pretext that, contrary to the ancient custom, the Duke was about to increase the excise duties, and, after the turbulent fashion of the Zealanders, the disturbance did not stop at protestations. The two commissioners of the Duke were seized, killed on the spot, and their corpses flung out of the windows of the Stadhuis; and the magistrate, who was much alarmed by the violence of the mob, was forced, in order to save his life, to humble himself before them, and deliver up the keys of the town.

Charles the Bold, whom Chastelain calls 'that creamy prince, and great lover of justice,' was not inclined to put up with rebellions of this kind. He summoned the town, 'under pain of fire and sword,' to resume its obedience. The chief ringleaders in the disturbance were beheaded, two hundred of the most deeply implicated citizens fled, and, the Duke having landed on the island, the whole Commune presented themselves before him, crying 'Mercy, mercy!' Their prayer was granted; the sentence was commuted into a heavy fine.

In 1491 the Duke of Saxony made a similar visit to the people of Zierikzee, and taxed them very heavily, 'intending to bleed them,' he said, 'because, during the war with the Flemings, they were for them rather than for their prince.' This time again they were obliged to pay thirty-six thousand German florins, a heavy sum for a town which had seen its best days, and was declining. The old chronicles make it plain that all the strength of Zierikzee was entirely maritime. In the twelfth century, at a time when history had as yet made no mention of their future rivals, ' the citizens of Zierikzee in the island of Schouwen, in Zealand, had begun to build large merchant vessels for trade in all the northern, as well as the southern seas, and to make their city famous on account of their seamanship, having fit and proper roadsteads.' But those 'fit and proper roadsteads' were by degrees choked up with sand, and the coming in of the sixteenth century saw the old city obliged to abdicate her ancient prestige, and to bow down before the maritime fortune of Middelburg, which then reached its apogee.

Although Zierikzee lost commercial supremacy, the town remained none the less in a condition to supply the fleet of the States-General with daring sea-captains, dauntless sailors, and intrepid heroes. From Zierikzee the mysterious and legendary army of the Beggars of the Sea drew its hardiest recruits. From Zierikzee Admiral Boisot obtained the greater portion of the crews for that extraordinary expedition which crossed an inundated country to revictual Leyden, and to inflict upon the Spaniards one of the most severe reverses they ever sustained.

It is well worth while to read the description of that patriotic band in the writings of the period, and how they went forth to face death that they might deliver their country. The graver of Callot has produced no such phantasmagoria as that, nor has the brush of Salvator Rosa portrayed an assemblage uglier or more heroic.

At Rotterdam and on the Maas two hundred flat boats, with ten, twelve, fourteen, and eighteen oars, were constructed. The largest of these carried two heavy pieces of cannon at the bows, and six pieces of smaller calibre on either side. It was necessary to man this flotilla with picked crews. Here let me quote from Meteren. 'Upon these boats were placed 800 sailors from Zealand—rough men, also austere, and terrible to see because of their scars and wounds, some having but one leg, others having but one arm, according as they had been maimed in the various sea-fights in which they had taken part, and nevertheless they were still able to defend themselves well, and to do good service.' Such was the troop of heroes whom Admiral Louis Boisot and Adrian Willemsen of Zierikzee led to the succour of Leyden. With such men everything might be hoped, and anything undertaken. They were in fact as hardy in mind as in body, and each wore in his hat a crescent with the device 'Rather Turk than Papist,' or upon his breast one of those medals which are still to be seen in the numismatic collections of the Low Countries, and which bore the significant words, 'In defiance of the Mass.' One example will show as well as a hundred of what these men were capable. The author from whom I borrow the following frightful story is above all suspicion. He was an accurate and painstaking annalist, a rigid Calvinist, and a stern patriot. His absolute truthfulness cannot be questioned. 'It happened here,' he tells us, 'that a sailor having cut open a Spaniard, and torn out his heart, took several bites out of it, and then flung it away.' Only conceive to what a height the passion of hate must have risen when it could impel a man to such an act! and, it is even worse to know, as we do know, that this action, which makes us shudder, did not then excite either indignation or disgust. For this same sanguinary hate was so general that the Sieur Noordwijk, a very accomplished man, recorded the noble deed aforesaid in Latin verse.[1] Another poet of the time, and no doubt an equally accomplished one, celebrated it in French.[2]

> Naguère un matelot arracha par envie
> Le cœur d'un Espaignol et puis l'ayant gousté,
> Le cracha de sa bouche et tout d'une furie,
> Il de donna aux chiens pour être dévoré.

Is not this a terrible example of what men may be driven to, by the fanaticism engendered by the great passions calling themselves religion and patriotism!

---

[1] The following are the lines of the Sieur Noordwijk:—

> Macro caro est nuper cum cor gustasset Iberi,
> Respuit et canibus nauta vorare dedit.

[2] Meteren, *L'Histoire du Bas Pays, sous le gouvernement de Philippe, roy d'Espagne.*

Happily, it is not to danger of this sort that men's hearts are exposed in our time. Anything they have to fear in Zealand is from the eyes of the women, and not the teeth of the men. The Zealand women are very handsome, lively, frank and pleasant. We shall have occasion to refer to them hereafter. At present we must finish our expedition into the city, for time presses, and our crew are waiting.

On entering Zierikzee by the Zuidhaven Poort, we come, as I have already said, to the quay of a superb basin shaded by great trees, and bordered with handsome houses, some very old, but the greater number dating back no farther than a century. This quay is called the Oude Haven, or Old Port. Formerly it was full of ships, now it is empty; but in spite of its melancholy solitude, it still retains sufficient grandeur to remind us of what the former power and riches of Zierikzee were. In olden times this great basin, crossed by a wide bridge, was prolonged on the other side of that bridge to nearly double its extent, and that large space, now reclaimed from the water, forms a broad and shady avenue, in which the girls of Zierikzee walk of an evening, two and two. A curious church, more like a temple dedicated to Plutus than a Calvinistic sanctuary, is erected in this avenue. Farther on, but on the same side, stands another edifice, of still stranger appearance. It is built of stone, its windows are defended by formidable bars, its doors are sheeted with iron, its aspect is fierce, like that of a knight of the olden time. The ancient maps of the city, that of Blaeu amongst others, call this frowning monument Gravesteen's, that is to say, the Castle of the Counts.[1] In our day its name is more prosaic, and too explicit to require that I should say more respecting its present uses; it is called simply the Prison. Our progress across the old city has brought us to its highest point—the primitive dyke or dam. Close to this stands the Stadhuis, surrounded by venerable houses, with pointed arches and elegant ogives, but in a state of decay, worn by years, sodden with the rain, and rasped by the winds from the sea. The Stadhuis is also venerable, but it is no more. Its architecture is mixed, and indeed fantastic. The two entrances on the ground floor, with their fine ogives, belong to the close of the fifteenth, or the opening of the sixteenth century. The windows of the lower storey are not of any definite style or precise epoch, and the two decorated turrets that face the street belong to the seventeenth century. Its composite façade is surmounted by an odd-looking clock-tower, which is Japanese, Chinese, Muscovite, and Byzantine, all at once; bulbous in shape, swollen in the middle, cut out on the edges, bristling with points, spikes, and pinnacles, abounding in unexpected curves and crooked out-

---

[1] In the fourteenth and fifteenth centuries, all houses being built of wood, the word *steen*, which signifies stone, was the synonym of château, and this is probably a fragment of the ancient château inhabited by the Counts Floris, Thierry, and Wilhelm.

lines, and terminating in a superb gilded Neptune, armed with his trident, who seems to fling an eternal and aërial *quos ego* at the waters that surround his curious Belvidere. In the interior of the Stadhuis are to be seen a fine chimney-piece, with heraldic shields (the arms are those of the towns and villages of the Island of Schouwen), a pirogue, a silver goblet, and the seal of King Louis, the brother of Napoleon I. Ten minutes sufficed for the expression of all the admiration to which these municipal treasures are entitled; and, having settled our account with the curiosities of the city, we were returning to our boat, when, by a side view from the main street, we espied the fish market. Do not imagine for a moment that this is an ordinary *halle*. Not by any means. The *vischmarkt* of Zierikzee is a peculiar and exceptional institution. It is a charming little market, just like a scene in a comic opera, with a court and a garden, a covered platform, porticoes and colonnades, and, to represent the flat scene at the back, a pretty little house daubed in yellow and green; exactly like the *poffertjes* shops one sees at kermesses. Add to this lofty trees, a handsome park-railing, which divides the market from the street; throw in, as accessories, benches of painted wood arranged in semicircles, and seeming to await the coming of the stage fishermen and fishwives. Whenever I recall this pretty little market, its general physiognomy and its special charm, the recollection rouses my imagination. I fancy I behold a procession of fishermen bedecked with ribbons, fisherwomen in short petticoats, and boatmen in red shoes carrying nets on their shoulders, and wearing the Neapolitan red cap. Then I observe the auctioneer standing at the central desk, with his white wig, and his black three-cornered hat, with his spectacles, and his neck-band; he is conducting, and all these people, elegantly posed, and artistically grouped, are singing in chorus:

> 'Pêcheur diligent,
> Quelle ardeur te dévore?
> Tu pars dès l'aurore
> Toujours content:'

or some other verse borrowed from a 'Robin des Ondes' of the future. Alas! even as regards its fish market, the halcyon days of Zierikzee are past. Formerly its fishing fleet was counted by hundreds. In 1640 its number was reduced to eighty; in 1740 there were only fifty fishing boats; ten years later but thirty. How many are there now?

CHAPTER IV.

THE ISLAND OF SCHOUWEN—THE RAVAGES OF THE SEA—THE VAL—BLAAS-POEPEN, AND BROWN SEALS—A DAUGHTER OF THE FIELDS—THOLEN—WAR AND FIRE—A SLEEPING CITY.

THE Island of Schouwen is rich. Madder is grown and soda made there. For centuries past these two articles have been exported in great quantities, and for centuries past they have had a preference in the market because of their excellent quality. The soil is fertile, easily worked, and admirably cultivated. The people are brave, intelligent, and industrious. In addition to Zierikzee, which may be regarded as its capital, the island possesses another town, called Brouwershaven, which is situated on the north side, and a good many villages, Koudekerke, Kerkwerve, Renesse, &c., consisting of a number of pretty little houses, inhabited by industrious peasants. One would think that an expedition into the island ought to furnish matter for a number of curious remarks, and interesting and characteristic observations. This, however, is not the case. Foreigners unaccustomed to the habits and customs of the Dutch people would find a good deal to surprise them in Schouwen, especially its scrupulous cleanliness. The *netheid*, as the passion for washing, brushing and polishing is called in this country, would certainly delight them, for throughout the whole extent of this great tongue of land a dusty tile or an ill-kept room would be looked for equally in vain. This is, however, the only speciality of the country. Schouwen, of all the Zealand islands, most resembles the Dutch provinces. With the exception of the peasants' carts, which are strange, unaccountable, and marvellous objects, I saw nothing there that differed essentially from what we had already remarked in other parts of the Netherlands. Nor has the language anything typical in it. The manners and customs of the place are pretty much the same as those of the banks of the Maas. The costume of the men is not remarkable. The headdress of the women is like those large veils which we descried in the environs of Puttershoek. We need not therefore make any delay in these villages. The country round, though fertile, is very tame; its picturesque aspect does not gain by its excessive richness. We shall, therefore, only glance at Brouwershaven, a duty which need not detain us long.

Brouwershaven is the birthplace of the poet Cats, a statesman, a writer more weighty than profound, more solid than elegant, and a superficial politician. This fact is the principal title of the old city to fame, but it also formerly possessed a certain commercial importance. Its name, which means the 'Port of the Brewers,' indicates that it once served as a storehouse to the brewers of Dordrecht and Delft, and as the Zealanders were always great drinkers of beer, the people of Brouwershaven had plenty to do in those days. Unfortunately, Cats has been dead, and the brewers have disappeared, for more than two centuries. We shall, however, be able to find some beer on our way. No trace of the poet is to be found in the city which gave him birth. His house has been pulled down, and a statue has not yet been erected. We should only be disappointed if we went to look for Cats in Brouwershaven. We shall, however, find him in another island, that of Walcheren, at the Château Overduyn, where dwells a fervent admirer and an ardent student of Cats; a Zealander of high rank, who has piously collected in his sumptuous residence all the precious relics of his illustrious compatriot in existence. Let us be off then, for we shall look vainly in the Island of Schouwen for the originality and poetry that we shall find elsewhere and farther on.

And now we will steer for Bergen-op-Zoom! At this word the schipper started. Again, a course so long! to reascend the eastern Scheldt without putting in anywhere or making any stay! Such an order astonished and disconcerted him. 'We shall never get there this evening,' said he, shaking his head. 'Very well;' I replied, 'then we will go on all night, because we must be there early tomorrow morning.' So the *tjalk* started, with the crew in a bad humour. As we did not care much about that, we settled ourselves very comfortably on the deck to enjoy the fresh air and the fine weather. It is five o'clock in the morning; the sky is clear, the atmosphere is absolutely still, not a breath of wind ruffles the surface of the sea. To advance towards the current we must wait for the tide. At eight o'clock it begins to make itself felt, and at the same hour the horizon becomes clouded, and the wind rises. Our mainsail swells out to it, the *tjalk* bends over and we begin to cut rapidly through the water.

We are now on an arm of the Scheldt, over which few have floated before us. How many tourists have sailed in these waters for twenty years? Not many, of a truth; and nevertheless it is a most interesting, instructive and curious voyage; for, to understand Zealand aright, one should sail up and down all its rivers and penetrate into all its bottomless gulfs. To discern the strange charm of this unique country, and feel the invisible attraction which rivets Zealanders to the unstable soil of their insecure territory, one must have sailed upon the inland seas, which wind, serpent-like, around the strangely formed islands. Those great flat green banks, Duiveland on the north, Noord-Beveland on the south, and Tholen in front of us, hardly rising above the white waters, and girding the flat horizon with an emerald band, look like the garden borders of a great lake, eternally calm and tranquil. A hundred clock towers, piercing the sky at all points with their spires as at Middelburg and Goes, or rearing their deep-coloured and massive bulk, like the colossi of Veer and Zierikzee, tell of an active, industrious and wealthy population, sheltered behind this narrow green rim. The scantiness of such shelter seems to indicate absolute security; everything in the picture is peaceful, and speaks of repose. The far-extending flat surface seems to relieve us from the burden of thought. Here one has only to let oneself live, and be hardly conscious that one does so. All in a moment, however, we remember that this apparent tranquillity is fictitious; that, in truth, the islands, the towns, the villages, the hamlets, and the green plains are at the mercy of the waters. All that we see might be swallowed up of a sudden, so that, under this idyllic agricultural surface we detect an existence of unceasing strife and everlasting anxiety. The life of a whole people depends on the solidity of the strips of earth which encircle these green islands. A broken dyke—and all is lost; and nothing short of perpetual vigilance, ceaseless care, and courage equal to every emergency, can avert a cataclysm.

Guicciardini, who sailed on these waters, and coasted these green isles, has written as follows :—

'It would be almost necessary to describe them one after the other, all the more that the greater part of them have been transposed by tempests and inundations of the sea, and have changed their bed, this one becoming larger and that diminishing, this one being swallowed up by the waters, and that being laid bare by them; for the country of Zealand, gaining on the one side, is on the other ravaged by the sea. The accreted land was for some time without fear of peril, but now the waters are beginning to eat into it. Under the dyke of Soudkerke there is so great a depth that it is feared the Island of Schouwen will, at some time, sink in from the middle on the north side.' And the old story of three centuries ago is true of to-day. That ceaseless strife in which the unexpected is always turning up, and man is pitted against the elements, has not abated for a single moment. Penelope's web is unceasingly woven here. The green fields, the meadows, the cities and villages, the villas, and the rustic dwellings are all built upon a bottomless gulf, an abyss which some day or other will yawn, and close again, after it has swallowed trees and houses, peasants and cattle, and substituted blank desolation for these fortunate isles. The terrible Val,[1] that mysterious canker, which eats away the life of this country, is awful to think of. One day the traveller may pass by a green expanse, with a flourishing farm-house; horses are neighing, children playing, the trees are bending beneath their weight of fruit, and the sweet-smelling hay has been

---

[1] The word 'val' is derived from the word *vallon*, to sink, and is used in technical language to express this sudden destruction by water.

made into large round stacks. On the following day everything will have disappeared, without leaving a trace. The soil has sunk away; the sea-green water gurgles tranquilly in its place. In vain should we look for a stone or a fragment—only nothingness is there; a hole, twenty yards, or perhaps fifty yards deep, and at the bottom of that hole not the slightest vestige to recall the fact that yesterday the place was full of life, health, hope, and prosperity.

What has become in one night of this little fragment of the human family, this particle of the soil, this atom of the country? No one knows, and science itself, reduced to conjecture, makes hesitating answer, and can suggest no remedy for an evil of which it can only register the facts, but cannot divine the cause. In the spot where we are now sailing how many events of this kind have taken place? That great sheet of water before us was once a fertile, rich, thickly-populated island, which formed an annexe of Zuid-Beveland, and the Scheldt flowed peacefully between two fertile banks, covered with rich crops, and populous villages, justly proud of their flourishing communities. In 1530, twenty villages disappeared totally in one night, with the island on which they stood. These were Schoond, Conwerd, Durven, Lodjik, Broek, Kreek, Ouwerringhen, Rilland, Steenvliet, Ewartswaert, Kravendjik, Moere, and Nieuwelandt, and they remain for ever under the waters. The place which they occupied —you can see it from here—is now that great arm of the sea, with its little shimmering waves glittering in the sun!

Who shall reveal to us the mysteries of that terrible night? Thousands of human beings were drowned. For eight days afterwards dead beasts, swollen, hideous carcases, gnawed by the new denizens of those new depths, floated to the surface of the improvised lake. A contemporary writer tells us that fifty persons, having taken refuge on the roof of the church at Moere, endured for three long days the pangs of hunger and thirst, and were afterwards saved by a ship. During this awful tempest the entire island trembled, 'just as if it had not been well and solidly founded.' It was twenty leagues in circumference, and to-day it is not one-half the size. The town of Borselen, at its other extremity, was submerged, with all the land which surrounded it, and in that immense expanse before our eyes but one town was saved, Rommerswaal.

Rommerswaal, then rich, famous, and powerful, proud of its fine public buildings, was opposite to Tholen, at the distance of 'the range of a musket shot,' and on the east was its rival, Bergen-op-Zoom. One fact will suffice to prove its antiquity and its importance. When in 1285 Floris the Fifth granted to the inhabitants of Middelburg the 'right of commune,'[1] which conferred municipal existence on their city, he followed Rommerswaal in the drawing up of the clauses and conditions: '*Also alse dit*

[1] See Appendix.

ruyt haven tote Reymerzwale;' or, 'thus it has been granted to Rommerswaal.' Such was the wording of this gracious act, which Middelburg regarded as its dearest privilege. It was, besides, in Rommerswaal that the Counts of Zealand were invested with their suzerainty. Within its walls the States assembled to take the oath of fidelity to their prince. In 1549 Philip the Second presented himself there to be acknowledged as sovereign count. The houses were decorated, the public buildings were hung with tapestries of great price, triumphal arches were erected everywhere. The city was dazzling to behold. Never had a more stately ceremony taken place within its walls.

This was, so to speak, the song of the swan, for from that day forth ill-fortune descended upon Rommerswaal, and clung to it with singular tenacity. The city was occupied by the Spaniards, and taken by Admiral Boisot. Cannon thundered upon its ramparts, blood flowed in its streets. To-day you may search in vain for any trace of its lofty walls, its dainty houses, and its proud monuments; nothingness has replaced them all. Its former place is indicated upon modern charts by a black spot, as a rock is marked; that spot is its ancient spire, now covered by the waters, an object of dread to seamen, and this novel kind of reef has been doubly dangerous of late, since a ship foundered upon its point. And now, floating gently between the land and the water, past these evergreen shores, dwell on these remembrances, let your mind wander from the placid scene which surrounds you, let your fancy revive the incidents of history which I have just recalled, while it contemplates the fair picture in the distance. Compare this absolute, actual repose, so complete that it seems as if it must last for ever, with those sudden alarms, full of anxiety, full of mortal terror, and you will have the exact 'note' of this strange and charming country, at once so joyous and so melancholy, the absolute contrast between that which one knows and that which one sees. But our *tjalk* is advancing, and we have come to Stevenisse Point. The passage which we are crossing is a famous place, for here it was that, two centuries and a half ago, the celebrated 'Battle of the Sloops' took place. Never, I believe, was a more complete and irremediable defeat inflicted upon the Spaniards. They were surprised by Martin Hollart, Vice-Admiral of Zealand, commanding the fleet of the States, and were all either taken prisoners or massacred. The conquerors took 76 vessels, small and great, and more than 4,000 prisoners, captured in that one day, to Bergen-op-Zoom. Of the whole army, only the two generals, John of Nassau and Albert of Barbençon, succeeded in escaping, with ten of their men. They got into a small boat, and, owing to the darkness of the night, eluded the victorious Zealanders. The field of battle is now quite deserted; nature is reposing everywhere to-day, and the midday sun is baking our deck. The spires of Saint Martin's Dyke and West Kerke rise on our left, dark, frowning silent masses; and the only living creatures in all this solitude are the brown seals at their lumbering gambols on the edge of the sandbanks, their shining skins glittering with sea water. The remembrance of the Battle of the Sloops has awakened our warlike spirit; we fire two shots, and two balls fall into the midst of the ungainly group; they disappear with a flop, but turn up again at 100 yards' distance. The *tjalk* pursues the fugitives, and when it comes within range of them, we send a fresh volley into the midst of the harmless enemy; and thus we pursue them, until they disappear altogether. At the same moment our attention is attracted by a distant sound of music. A light column of smoke rises above the wide horizon, and a little steamboat, following the same course as ourselves, advances rapidly. On board are the *virtuosi* whom we heard the other day at Zierikzee. In a quarter of an hour the steamboat is alongside. It passes us closely, and hoists its flag to do us honour. We return the salute, and, borrowing a speaking trumpet, I shout through it with all my might, '*Blaas-poepen, een beetji musick, asje blieft.*'[1] Our appeal is heard, and the wandering orchestra begins to play that celebrated waltz, the 'Blue Danube.' Presently the music ceases, the little steamer turns to the left,

---

[1] '*Blaas-poepen*, a little music, if you please.' In all Zealand and Northern Holland the name of '*Blaas-poepen*' is given to the bands of German musicians who cross the frontiers to perform at the kermesses.

enters the Mast Zipje, and disappears from our eyes. This evening her noisy passengers will land at Rotterdam. Now we are advancing with difficulty, and we are soon obliged to cast our anchor; the tide has fallen, and the wind has ceased to blow. The *tjalk* has reached Poortvliet.

The sky is blue, the weather is warm; what should we do on board? Quick, let us lower the boat and land. We will go and visit the island of Tholen, which stretches out before us, and the little city whence it takes its name. Having ascended the steep dyke, we come upon a charming spectacle. No great cultivated park, no prize farm, no village paradise, ever presented a more pleasing aspect. On all sides are rich crops, golden fields or grassy meadows, intersected by broad alleys of great trees, curving gracefully away into the distance. On all sides is abundance, wealth, even profusion. The harvest is near, and the full ears bend their long golden stems towards the earth; this is the boasted wheat of Zealand, 'the fairest and the sweetest that can be seen,' the grain that was famous in the Middle Ages, celebrated even in Italy, and which astonished Guicciardini. How right was Hofler, the maker of Latin verses, when he lauded the fertility of this exceptionally generous soil, which refuses nothing to those who bestow their care upon it:—

'*Fertilis est frugum pecorisque uberrima tellus.*'

A dozen young girls are working in the fields in

front of us. Their arms are bare, their petticoats are short, the straw hats shading their eyes are trimmed with blue ribbons crossed over the back. One of these girls, standing on the ridge of the dyke, and quite surprised to find us in that place, salutes us with her voice, and waves her hand. 'Good morning, gentlemen.' 'Good day, fair ladies.' 'Whence come you then?' 'From a very distant country, which none of you have ever seen. Which is the road to Tholen?' 'Many others have found it who came from as far as you.' 'Will you show it to us?' 'What! Do the girls in your country lead the men?' and then a burst of clear and silvery laughter runs from lip to lip among the whole group, like fire along a train of powder. 'Good-bye, you saucy girl; at least, tell me your name.' 'My mother knew it before me; go and ask it of her.' 'Well, then, where is your mother?' 'Where a woman ought to be—beside her husband.' Thereupon the laughter is renewed; we take our share in it, and wave our hands to the girls, who return the salute with interest. A little farther on, the workmen engaged on the dyke give us the information which the merry girl whose mother knew her name so well had refused. They point out a shady road, which, after a few windings and half an hour's walking, leads us to the wide old moat that formerly encircled the ramparts of Tholen. Never was I more delighted with the entrance to any city. In a moment we seemed to be transported to one of the great English parks, or a beautiful suburban domain in the vicinity of London. The old city, shaded by immemorial trees and surrounded by rich plantations, seems to nestle luxuriously amid all this verdure. Limpid waters lave its sides. Its antique bastions, converted into gardens, are reflected in the tranquil flow, while a great mill, painted white and streaked with the brightest hues, strikes a lively note in this concert of harmonious colouring. Every object adds to the singular aspect of the scene, even the iron railing which replaces the Oudelandschepoort, or ancient gate of the city. The interior of Tholen is in harmony with its artistic exterior. It has rather the aspect of a large village than that of a once powerful city, for the houses are detached, and its extent seems far too great for its population. Nevertheless, Tholen was a populous place in old times, when it held the fourth rank in the councils of the Provinces, its deputies taking precedence of those of Flushing. Its name, which signifies 'toll,' indicates that at the period when the islands of Zealand were not separated from the continent, it formed a place of passage where merchandise paid certain duties. Tholen early became an important place; it certainly was fortified, and although, as Blaeu states,[1] nothing is known of its foundation, at least we may admit, with the eminent geographer, that the city is of great antiquity, and that it attained eminence in more than one respect. Another indication of its past grandeur

---

[1] Blaeu, *Theatrum Urbium*, op. cit.

is its division into three quarters; or, indeed, into three towns; and this division is at least nominally retained at the present time. Tholen, in fact, is composed of an old city (Oudestad), of a new city (Nieuwestad), and of an external city (Buitenstad), the whole comprised in barely two hundred houses. The ruin of the triple city and its shrunken condition are attributable to a fearful conflagration which occurred in 1452. Tholen was then completely reduced to ashes, and the memory of that awful disaster is preserved in the names which strike one at various points. We pass through the burnt street (Verbrandestraat), and see the place where formerly stood the ' burnt gate ' (Verbrandepoort).

Philip the Good conferred several privileges on the city, hoping to retrieve its fortunes, which had vanished in flame and smoke; other citizens came thither to replace the former inhabitants, but the 'good pleasure' of the old duke had not such efficacy as he expected, and it may be that the transformation which the whole country underwent at the commencement of the fifteenth century was the chief cause of the failure of his endeavours. The *raison d'être* of the toll no longer existing, Tholen could not possibly resume its former importance.

We must not, however, conclude that Tholen became all at once a despicable place. The determined obstinacy with which the different parties contended for the mastery of it at the epoch of the War of Independence, is sufficient proof that the city was important in their eyes. In 1573, in fact, we find the Zealanders under Rolle vainly endeavouring to seize the 'Beggars' Hole' by main force. Champigny was more fortunate; he surprised the town in 1577; and in 1588 the Spaniards in their turn besieged it in vain. If the memoirs of the time are to be believed, Tholen was preserved from capture by its dams. The city is, in fact, so packed away behind those curious ramparts that the enemy's projectiles, passing over its roofs, spent themselves in the plains beyond, where, no doubt, they assassinated some peaceful, ruminating animals who had no share in the quarrel, while the people of Tholen, in safety behind their dams, directed a murderous fire on the Prince of Parma's musketeers, and decimated them at their leisure.

Another indication of the importance of Tholen, subsequent to the great fire, is the Church of Our Lady, which was rebuilt about that same period, and is quite befitting a great city. It is built of white stone, is of imposing size, and has a lofty steeple and a fine portal. It stands upon a vast square, planted with great trees and surrounded by small houses, which are like a Béguinage. The whole effect is singular; the contrast has something strange and discordant in it, for the houses appear smaller than they are, and the church looks larger than it is. If it were in better preservation, Our Lady of Tholen would be a fine object. The nave, which rests upon twelve substantial pillars, is, so far as the transept, in good preservation, but the vaulted roof of the building was destroyed, and the enclosure of the choir has been removed. Rough plaster has been employed to fill up the rents made by the ravages of time or of man, and which were not anticipated by the architect. I shall spare you a description of the pavement of the choir, of the slabs with their pompous heraldic bearings and their eulogistic epitaphs, celebrating the virtues and the merits of forgotten nobles. I dislike nothing more than this misuse of heraldic shields, and funereal eloquence, in the laudation of contraband heroes, whose names posterity ought to ignore. The most illustrious sleeper in this place is Guy, Bastard of Blois, the last seigneur of Tholen.

We have now to walk through the streets and to visit the Stadhuis. The streets of Tholen are neither wide nor much frequented, consequently they are rather dull. Our solitary promenade reminds me of an anecdote told thirty years ago by one of the high officials of the Netherlands Government. 'It was on a Sunday,' said he, 'that I arrived at Tholen. At the city gate (the Oudelandschepoort) we observed about fifty young fellows, all tall, all healthy, all pensive, silent, and melancholy, contemplating with fixed attention the smoke which issued from their pipes and rose into the air in white spirals. We crossed the city, and at the other end we found a number of young girls, in Sunday attire, all fat, all blooming, all pensive, silent, and melancholy, who were regarding with fixed attention the flowing water. We crossed the river on a ferry-boat, we walked about half a mile, and we found ourselves in a hamlet where the girls and the young fellows were gathered together, laughing and talking, as happy as kings, and dancing merrily to the sound of a village hurdy-gurdy.' 'We had quitted Zealand for Brabant,' added the old statesman; 'all the difference of the two people is told in that contrast.' I do not know whether this preliminary hint helped me to the discovery that the streets of Tholen were rather too empty, but my own impression of that town greatly resembles the reminiscences of my venerable friend. Tholen, although it is upon the frontier, exhibits the characteristics of its own province only. The respectable old houses, with their brick façades, their gables, and their windows inserted in an elliptical arch, are distinguished by the marvellous cleanliness and scrupulous care, which may be called the livery of Zealand. The window panes are spotlessly clean, the shops are neat and well arranged, the paint is always fresh, and that is something, is it not? The Stadhuis, built of stone, like the church, although more curious than pretty, and odd rather than elegant, is nevertheless picturesque. It is composed of a lofty ground-floor storey, with two storeys above, a small belfry adorns the roof. The lower storey has trefoiled windows, those of the second are square, and the third storey is crenelated. Between these windows are projecting niches with consoles, and carved pinnacles.

The entrance has been modernised, and is adorned with four lions, each holding an escutcheon; the first bears the arms of the House of Orange, the second those of Zealand, the third those of Tholen, and the fourth those of the Ambacht of Shakerloo. While we were studying this fantastic Stadhuis, a groan issued from the roof, followed by a significant rasping in the belfry, and a cracked, dislocated carillon began to drone a melody so discordant, so harsh, and so incoherent that it put us to flight. In 1712 a detachment of French soldiers, commanded by Brigadier Pasture, made what, sixty years later, would have been called a 'raid,' that is to say, an expedition across the Dutch Provinces, and, in return for similar proceedings in France on the part of the Allies, he put Tholen to ransom. It is a pity that the carillon was not then in its present condition, for it would have sent our compatriots back again more quickly than they had come. But what is that other and deeper sound? It is the report of a gun, it is the appointed signal; our boat is all ready, and it waits for us at the turn of the river. Come, let us embark.

We have hardly a moment to glance at a novel kind of pisciculture which has been introduced here of late years, and has replaced the old fishery. The oyster parks of the Scheldt are still in their infancy, but the results are already satisfactory, and they probably have a prosperous future before them, from which the industrious population of Tholen will derive renewed wealth, comfort, and prosperity.

We are again on board. As the crow flies we should have only one league to make, but that league will be at least doubled by our inevitable tacks. No matter; we are now certain to arrive this evening, for Bergen-op-Zoom is visible, its towers and spires shining like gold in the distance. We shall not miss the promised land. The evening is magnificent; the sunset one of the most splendid which I have ever seen; I can give you no idea of the marvellous spectacle that spreads before us to the horizon. No words could convey the delicacy of tint, the softness of tone, the colouring at once brilliant and mellow, shading from intense red into celestial blue, following all the grades of the prism, alike in the sky and in the water, and coming to us strained through a warm and glowing atmosphere, so vital and so real that it seems impossible but that it must feel something of the pleasure it imparts to us.

CHAPTER V.

BERGEN-OP-ZOOM—A MILITARY RECEPTION—THE SCHUTTERIJ—THE CAMP—THE HISTORY OF A WARLIKE CITY—MARSHAL VON LOWENDAHL—THE GREAT SIEGE OF BERGEN-OP-ZOOM.

OUR resolution to arrive on a certain day at the old capital of the Counts of Bergen, was not dictated by mere fancy or caprice. We had, or at least one of us had, duties to fulfil there. Constant de Rebecque has the honour of being a major in the civic guard, and this distinguished rank involves certain obligations. He was bound to be present at a shooting match, which was to take place on the following day; consequently, although we arrived after dark, no sooner was our *tjalk* moored than my amiable fellow-traveller proceeded to attire himself, and one of our sailors was despatched on a voyage of discovery to find out where the colonel-commandant lived, as we wished to pay our compliments to him without loss of time. A quarter of an hour afterwards a great clanking of swords and the sound of voices summoned me to the deck, to behold no less a person than Colonel Van Beusekom, who, laying aside all rules of etiquette and strict precedence, had come down, with several officers of his staff, to bid us welcome.

As may be supposed, the meeting was exceedingly cordial on both sides. All these brilliant uniforms crowded into our little saloon! never had the *tjalk* beheld such a spectacle! Champagne was speedily sparkling in the glasses; friendly toasts were drunk; and then we were carried off to the camp, which, notwithstanding the late hour, was still full of life and stir. This camp, at which the shooting match was to take place on the morrow, was upon a wide esplanade, which had been a famous bastion in the old warlike days of Bergen-op-Zoom. The tents had been pitched, and the cafés and restaurants erected a fortnight previously. In the centre stood a kiosk, which was lighted up in the evening, and occupied by an excellent band; and as the camp was just about to break up, all its inhabitants were enjoying themselves as much as possible. The dispensers of victuals and drink were overcharging their customers for the last time, and the population of Bergen, to whom the camp and its accessories afforded a rare recreation, swarmed about them as eagerly as the troopers themselves.

When we arrived, the enclosure was crowded. The kind Colonel, to put the finishing touch to his cordial reception of us, strangers, made the band strike up in our honour; and the gallant Captain

Koorevaar undertook to make me tipsy; a truly soldierly manner of testifying to the cordial regard with which I inspired him.

I have no intention of discussing the army of the Netherlands, of explaining the part which the *Schutterij* plays in it, or even dwelling upon the advantages of that institution. I shall merely say that the *Schutterij* is somewhat analogous to our old National Guard, but that it is more strictly disciplined, better organised, and has more cohesion about it, because it is composed partly of men who have already served in the army, and especially because it is regarded in a serious light by those who belong to it.[1] All who have any knowledge of military matters will agree with me that a concentration of troops of this nature, taken away for a certain time from their homes, obliged to live under canvas, to observe discipline, and to undergo drill and obey orders, cannot be other than an excellent institution. The officers and soldiers come to know one another, and there arises from this obligatory association a valuable spirit of comradeship, which pervades their future mutual relations. The practical use of fire-arms is also useful to novices, and makes better soldiers of

---

[1] The *Schutterij*, which was instituted by the law of April 11, 1827, is intended for the defence of the territory and the maintenance of order. It is divided into active and stationary corps. It is composed of three divisions: the first comprises unmarried men and widowers without children; the second and third, married men and widowers with children. The force of the *Schutterij* is, in round numbers, 90,000, of whom 25,000 are in the active and 65,000 in the stationary corps.

them, when they pass into the regular military service. It seems to me therefore that these periodical exercises are highly to be commended, and, for my own part, I take a great interest in them.

Every hour of the following day was filled with occupation. In the morning, we received a brilliant staff, who condescended to share our breakfast; in the evening, we were invited to the farewell banquet given to the authorities of the city and to the garrison by the officers of the *Schutterij*. We were also present at the fête which followed the banquet, and between times, Constant contrived to cover himself with glory by carrying off one of the palms of the tournament, that is to say, one of the prizes of the shooting match. Far be it from me to relate in detail the events of that great day. My narrative would, however, be culpably incomplete, and I should be guilty of ingratitude were I to omit one impressive incident. First, the president of the banquet, in the kindest and most gracious manner, proposed the health of the French author who was present at this great family festival, and secondly, 'France' was proposed by the gallant Colonel Knyght, in one sentence of heartfelt eloquence. 'To that great and noble country to which we owe so much,' were his words, and although I thanked him for them at the moment by drinking to the Netherlands, I wish now to prove to him that I have not forgotten them. That our first experience of Bergen-op-Zoom should be a military fête is surely appropriate, for in the history of that martial city all things warlike hold the foremost place. The name of Bergen would, in fact, be hardly known, were it not for the sieges which the city has stood, and the deeds of arms which have been achieved beneath its walls. If the name of Bergen be more popular than that of many another great town, the fact is due to the incomparable bravery exhibited there in old times, in the attack as well as in the defence of its ramparts.

Bergen, although of great antiquity, made no name in history until it was fortified. The town, according to the old annalists, owes its origin to a little colony of fishermen, who established themselves at the mouth of the small river Zoom. The height of the land above all the surrounding country, which would place them in security from inundation, had attracted them thither. *Berg*, a mountain, *op-Zoom*, upon the Zoom; the etymology of this name is too clear to require interpretation. In 654 Saint Gertrude, the eldest daughter of Pepin of Landen, came to visit the place. The pious princess took up her abode in a little hamlet in the neighbourhood, which afterwards bore her name, Sankt-Geertruidenberg. From thence her benefactions were distributed over the surrounding country, for she devoted herself to ameliorating the lot of the still primitive population, and the result of her coming to Bergen was the foundation of a church which was afterwards consecrated to her. At the death of Saint Gertrude, the little new-born city was included among her patrimonial property, and added to the Barony of Breda. Thus it formed a detached portion of Brabant. In 1287, John I. having divided the Barony of Breda into two portions, handed over Bergen and its territory to Gerard, Seigneur of Wesemael; the new suzerain enclosed it with walls, and built a castle. The entrance of Bergen into history dates from that period. I shall not endeavour to follow the city through all its successive stages of development; for only one event, presently to be recalled, is of any importance to the French in the long lapse of three centuries.

The great church founded by Saint Gertrude was destroyed by fire in 1397. In 1442 it was rebuilt by the order of John of Glimes, who erected it into a collegiate church, with eight canons. I am particular about this date, because I shall have something to say concerning the monument which records it. After 1287, Bergen had its own special seigneurs, who bore the title of baron. In 1533 it was erected into a marquisate by the Emperor Charles V.; and, curious to state, the town, which until then had remained in the possession of one and the same family, changed hands from that time forth so often, that in less than two centuries its title fell successively to six houses, all different, and of divers nationalities! In 1558 it passed into the family of Mérode, in 1577 into tha of Wethem, in 1625 into that of Heerensberg, in 1641 into that of Hohenzollern, in 1652 into that of Latour d'Auvergne, and in 1722 into the palatine house of Pultzbach in Germany, which retained its title until 1801. I say 'its title,' because, from 1577, when it was surprised by Champigny, it was taken away from its hereditary suzerains, and remained annexed to the United Provinces. Before that date Bergen had witnessed a great feat of arms which proved disastrous to the Spaniards, to whom indeed the town seems always to have been fatal; and as its military reputation dates from that time, I will briefly relate the incident.

In 1574, Requesens, being resolved to force insurgent Zealand into obedience, had collected under the walls and in the port of Bergen-op-Zoom an armada which his Castillian pride believed to be invincible. His most able captains, John of Glimes and Julian Romaro, had taken the command of this fleet. On January 25, persuaded that they need only show themselves in such terrible array, to make the whole country tremble, and re-establish the authority of the King, they marched out in good order, and advanced upon the Scheldt; but hardly had they passed the point of Bergen than the 'Beggars of the Sea,' who were lying in wait, fell upon them. The first shock was terrible. The Spanish artillery was very superior to that of the Zealanders, and made great havoc in their ranks. Admiral Boisot, who commanded the fleet, lost an eye at the first volley; Captain Claessens had both his legs carried off; Captain Schott and Captain Valentin each lost an arm; but those gallant heroes, encouraging their men by voice and gesture, hurled them upon the enemy's ships, and in a moment the *mêlée* became general. The action was fought on both sides with equal determination. It was one heroic deed which inclined the balance in favour of the Beggars, and decided the fate of the day. Admiral Boisot was not only a very brave seaman, but he had a practical mind, and he had promised the men of his fleet that he who should carry off the enemy's flag during the combat should have a new coat.[1] It seems this was a tempting promise, for a young man from Souteland, near Flushing, named Jasper Leynsen, profiting by the fact that his comrades were occupied by a hand-to-hand fight with the Spaniards, scaled the sides of the Admiral's ship, climbed the mast, tore down Glimes' flag, and having tied it round him, let himself drop on the deck. On beholding this, all the Spaniards on the ships believed that the Admiral had struck his flag, and that the battle was lost. The rout was general, nothing but flight was thought of; but the Zealanders fought with redoubled fury, and the engagement became still more sanguinary. Admiral Glimes, Perenot, cousin to Cardinal de Granvelle, Captains Gaglia, Acugna, Meto and Elfiero were killed upon their decks. The massacre was terrible. 'No mercy was shown to those who were found alive, the half-dead were thrown into the water without being stripped, although they had chains of gold on their necks.' The Zealanders captured ten ships, and burnt as many more. Julian Romaro only

---

[1] Meteren.

escaped by throwing himself into the water, and thus gained the dam of Shakerloo, from whence Requesens in person had witnessed this terrible rout. 'You knew,' said he to the Commander, 'that I was not a seaman, but only a land soldier; it is not surprising that we have lost this fleet, for if they gave us a hundred, we should lose them all.' To which Requesens made answer, 'Let us thank God. The fault of this disaster rests neither with you nor with these brave men; it is to be imputed only to our sins.'

After Bergen had been surprised by Champigny, the States placed an English garrison there, under the command of a leader called Morgan, a man of tried courage, uncommon ability, and sufficiently easy conscience. His soldiers, much given to pillage, daring marauders, and in fact, generally speaking, a bad lot, took advantage of the liberty that was given them to make expeditions, which rendered the roads between Bergen-op-Zoom, Antwerp, and Malines, unsafe. 'They seized convoys of merchandise, robbed travellers, and made prisoners of the unoffending citizens, whom they afterwards put to ransom.' We cannot form any idea, in these days, of what those wars of brigandage were. One example among many will show to what a point the 'overrunners of the country' pushed their daring, and the absence of any kind of scruple. One day, under the leadership of two adventurers, Captains Cotwis and Augustin, they sallied forth to the number of three hundred, their intention being to push on to Antwerp, and to carry off some of the citizens—a number of whom were in the habit of walking every day on the promenade of Borgherhoudt, at the farther end of the city. This plan was cleverly contrived: one hundred of their best horsemen were to pass under the walls, to seize upon the passing promenaders from the rear, and drive them before them in the direction of Dambrugghe, where the water was very deep; there the others, who would have time to throw a bridge over the river, were to wait for them, and, having forced the unlucky citizens to cross, were to destroy the bridge, when being safe from pursuit, they could regain Bergen-op Zoom with their prey. 'The design was good,' says the old annalist, from whom I borrow the recital of this noble feat; 'but on the preceding night it had rained heavily, and the water had risen so much, that of the hundred horsemen, twenty could not pass, and those who passed took no more than three or four prisoners.' This insignificant result amounted to a failure; but the alarm being given in the town, the citizens came out in great numbers to deliver their fellows, and fell into the ambuscade at the bridge, where 'those of Bergen' seized about forty of them. Among the captives there were some rich merchants and bankers; but the honest marauders, who were quite men of business, refused to put them to ransom separately; they simply required 50,000 florins for the lot. We may picture to ourselves the dismay which this adventurous proceeding spread over all the country, and to what urgent solicitations the Prince of Parma yielded when, on September 24, 1588, he came, with 'much artillery, many gabions, masts, planks, carpenters, and boats, to lay siege to Bergen-op-Zoom.' The reputation of the place was, however, already so well established that the Prince did not expect all this display of troops and engines would be sufficient to carry it immediately, and he therefore had recourse to treason. Two Englishmen, who were brought into his camp, promised him that the gate should be delivered up by the disaffected garrison; and while he believed himself certain of the assistance of the two traitors, those honest fellows, selling him in his turn, led his best officers into an ambuscade, and caused 1,500 of his bravest soldiers to perish in an ill-conducted assault. Having failed in this enterprise, the Prince abandoned his design. It was, however, resumed in 1605, by the Sieurs de la Biche, du Terrail, and d'Elte, who on two several occasions, with an interval of two months between them, endeavoured to surprise the city, and carry it by a *coup-de-main*. The first time they came in small numbers, the second with a large body of troops, and both times they were very soundly beaten, and obliged to take ignominiously to flight. They had reckoned upon an easy capture of the fortress, because of its small garrison; but the citizens came to the aid of the soldiers. The conduct of the population was indeed admirable; everybody fought with extraordinary bravery; in the presence of danger which threatened the common country all differences of creed were forgotten. 'The citizens and inhabitants, who were known to be of the Roman Religion,' writes a contemporary, 'acquitted themselves of their duties upon the ramparts no less well than the others; rushing with cries as loud as theirs to the destruction of their enemies.' The bearing of the women was above all praise. 'It was an admirable thing to see with what courage the women and the children assisted the combatants, carrying powder, balls, tar-hoops, stones, and even the straw of which their own beds were made. Others took their children out of their cradles, so that they might use the latter to drag stones to the ramparts.' This double victory greatly magnified the military renown of Bergen-op-Zoom; but that which put the seal upon its reputation as a fortress was the defeat sustained by the Marquis de Spinola, 'the great taker of cities,' under its walls. During eleven whole weeks that celebrated man of war besieged Bergen in form, without obtaining a single important advantage—without being able to carry even one of its outworks, notwithstanding his repeated assaults. At the end of September, after two months of daily fighting, the fire from the place was still so steady and continuous that the Spanish general, wanting to erect heavy batteries at any cost, was obliged to give eight and nine crowns per night to the men who levelled the ground for the earthworks, and even at that high price he could not get sufficient hands. A few days later, on the 20th of

October, Prince Maurice came with his army and took up his position in the environs of Rosendaal, three leagues from the besieged city, and at noon of the same day, the sentinels of the besieged, upon the most advanced outworks of the place, apprised those who were commanding in the town, that the Spaniards were packing up and departing. Spinola thought he had gained enough honour by retiring in good order, without trying to push matters further.

This succession of glorious sieges caused the States to appreciate the sterling worth of the city of Bergen-op-Zoom, so that they resolved to make of it an exceptional place of war, and the illustrious Menno Coehoorn, Vauban's rival, employed all the resources of his science and his genius upon its defences. From that time forth Bergen was considered impregnable; covered by the Scheldt on two of its faces, easily revictualled from that side, dominating the surrounding countries, capable of being isolated by inundation, defended besides by formidable works, it seemed to defy surprise and render all attacks useless. It was, then, with disdainful astonishment that the allied army learned, on the 2nd of July 1747, that the French troops, under the command of Count Lowendahl, had received orders to march upon Bergen-op-Zoom, and take the place. Voltaire has given a concise history of this great feat of arms, in his 'Siècle de Louis Quinze.' I was about to refer the reader to that narrative, when an unpublished and unknown document came into my hands. It is the journal of Baron Samuel de Constant, a general in the besieged army, written on the spot, day by day, and almost hour by hour. Need I say that it was among the family papers of my travelling companion I made this valuable and doubly opportune discovery? I am sure that a few pages of the journal will be acceptable to my readers. This account, given by an eye-witness, proves that extraordinary carelessness had been shown with regard to the state of the fortress at the time.

It was so firmly believed that Bergen could not be taken, that none of the preventive measures customary in the defence of military works had been resorted to. Much care had been bestowed by the engineers upon the fortifying of Sandvliet, which the French took in twenty-four hours, 'but it is remarkable,' the Baron writes, 'that no precaution or measure for defence has been taken either inside or outside the fortress. The houses, woods, and hedges are left in their entirety, no battery had been mounted, nothing was prepared in the city, there were hardly any artillery, and at most six miners; in fact, everything is in so pitiable a condition, that if the town could be completely invested, this formidable fortress would hold out about ten days at the most.'

On the 14th of July Cromström arrives, and takes the command of the army, and also of the town.[1] He leaves the details of the interior to the Prince of

---

[1] He had been appointed by the Prince of Orange Commander-in-chief from the Scheldt to the Maas.

Hesse, Governor of the town, and its exterior to the Prince of Saxony. He hurries up the supplementary troops, the besieged may count on two armies of succour. During the night of the 14th to the 15th, the French open the trenches; during the 18th to the 19th their first parallel is finished. On the 20th, in the morning, at daybreak, they begin to fire on the town. They had thirty pieces of artillery and twenty mortars. The first bomb which fell upon Bergen set fire to the great church, and burnt it to ashes. From that moment the artillery duel was incessant, and under its shelter the French pushed on their works with surprising rapidity. 'Their works advance marvellously, the trench also advances considerably on this side; they push their saps with much speed and facility on the glacis; they already approach the palisades, and have traced the third parallel.' Such are the comments which I find under the dates of July 23rd, 28th, and 29th. The fire of the besieged, on the contrary, is irregular. Two sorties, one on the night of the 15th to the 16th, the other on the night of the 29th to the 30th, are ineffectual, and the men return 'in some disorder.' On the 26th and the 30th the besiegers unmask new batteries. On the 1st of August they push their saps to the palisades; on the 4th they effect a lodgment in the trenches leading to these, and in the night of the 5th to the 6th, at midnight, they assault, and gain the ridge with five salient angles. The assailants advance, but only step by step. so that the fight is about to become hand to hand. We need not follow them through this prolonged battle; but I wanted to give these first exact, and, so to speak, official indications, in order to show with what rapidity the operations were carried out, with what vigour the siege was conducted. Nothing can stop the advance of the besiegers. In vain, on the 10th does General Swartzenberg, who commands one of the armies of relief, attempt a diversion. On the 12th, reinforcements of artillery, artificers and miners from England, and a detachment from the great army, arrive; on the 13th, eight battalions come up. Each day is marked by a step in advance, each hour by progress. On the night of the 15th to the 16th, the French, having constructed a mine under the Zealand lunette, assaulted. On the night of the 16th to the 17th a sortie was made on the new position of the French, who were driven back a little, at a cost of many men. On the night of the 17th to the 18th, such alarm reigns in the city that the Commander-in-Chief makes arrangements for retreat; on that of the 19th to the 20th the French blow up the corner of the Utrecht lunette, and occupy its rear; on that of the 20th to the 21st they destroy a portion of the gallery. From the 21st to the 22nd they fill up the Dedem moat. And the brave soldier, who witnesses this progress of the enemy, becoming more marked day by day, betrays his grave fears and disheartenment in the following lines:—' The enemy's miners have completely got the better of those of the town, and in general the defence of the place is very weak, considering all the advantages which it possesses. The enemy's works are hardly delayed at all, the most considerable obstacle to them is the excellence of the fortifications only.' Nothing can be more interesting than to trace the vicissitudes of the attack and defence throughout the course of these notes taken on the spot. It is deeply impressive to watch the ring of fire and iron closing round the city day by day, to see its famous bastions crumbling one by one, and the ground, disputed foot by foot, drinking the blood with which it is wet.

But why should I linger over these details? My object was to prove that the taking of Bergen was not, as so many have said or repeated, a fortunate *coup-de-main*, a sort of audacious adventure, chiefly due to the *furia francese*. General Constant's statement is sufficient to establish that it was, on the contrary, a siege of the most formal kind; complete, deliberate, strictly conducted, in which nothing was left to chance, and the besieged could neither find fault with the tactics of the besiegers, nor accuse them of a single act of imprudence or miscalculation. I am anxious to arrive at the conclusion of the great military drama, and will only dwell on an episode in this technical narrative, which conveys some idea of the extraordinary obstinacy of the combat on both sides. The following is one of those facts which do not admit of comment: 'On the 13th (September) towards morning, the French blew up a mine under the Utrecht lunette on the right; the explosion destroyed the small portion of the gallery which still remained. Two officers and thirty men were buried under its ruins. No assistance could be given them, and it was necessary to abandon them alive to their terrible fate.'

We now arrive at the famous day, the 16th of September, and here, allowing the narrator to speak, I shall be careful not to change a word of his recital. 'On the night of the 15th to the 16th, the fire of the enemy was extremely rapid, that of the fortress had never been so bad. In the town less precaution was taken, and more security was felt than ever before. On the 16th, at five o'clock in the morning, after three discharges of bombs, the last of which were not loaded, the French mounted to the assault by the breach of the demilune, and also those of the Pucelle and Coehoorn bastions. So little were they on the alert, and so badly guarded were the approaches, that the enemy reached the ramparts without serious difficulty, and had no trouble in gaining the entrenchments, and occupying the ramparts on the right and on the left. The alarm was not given in the city until very late; everybody was asleep, all was in profound security; we may therefore judge whether proper arrangements had been made. Cromström could not believe in what was happening. The troops, stationed in the ditches on the side of the Steenbergen Gate, could not reach the city until after the enemy had taken the ramparts and were actually in the streets. The French had already passed the Fort, and entered the Steenbergen Street, when the troops of the garrison drove them back upon the Fort, where the battle began, and raged for two hours. It soon became so general throughout the whole extent of the city, that the French occupied the houses and gained the ramparts, even down to the Steenbergen Gate.

Retreat became inevitable; Cromström defiled with his troops out of the Steenbergen Gate; the enemy pursued the garrison as it retreated. Two Scotch battalions, who from the beginning had made the best possible face, closed the retreat, and were severely harassed. At the Steenbergen Gate the carnage was greater than anywhere else, and there was the close of the assault. The French shut the gates upon the garrison, and the drawbridge was taken up. They snapped their fingers at Cromström; they took prisoners all the soldiers who, being cut off, could not escape them. While this was passing in the city, the alarm reached the camp. The French had made a feigned attack on the lines at the moment of the assault in order to distract the troops, and discover the movements of the Prince of Saxony. The latter was as full of security and tranquillity as the town had been, and his dispositions were no better made. The French were masters of the Fort before the alarm was given in the camp, and a retreat was speedily resolved upon and accomplished with all imaginable disorder. Every post from the Wouw Gate to Fort

Pinson was abandoned with such precipitation, that time was not given¹ . . . the regiment retired to the highest . . . joined with the troops who had come out of the town, they . . . better order, the road to . . . where the following day they joined the army of Oudenbosch, of which Cromström took the command-in-chief.'

I have now exactly reproduced the details of this enterprise, whose conception, and still more its success, astonished all Europe.² This narrative, written by a general officer, who was as highly informed as he was loyal and brave, throws a strong light upon the *dénouement* of that epic siege. The contemporaries of the great event did not hesitate to apply that fatal word to it which is so often used to explain the disasters of war. We need not be angry with them that they have cried 'Treason!' But we may be astonished³ that the historians of our own time, that writers of our own day, should repeat the coarse calumny. Either partiality has blunted their conscience, or they must be very ill-informed. For my part, I can recognise no place for treason in that uninterrupted succession of murderous operations, planned with admirable skill, and conducted with implacable precision. Had there been any other means of carrying the citadel, exhausting efforts of

---

¹ The manuscript is injured at this place and several lines are missing.
² Van Hassell, *Belgique et Hollande*.
³ Especially M. Schwartz, in his work *Le Pays Bas, considérés au point de vue historique, politique, et topographique*.

this kind would not have been resorted to. In the street fight, after the invasion of the city, in the butchery of the great square and the Steenbergen Gate, I also look in vain for treason; I can only find brave, determined, and resolute men on both sides, who heroically did their duty. Another accusation, from which the narrative of General de Constant completely clears not only the conquerors, but the conquered, is that of a general massacre of the soldiers and the inhabitants of the city by order, which, with the systematic pillage of the town, or rather of its remains, has been gratuitously attributed to them. That in the fury of that street-battle, there was little mercy shown on one side or the other, I cannot doubt; that the inhabitants perished with the soldiers, that women and children were put to death in that house-to-house fight, is very probable; but, between such grievous and deplorable accidents, the inevitable consequence of so obstinate a fight, and a deliberate massacre, there is a great gulf. And that phrase 'they took all the troops, who, being cut off, could not escape,' also proves that quarter was given to the conquered, and that the lives of the prisoners, and consequently those of the citizens, were spared. In support of the journal of General Samuel de Constant I have found among the same archives another document, which is indeed an absolute confirmation. This is a letter, or rather a report, addressed to the General by Captain-Lieutenant Philippe Germain de Constant, his second son, who was also present at the siege of Bergen-op-Zoom, and its purpose is to relate his own acts during that terrible day to his father, who was at the same time his military superior. He relates that, being detached at Fort Pinson, he was cut off from head-quarters, and without orders. He would not abandon his post, was surrounded by the enemy, resisted to the last, and was then made prisoner.

'Although I must lose many of my men, and that I had no hope of being able to save myself, I made my arrangements to defend myself to the last, and to render myself up honourably. I divided my men on the right and on the left of the barriers, to defend a kind of dyke, by which the enemy could get to where I was. At the end of a quarter-of-an-hour, the enemy debouched upon my post with a great noise and in strength, and came on without difficulty to surround and overthrow me. I was taken with two officers and those who remained of my men. My two sergeants and fifteen men lost their lives. Monsieur de Gustine, who commanded, prevented the continuance of the massacre at the risk of his own life.' The reward of this great deed of arms was a Marshal's bâton, bestowed upon the conqueror, who indeed deserved it well. Count Lowendahl now became one of the most popular heroes in Europe, his name was upon every lip, and his heroic victory was celebrated in song. Another result, which was more unexpected, was the exaltation of the House of Orange. The hereditary Stadtholdership being instituted in the family, and that high station being combined with the control of the army, it found itself, in the person of William IV., in the possession of almost royal power. Lastly, as a final result, Bergen-op-Zoom lost on that day the reputation for inviolability which the city had so gloriously acquired. In vain, in 1813, did the French troops inflict a grievous defeat upon the English troops who opposed them, and restore to its ramparts a portion of their ancient renown—the virgin wreath of the city of Bergen had faded for ever.

CHAPTER VI.

AN OLD COMMERCIAL CITY—STREETS AND BUILDINGS—THE LAND OF SAINT GERTRUDE—EPITAPHS AND TOMBS—'JAN METTE LIPPEN'—THE PORTER OF THE STADHUIS.

ALTHOUGH Bergen-op-Zoom has utterly and for ever renounced military renown, and as much zeal and energy have been displayed in sapping its ramparts, levelling its ravelines, and destroying its bastions and lunettes, as were devoted in Coehoorn's time to the construction of those works; we ought not to be deterred by the vanished splendour of its past history from paying a short visit to the quaint city.

'Bergen has a very fine port on the Scheldt,' says an author of the seventeenth century.[1] We inhabit this port at present, and that pretentious epithet applied to a narrow passage of no great depth, adapted indeed to the flyboats, hoys, and Flemish sloops of Admiral Boisot, but which could not accommodate a modern brig, may suffice to give us an exact idea of the old Zealand navy. We are, in fact, in the habit of exaggerating to ourselves the importance of those

[1] See *Les Délices des Pays Bas.*

expeditions, armadas, and sea-fights for want of a standard of comparison, of an exact measure. The fleets, consisting of fifty, one hundred, or even two hundred vessels, which took part in them, are in our imagination composed of ships of the line, frigates, and even three-deckers. Nothing of the sort was the case. The missing standard of comparison and the exact measure are supplied to us by the 'very fine port' of Bergen-op-Zoom; let us bear them in mind henceforth.

We will now leave the harbour, in which there is nothing curious or remarkable to detain us, and walk along the margin of the great basin, whose quay leads straight into the town. What a change in everything! It is easy to see that we are no longer in Zealand. The aspect both of the people and of their houses is totally different. No more do we behold those dwellings of brick, with sombre walls, carefully polished woodwork, bright pretty blinds, and spotless window-panes. Brick is still indeed the material used in building, but here it is bedaubed with the greyish blue colouring so dear to the Belgian heart. Window-blinds have given place to shutters; gay woodwork no longer breaks and brightens up the dull façades; the modest shop-fronts are carelessly set out; the interior of the houses are carelessly kept, and at their thresholds sport big lubberly brats, fat, flourishing, dirty-faced, and happy, who paddle about, with unmixed delight, in the thick coaly mud of the street gutter.

The people themselves are of quite another race. The men are bigger, fairer of complexion, less red and less grave. The women are of larger build and not so slim; their skin, whether pale or high-coloured, has not the delicate transparency of the Walcheren faces; their hair is more abundant and less sleek; and the curves of the boddice and petticoat indicate strength and solidity, which we should look for in vain in the Islands of Tholen, or Schouwen, or even in Beveland. There the Zealand blood is found in all its purity; here, the blood of Brabant in all its vigour flows in a full tide through the veins of these people. Under those hardy muscles, those swelling boddices, those rounded cheeks, we feel that it courses and filters. The first glance shows us that we are among a people of the sanguine temperament; and further acquaintance with their character and customs confirms this impression. Independently of these general indications proper to the whole country, some officers, whom we met there, assured us that the women of Bergen-op-Zoom have a special and well-deserved reputation for exceptional good looks.

We find our course arrested by a venerable building. It is 'Our Lady's Gate,' the last remnant of those old ramparts so often attacked and so bravely defended. This sturdy edifice was surrounded in former times by a broad ditch, full of water, and then its aspect was more imposing. The ditch is filled up now, and the street crosses it; but the old gate, still at its post like a sentinel, has lost nothing of its proud, martial, and repellant aspect.

Two huge towers, sturdy and valiant, surmounted by long roofs, with pepper-castor turrets, and pierced with openings, small, narrow, strongly barred, which might safely defy all attempts upon them, stand out on either side; and, at the base of the main body of the massive building is a large ogival bay, with a little trefoiled niche, despoiled of its Madonna. This affords an extensive view of the inner street and gives access to the heart of the city.

When, having passed through Our Lady's Gate, we contemplate it from the other side, although it is equally coloured, bronzed, and spangled by the action of the ages, the ancient structure presents a different aspect. Here, it is the main building, surmounted by a tower with redans, and flanked by two octagon turrets, which stand prominently forward, while the great towers are in the background. And, although this new aspect of the Gate is less warlike and imposing, it is not less picturesque than the first.

On the right of the centre building, and on the inner side, is a steep and narrow external staircase. It consists of rough stone steps, which have been worn by many feet during the long years, and are now slippery and unsafe. A sort of pent-house protects this staircase, which gives access from the first floor to the interior of the old tower, now converted into a prison; not indeed a house of correction and detention such as are built in the present day, but a prison of the

OUR LADY'S GATE AT BERGEN-OP-ZOOM.

olden time. A real prison of romance and melodrama, with a vaulted roof, walls two yards thick, windows with triple bars of iron, creaking bolts, grinding locks, groaning doors, and all the paraphernalia of bulky chains and keys, of locksmiths' work and ironmongery, which explain the old French term 'écrouer.' After ten minutes passed in this place, a crowd of extravagant recollections and farfetched ideas are borne in on the visitor's mind, and all the celebrated escapes from dungeons of which he has read in history or fiction recur to his memory. A little more, and he, in his turn, would be tempted to escape, to saw the triple bars with his watch-spring, to make a hole in the ceiling with his penknife, to open a way through those thick walls with his pencil-case, so that he might escape down a rope ladder formed by patient industry out of candlewicks. But the jailoress, a plump and placid person, who keeps the key of this sombre dwelling, does not give one time to put such foolish ideas into execution. The supper is on the fire, the children are crying, and the visitors are requested to retire in prosaic fashion, to go out by the common door, and to descend into the street, by the same little staircase that has given them access to the famous tower.

We are in the street again, and it has assumed a different aspect. By degrees, as we approach the centre of the city, the Dutch influence makes itself more and more felt. The officials, the garrison, the municipal officers, have transplanted into this part of the city some of the habits and customs of the Northern province. Cleanliness, that primary need of the Dutchman, that quality *par excellence* of the Batavian housewife, here resumes its empire and all its rights. The shop-fronts are well arranged, everything is freshly painted and freshly varnished, and dark bricks re-appear in the façades of the houses. Some of these façades are ornamented with carvings. Formerly these archaic houses were numerous, but since the hecatomb of 1747, only a few remain. Walking straight on, we arrive at an ancient building, the Markiezenhof, or the Court of the Marquises, now transformed into a barrack. This is a huge edifice of brick and stone in the grand style, and which has unfortunately suffered much by adaptation to its new purpose. Its mutilated façade, and its spacious inner court, have preserved an impressive character, and a stamp of distinction, in spite of the hand of man and the action of time. The Dutch architects would find scope for their skill in restoration in these princely habitations, which are all the more interesting, as heraldic dwellings are rare throughout the Low Countries, and of all those which once adorned the land very few remain. 'Every popular revolution,' as Polybius says, somewhere, 'brings about with it a displacement of influences and of fortunes:' the tempest that emancipated the United Provinces obeyed this general law, and bore within itself a social transformation. The destruction of the Spanish rule struck the last blow at feudalism in all this part of Europe, and the castles disappeared together with their privileged possessors.

At length we have reached the great square, the scene of that terrible fusilade on the 16th of September 1747, and the hand-to-hand fight of which we have read the account. A fatal year, cruel days, and grievous hours for that poor city, whose wounds are still visible. The mutilated sanctuary that adorns one side of this once handsome square, suggests a succession of melancholy reflections. Is this the great church, the monument built by John of Glimes, and placed by the Seigneur of Bergen under the invocation of Saint Gertrude, whom he regarded as the celestial protectress most interested in preserving his pious work. '*Sancta Gertrudis, hujus terræ quondam Domina! Interveni pro populo tuo.*' 'Saint Gertrude, once lady of this land, intervene in favour of thy people!' Such was the dedicatory inscription traced by a reverent hand upon the portal in letters of gold. Vain was the dedication, no heed was paid to it; the invocation was unheard. In 1587, two hundred and forty years before the French cannon laid waste the sacred building, the 'Reform' effaced the inscription; and, having despoiled the sanctuary of its treasures, converted it into a barrack. It was restored at a later period to public worship, but again destined to terrible experiences. 'The first bombs which fell upon Bergen set fire to the great church, and reduced it to ashes,'—that phrase which I read a little while ago—rings in one's ears like a funeral knell, terrible in its distinctness.

No description could give an idea of the condition of the city when the French got into it. A clever artist, who was an eye-witness of these events, has left us a series of drawings, representing the city of Bergen after the siege, and I do not know anything more painful to look at than they are.[1] The ruined houses, the mutilated buildings, the torn-up squares transformed into pits and holes, all form a hideous scene of ruin and devastation; and in the midst of it all, the author places a group of pretty girls, in the widely-hooped costume of the period, laughing behind their fans at the indiscreet speeches of a gallant cavalier. Perhaps he wants to make the frightful picture that he places before our eyes seem more striking from this contrast.

The interior of the vast and ancient church presents a mournful aspect. Its wide nave terminates in a ruin; it is separated by a wooden partition from a gigantic transept; and the latter, transformed into a covered passage which leads from one end of the quarter to another, opens upon a space once occupied by the choir, which has long since disappeared. Nothing can be more impressive than this great empty piece of ground covered with briars, where there are a few great trees, where the grass

---

[1] These drawings by Pronk were engraved by S. Fokke. I was fortunate enough to find the entire series, which has become very rare, in the portfolios of the War Office at the Hague, and the Minister kindly permitted me to study them at my leisure.

grows hard, dry, and scanty, as though in a cemetery, and where the eye seeks in vain among the undulations of the soil for traces of the vanished choir. Those great ogival bays, now masked by common masonry, and those majestic arcades, whose fine architectural curves remain unfinished, produce a dreary effect. Still more melancholy is the transept, which has been transformed into a passage, and is now a receptacle for mutilated tombs, headless statues and broken grave slabs. A great company of heroes have been laid to rest in this noble sanctuary. The ancient Seigneurs of Bergen had their place of sepulture within its precincts; and after them, the Governors of the city. Morgan, who repulsed the Duke of Parma, Louis of Kethel, who opposed Spinola, were interred here. The gratitude of the inhabitants had decreed pompous inscriptions, bas-reliefs and statues to these valiant heroes; they rested under the shadow of great porticos of marble; but the cannon of 1747 disturbed their eternal slumber, and mingled their ashes, by breaking into their tombs. Of all these superb monuments, there remain only a few fragments, and we may think ourselves fortunate to be able to make out from whence they came. On the tomb of Morgan, we can still trace the figure of the old soldier clad in his armour, sleeping under the shadow of his trophies, whilst his mourning daughter casts a last glance upon her father's corpse. A mortuary medallion in the grand style shows us the name of Adrian of Reymerswaal, and we can also distinguish the slab which covered the remains of Jérôme Van Tuyl and Dame Leonora Micault, his wife. Pious hands have replaced the ashes of William of Ryede and Judith of Brakel under their marble portico; but the arch of triumph under which the brave Louis of Kethel rested has been robbed of its statues. Let us escape from this funereal passage, from this last refuge, so ruthlessly violated by war that it is no longer a place of repose even for the dead.

The great square to which we have now returned, boasts, in addition to the old church of Saint Gertrude, two other monuments belonging to different periods, and of very unequal architectural value. These are the Stadhuis and the Catholic Church. The latter is important because of its size; the great majority of the inhabitants of Bergen belonging to the Catholic faith, as indeed do those of the States of Brabant generally, it was natural that the sanctuary should be proportioned to the number of the faithful. Unfortunately, this church, which was recently built, dates from a tasteless epoch; in this instance, the architects of 1829 have displayed their debased style to perfection.

The Stadhuis, on the third side of the square, is a pretty, simple, even modest little edifice, but not wanting in elegance or character. It was commenced in the fifteenth century, and built at first in the Gothic style; then restored at different periods, notably in 1610, as we learn from an inscription upon it, but it was tastefully restored. It is three storeys high, and each storey has eight openings, four on either side of the roof, separated by a vertical line of niches, which enclose emblematical statues of Justice, Prudence, etc. This central portion is surmounted by a tall turret, terminating in an attic in the style of the seventeenth century, and the rest of the façade has a heavy roof, pierced with dormer windows, and partially masked by a row of battlements. The tower is not in the centre, but on the left side, and is reached by a flight of granite steps, quite modern, but very well adapted to the building. On the front is the device, '*Mille periculis supersum*,' which in any other place might perhaps be ambitious, but which here, after so many perils faced and conquered, is only just.

Having passed through the entrance, we find ourselves in a vast ancient chamber, a sort of ante-room, which has preserved a purely Gothic aspect, and we descend by a staircase into a little court below, where some remnants of very interesting architecture may be traced. These consist of an ancient tower, bearing the date of 1389—which was probably added after its erection—and the columns and capitals in a very good style, mixed up with more modern masonry, which formerly made part of the Exchange of Bergen. The little town of our days, was, in fact, a very important commercial city in the fifteenth century. 'Fairs were permitted in this place by privilege from all antiquity,' says Guicciardini, 'and were very frequent there.' The English especially brought their woollen goods; their counting-houses were more numerous here than in any other town in Zealand, and even now there is a street (the Engelsche-straat) which bears their name. In 1495, the inhabitants of Bergen-op-Zoom obtained from Philip the Fair an ordinance, which gave their city the Staple of all the woollen goods imported into the country from England, Ireland, and Scotland.[1]

All cloth goods, no matter what their destination, had to be produced, in the first instance, at the market of Bergen-op-Zoom, and there to receive the seal of the city. Any cloth goods offered for sale without this preliminary operation were confiscated to the Duke, and we find the latter menacing the inhabitants and the Council of Middelburg with his displeasure because they refused to submit to this exorbitant privilege. They never did submit to it completely, in fact; for twenty years later, in 1537, ' Jehan Hutton, governor of the English nation' at Bergen-op-Zoom, made his protests and complaints to be heard by the recalcitrant Middelburgers, and in 1552, the latter negotiated with James Henrison of Edinburgh, to prevent the inhabitants of Bergen and Kampveer from endeavouring to retain the Staple among them.

This commercial struggle was soon to come to an end. The sixteenth century was destined to be fatal to Bergen-op-Zoom. The city, which had seen not only English, Irish, Scotch, and Danish traders, but Spanish merchants and the 'factors of Portugal' within its walls, had arrived at that critical period through which so many other commercial cities of

---

[1] See *Inventaris van het oud archief van Middelburg*, No. 724.

that time passed, and which was about to be followed by a fatal decline. Antwerp had developed commercial activity which was destined to place it in the first rank of the trading towns of the north. The 'heiress of Bruges' speedily attracted to itself all the merchants who traded with those secondary places; it absorbed the traffic of the neighbouring and rival cities; and according to the testimony of contemporaries, it was not long before foreign merchants preferred the ordinary market of Antwerp to the extraordinary fairs of the small surrounding towns. From that moment dates the commercial decline of Bergen-op-Zoom, and, very probably, the abandonment and ruin of its Exchange.

The Stadhuis, which we are about to re-enter, contains some curiosities of unequal value and of different kinds. Among the number, are two fine chimney-pieces; one in carved wood, resting upon columns of marble, the other in stone, somewhat coarsely carved, but very Gothic and strange in design and ornament. The latter comes, if I remember aright, from the Markiezenhof, of which it was a chief ornament. Add to these an interesting staircase and some second-rate pictures, among them the portrait of a Republican general, with his tri-coloured scarf and plumed hat, whose name I do not know, and one of a certain 'Jan mette Lippen,' or 'John of the thick lips,' who in 1494, when his portrait was taken, had endowed his country with fifty-four little sons of Brabant.

And now let me present to you a curiosity of

another description, but one to my mind superior to all past and future thick-lipped Jans—a curiosity in flesh and blood, no other than the porter of the Stadhuis. He is a fat man; he has a broad and honest face; he has a kindly smile and a cheery bearing. In the sphere in which he gravitates, he is a veritable *savant*. If his destiny had not decreed that he was to be born in so modest a state of life, he would certainly be at present one of the lights of palæography in the Low Countries. Mere porter though he be, he has rendered greater services to his natal town than many of his more fortunate and famous fellow-citizens. I am about to tell you what he has done; judge and see whether I exaggerate. He was engaged to fulfil the functions of porter; that is to say, to sweep out the Stadhuis, to dust the chairs of the worshipful councillors, to watch over the ink-bottles and pens, to have an obsequious smile for the authorities, and a stern frown for the poor devils—to perform, in fact, all the offices of the little-lucrative post of a municipal doorkeeper. One day, his conscientious taste for cleanliness led him to a vast garret, where within the memory of man no one had ever set foot. In this dark and dusty place, lay, pell mell, a great mass of papers, large and small, registers, ledgers, and daybooks. These were the archives of Bergen-op-Zoom. Our brave porter opened books, turned over registers, looked through ledgers, and endeavoured to decipher the antique writing. At first he got on very badly, the strange characters puzzled him, the old texts were too much for him, but going from one to the other, from those which were well written to those which were badly written, from the simple to the complicated, he learned to read and to understand, and, when he understood, he was struck with the importance of the dusty lot of waste paper which lay before him. A sort of revelation of its value to the history of his native city came to him. Then he took an audacious, extraordinary, and unheard-of step; he asked for permission to put the archives into something like order. The Burgomaster and the Aldermen of that epoch believed that he meant simply to go at them with his brush and his duster, the request seemed natural, and they granted the required permission without any difficulty. This made him perfectly happy. If they had suspected the project which their porter nourished in the secret recesses of his heart, it is to be presumed that they would have refused him—and which of us have a right to throw a stone at them? Who could have supposed that a porter was a fit man for such a task? From that day forth he was seen at work at all hours, sawing laths, planing planks, hammering and nailing. Everybody was astonished at this carpentering fit which had seized him, but he was a trusty official, punctual in the discharge of his duties, and his harmless mania did not injure his good name, any more than his request to be allowed to put the archives into order had injured it. Months, years doubtless, passed away: at length our porter left off his carpentering work, his large cheerful face assumed an air of beatified satisfaction, his task was ended, the archives were in order! Then did the Burgomaster and Aldermen open their eyes, they saw what nobody suspected, what I could not contemplate without surprise, and what I advise you to see, if ever you go to Bergen-op-Zoom. Instead of a bare dusty garret, they saw a large room, entirely furnished with bookshelves; in place of a shapeless mass of dirty waste paper, they saw large manuscript books, chronologically classified, and archives arranged in perfect order. In one corner there still remained a great heap, which the improvised archivist had not been able to decipher. It consisted of Latin and French texts which, for a good reason, he did not understand, but the greater part of his work was done. From that day the man began to learn, he informed himself, consulted others, and the heap diminished. It is now reduced to a few documents. What treasures would have been lost if this odd palæographer had not turned up so appropriately! Thanks to this unhoped-for chance, the archives of Bergen, from 1313 down to 1800, are now in a state to be consulted by all who are interested in them; and their preserver goes straight to the document you require, and puts it into your hands without any difficulty or hesitation. I wanted to see the book of the Resolutions of the 'Magistraat,' his *dagboek*, or journal at the epoch of the siege of 1747, with which I was much engaged at that time. The porter found it for me immediately, and I read it with the greatest curiosity. Up to the 15th of September, inclusive, all the pages are filled. At the date of the 16th and 17th, two blank pages occur, surely more eloquent than those which precede and follow! I wanted to say all these things because it is well when one finds such an honest and remarkable person to proclaim it aloud. Some time ago, a man of talent and humour, aide-de-camp to a prince of the blood royal, asked me whether I knew anybody at Bergen-op-Zoom? 'Certainly,' replied I, 'there is a man there whom I esteem much, and for whom I have a quite particular veneration.' 'And who is the man?' asked he. 'The porter of the Stadhuis!' He opened his eyes, seemed scandalised, shrugged his shoulders, and turned on his heel. He thought I was jesting, but I had spoken quite seriously; and I repeat the sentiment now and here, because I hope that it may be better understood.

CHAPTER VII.

BAD WEATHER AND A DULL VOYAGE—THE VILLAGE OF WORMEL-
DINGEN—POLITENESS IN ZEALAND—GOES—THE SUSCEPTIBLE
JACQUELINE AND THE SEIGNEUR OF BORSELEN.

E left Bergen-op-Zoom early in the morning, much to the displeasure of our crew, who had been drunk on the previous day. The weather was dull, cold, and dark; a small, penetrating, icy rain was falling, and as there was hardly any wind, we were three mortal hours without making any perceptible advance. We had to wait for the current; and, to avail ourselves of it, we had to retrace the route which we had taken a few days before. We saw Tholen once more, but from a distance this time, and indistinctly through the mist. We sailed past the place where brilliant Rommerswaal formerly existed, and we doubled the point of Oostkerke. By this time the weather had become very bad indeed; the rain, which fell in torrents, was hissing upon the deck, and making its way through every crevice. Almost at the same moment we perceived that the water was coming into

the boat from below. Our sleeping quarters were inundated, our boots and slippers were sailing gaily about, going from one end of the room to the other with each movement of the *tjalk*. We sent our two boys to the pumps, but then the working of the boat suffered. At two o'clock a breeze began to blow; but the wind was contrary, so that we were obliged to take refuge at Wormeldingen, where we cast anchor. The wind, which now blew with violence, had cleared the atmosphere, but it obliged us to put the boat under shelter; so we resolved to avail ourselves of the state of the weather to land for a while, to visit the dams in the first place, and afterwards the village of Wormeldingen.

The dams are most interesting. These engineering works, which would seem gigantic in any country, are truly marvellous in this. We know what the Zealand soil is, how uncertain, changing, and mutable; nevertheless, a construction is placed upon it, one hundred and twenty yards long, sixteen yards wide at the entrance, and more than seven and a half yards deep below high water. Add to this that the enormous basin (1,900 square yards) is enclosed within granite walls of extraordinary thickness, formed of solid blocks of stone of tremendous weight. To what depth must the daring workmen who undertook the Cyclopean task have gone in search of a stable standpoint, on which to lay the foundation of such a mass? in what subterranean layer could they have had such confidence, in this country where the earth sinks in all of a sudden, where islands disappear without leaving a trace, that they ventured to build upon it so mighty an edifice? And, observe, that not only one dam is thus built: in the two islands of Zuid Beveland and Walcheren a dozen have been constructed. There are two at Wormeldingen. In the presence of these achievements, of problems faced with such courage and solved with such success, one is almost bewildered. We remained for nearly an hour contemplating these enormous works from every side; then, as the wind was still against us, we went on to the village of Wormeldingen, a few yards off. We hoped that we might be able to push on to Kattendijk, whose church steeple we descried at about a league's distance.

Wormeldingen is a curious village. Its trees and houses closely resemble a big box of Nuremberg toys just unpacked. Imagine a double row of dwellings, all squat, all pretty, all spotlessly clean, all painted in vivid colours, all built exactly in the same way, with the same materials, placed in two long lines, symmetrically intersected by straw-coloured woodwork. Before these two lines of houses, plant two rows of little old trees, with thick trunks and sparse foliage, all clipped, shaped, and pointed; all of the same size, and forming a kind of screen, no thicker or higher at one end than at the other, nor in the middle than at the two extremities. Then, in the street, dusted, cleaned, scraped unremittingly, where the houses are washed, and waxed, until you could not find a spot upon them, nor so much as a straw lying about, where the trees have a combed and brushed look, and not a leaf is out of its place, picture a population of honest folk, all dressed after the same fashion, the son like the father and the father like the grandfather, the little girl like the grown-up girl and the mamma like the old grandmother; and you have Wormeldingen as nearly as I can give you an idea of the place. Be careful to remember that each little house taken separately is a pretty bonbon box, and that the costumes taken separately are charming. These peasants, great and small, dressed entirely in velvet and black cloth, with their knee breeches, their coarse stockings, their shoes with silver buckles, their high waistcoats with double rows of buttons in filigree silver, their coats cut into their waists, their belts with silver clasps, and their gold buttons at the neck, look remarkably well. Complete this costume by a gracefully shaped felt hat, the brim raised behind and sloping in front, so that it forms a sort of visor, and you will have a notion of the dress which is worn in Zuid Beveland. This costume looks pretty on the children, elegant on the men, and picturesque on the old people; and it is always and everywhere most original and characteristic. The uniform of the women—for I really must call it so—is equally curious, and equally tasteful. From their most tender youth to the pitiless age at which the body bent by years, is bowed down towards the earth soon to be its last resting-place, the form and arrangement of the women's attire are unvariable. From the cradle to the tomb all these stout peasants have bare arms, the bust confined by a very tight bodice, over which lies, in graceful folds, a handkerchief, fastened by a coral brooch. The face is framed in a coif, with wide borders, which resembles a veil rather than a cap. A flat piece of gold hangs down on the forehead, corkscrews of gold adorn the temples, on the neck is a coral necklace, rings and brooches abound—in a word, these women wear a profusion of valuable ornaments. So much for the upper part of the figure, which is highly adorned, and generally slim and delicate. The slenderness of the women's figures is rendered more striking by an enormous petticoat, three yards wide, which is held out by a monstrous hoop resembling a bell; the body, from the waist up representing the handle, and the two slender legs the clapper. When seen from a distance thus attired, and standing still, the women might easily be taken for large dolls, but, also, for pretty dolls, perfectly new, quite uninjured, just taken out of cases, in which they have been packed so carefully that their complexions are not injured, nor their dress crushed. At Wormeldingen, at the end of the village near the church, we were surrounded by a bevy of girls, who had just come out of school. They were all white and pink, they were all dressed in this identical costume, every girl was exactly like her neighbour, and had a flower in her mouth. I felt as if some magician had suddenly opened a gigantic box of living toys before our eyes. To complete this amusing and truly picturesque scene, it must be remarked that the whole of this population is 'bon enfant,' very cordial and very hospitable. The men have always a kind word for the stranger, and the women a pleasant smile. You would never meet a peasant or a village girl upon the road without having a cheerful ' good day ' from them, and if there were many of you, they would not only say *'Goeden day'* in the singular, but they would give you a complex and plural greeting : *' Day drie,'* if you were three ; *' Day vier,'* if you were four ; that is to say, 'Good day to the three of you,' 'Good day to the four of you,' and *' Day zamen,'* which means 'Good day together,' if there were but two. Sometimes a roguish boy (there are such in every country) will salute a traveller who is going along with an ass or a dog with this *' Day zamen,'* but we must not grudge people their harmless joke, and this one is too inoffensive to vex anybody. The Zealand peasant is very polite and kind, cordial in his welcome, much less given to mocking strangers than is the Dutch peasant. If he meets a foreigner, he makes every possible effort to understand him, and to make himself understood by him ; he takes an interest in his visitor, questions him, and informs himself about him; but he never departs from the laws of politeness, or commits an indiscretion. He has an innate sense of good manners, he possesses tact which we look for in vain in many other countries, but which does not exclude frankness, for he will at once give you his hand, and open his house to you.

Two years ago, I was travelling on foot with one of my friends, a Frenchman, and indeed a Parisian, in this same island of Zuid Beveland, but down below Goes, consequently much more to the south. We two, quite alone, without a *cicerone* and without a guide, visited the delightful villages which are called Heer Hendrik's Kinderen and Heer Arendskerke's. During our long excursion, we never met any but kindly folk, ready to be useful to us and well disposed to make things pleasant. The Burgomaster of Middelburg gave me his card for one of his farmers. We had the rustic habitation of this good fellow pointed out to us, and ten persons offered to conduct us thither. The old peasant, a true gentleman-farmer, received us as a nobleman might have done. He introduced us to his family, and showed us his farm, buildings, and machinery. His wife and daughter offered us a choice little collation, and all this with perfect politeness. He was easy without being familiar, talkative without being importunate, and assiduous without being obsequious. My friend had hurt his foot, and our kind host took infinite trouble to find a vehicle for us, but every sort of carriage in the place had been requisitioned for the kermesse at Middelburg. The young men and the maidens had departed thither in the vehicles, and we had to walk half a league to the station. The good farmer was not satisfied with showing us the way, he insisted upon accompanying us to our destination; a little more and he would have carried my friend on his back. When the train arrived, he shook hands with us warmly, and remained on the platform making signals to us, and calling out farewells as if we had been old friends. Two months afterwards he went to see his Burgomaster, and related the incidents of our visit. 'They are very good people, those French,' said he, then after a moment, he asked: 'Are they all as tall and as healthy as the two who came to see me?' It appears he had been struck by our height and appearance.

These recollections are, however, taking us far away from Wormeldingen; we must come back thither, and all the more quickly, that we need not have gone so far to learn how hospitable is the disposition of the people of Zuid Beveland. At the door of the second house in the village, we saw one of those strange little children, dressed like an old grandmother, who are so amusing to observe. I drew near to look at her more attentively, but she, alarmed at the approach of a stranger, ran into the house. Her mother, a handsome young woman, had observed the fright of the child, from her *horretjes*; taking her in her arms, she advanced towards me, and said, 'Give your hand to this gentleman, it is very wrong to run away like that. The gentleman will have a bad opinion of you.' The child, only half reconciled to me, gave me a queer glance from the corner of her eye. I took her in my arms, and we were soon good friends. She was particularly amused with my eye-glass, made me look through it, tried to fit it to her own eye, and went into fits of laughter. 'There now, you see that this is a kind gentleman,' said the mother smiling, and then addressing me apologetically, she added, 'children are always a little shy.' 'Would a kiss do any harm?' said I. 'Not in the least,' said she laughing, 'but such young children are frightened by a mere nothing.' I felt strongly inclined to ask the pretty young mother whether timidity of this kind passed away from the Zealanders as they grew older, but I thought the question might be indiscreet, and so contented myself with two kisses from the child, and a smile from the mother. Was not this a good deal for a poor foreigner who had lost his way in the country? Then we left the mother and child, and waved our hands in farewell as we disappeared from their view. I recalled La Bruyère's saying: 'One should never give with a bad grace, the gift is the whole trouble; what does it cost to add a smile?' In Zealand the smile is never wanting.

At the far end of the village of Wormeldingen is the Church. On our way to it, we passed a fine modern house, surrounded in true Dutch style by a beautiful garden, full of flowers, with yew trees, clipped in quaint fashions, in the shapes of birds, flowers, and buildings. This, no doubt, is the pastor's residence; its modern style and its pretty garden add to the austere and venerable aspect of the old church. A lofty tower, flanked at its summit by four decapitated turrets, gives the sanctuary the appearance of a fortress. The interior has been so completely restored, that he would be a clever man who should determine its primitive form. It is fitted up with the utmost simplicity and plainness; its sole adornment consisting of two pictures, very ill-painted indeed, but remarkable because it is strange that their presence should be tolerated in a place of worship belonging to the Reformed religion. On one of these pictures is inscribed, '*De Wet is door Moses gegeven*,' and on the other '*De Genade en Waarheid is door Jesus Christ gewoorden.*' These two legends sufficiently explain the subjects.[1]

The village ends with the church. We had intended to push on to Kattendijk, but the quickly approaching darkness made this impossible. We returned by the school-boys' road, that is to say, the longest way, passing behind the houses, and thus we saw Wormeldingen under a totally different aspect from that which it presents from the main street. On the outer side, the heavy thatched roofs, thick hedges, old trees, and spacious barns form a series of charming rural pictures. We were no longer in the midst of a box of newly unpacked toys, but in a rich and prosperous country, covered with thriving farms and all the tokens of busy agricultural life.

The night that followed this excursion was very

---

[1] 'The law is given by Moses,' and 'By Jesus Christ come grace and truth.'

boisterous, the wind rose to a tempest, the rain fell in torrents. At about two o'clock the water got into the boat both from above and below; our beds were flooded, all our bed covering was soaked, and we were obliged to take refuge in our little saloon. Towards morning the storm abated; but we had to repair the damages, to have our beds dried, and our sleeping quarters mopped, so that the hour of high tide passed by before we were in a condition to take advantage of it. The day was lost to us.

We availed ourselves of these little misfortunes to make a trip to Goes, which is situated in the interior of the island at the distance of one league. Guicciardini said of Goes in the sixteenth century, 'It is a good little town, which enjoys several very profitable privileges.' And if the Venetian traveller could visit Goes to-day he would find no cause to rescind his judgment. If a magnificent church, its principal adornment, and the marvellous richness of the land that surrounds it, may stand for 'profitable privileges,' Goes is to-day what Goes was three centuries ago, ' a good little town.' And although it is now the only place in the island that can boast the title of a town, although like every other Zealand city it has its inheritance of glorious memories and lofty deeds, its name would be no more known than that of any other large village, were it not for the poetic halo with which the love borne to Goes by Jacqueline of Brabant has adorned it.

That strange and melancholy personage, that

princess at once guilty and interesting, upon whom history has not yet passed a definite judgment, had an especial tenderness for the good town of Goes, which was to some extent founded by her family. One of her ancestors, William of Brabant, invested it in 1350 with several privileges. Jacqueline herself strengthened its fortifications, rebuilt its walls, and instituted a fair, which enjoyed great celebrity for more than a century. When she became a widow for the third time, though only thirty-two years of age, the romantic princess sought relief from her private sorrows at Goes, and a brief respite from the terrible difficulties in which she was placed by the machinations of the Duke of Burgundy. There she believed herself doubly in safety, sheltered at once from the dangers of love and the complications of policy; for Philip the Good, who had already laid hands on her county and her domains, and constituted himself her heir, by the right of the stronger, had craftily combined the two. He had imposed on the princess the strange condition that she should not marry again without his leave and consent, if she wished to retain her possessions. In making her accept such a stipulation, Philip acted a very cunning part, like a knowing fox as he was. Meanwhile, Jacqueline led a calm and peaceful life at Goes, and there was no reason to suppose that she had any intention of venturing upon matrimony for the fourth time, when an apparently trifling incident set fire to her inflammable heart. 'Now it came about,' say the old chronicles, 'that in the year 1432, our Lady, the Duchess Margaret, her mother, sent her by certain gentlemen and noble personages some rich jewels, with several horses.' This present gave great satisfaction to the Countess Jacqueline, but as she was extravagant and had a numerous court, but only meagre revenues, she found herself 'denuded of money, and had not wherewithal to honour by presents and satisfy by gratuities the people of the Duchess.' She first applied to the Vicomte de Montfort, who had been her lieutenant, and afterwards to other friends, for the loan of some unimportant sums, but they were afraid of compromising themselves with Philip, and so made excuses, refusing the Countess the assistance that she required; 'wherefore she was so grieved, that she retired all in tears to her chamber, complaining of the ingratitude of her friends and servants, and of the shame which she would be forced to incur, if she were constrained to let her mother's people depart empty-handed.' At this crisis, William of Bye, one of her gentlemen, intervened, and proposed to represent her needs to Franck of Borselen, lieutenant of Philip the Good in Zealand. That a servant of the Duke would prove more compassionate than the Countess's own friends seemed hardly credible; Jacqueline, nevertheless, permitted William of Bye to take this step, and to her great astonishment, that faithful servant brought her back a favourable answer. Franck of Borselen handed over the money which she asked to the envoy of the Countess, and dismissed him with these words, 'Go, say to your Lady, that not at this present only, but all the time of my life, she may dispose, according to her good pleasure, of me and my goods.' The princess was touched to the heart by this chivalrous message, and from that day forth she held Borselen in esteem, which soon became affection, and eventually love, ' even to the point of her wishing to make him her husband, which she afterwards did, being married to him, secretly, in her chamber, in the presence of her servants.' Who it was that betrayed the secret of that clandestine union was never known; but Philip was informed of the breach of the treaty that bound the heart and hand of Jacqueline, and he landed unexpectedly in Zealand, caused Franck of Borselen to be arrested, and had him taken as a prisoner to Rupelmonde. 'The said lady, seeing this, followed the Duke, insisting upon her husband being restored to her.' To procure his liberty, she had to renounce her States, and hand over to her stern cousin her countships and lands of Holland, Zealand, Friesland, and Hainault. When she had despoiled herself of these, the old Duke permitted her to 'marry solemnly, and enjoy freely and peacefully the society of the said Borselen, her husband.' He even made him a Knight of the Golden Fleece and Count of Oostervent. But neither the restoration of the husband for whom she had made so great a sacrifice, nor the dignities with which he was invested, was to bring peace to that sorely troubled heart. Shortly afterwards Jacqueline fell sick; Borselen himself, whose part in all this matter does not come out satisfactorily, did not prove himself so kind a husband as she had hoped; and, 'in the year 1456, on the vigil of St. Denis, died this Lady and Princess Jacqueline, at the Castle of Teylingen, of chagrin at beholding herself thus despoiled, after having been Lady and true heir of Holland, Zealand, and Hainault, and the seigneurie of Friesland. She died aged thirty-six years, and she lies at the Hague in the Chapel of the Court.' So ended the romance that began at Goes. Thus, in the prime of life, and in the lustre of her beauty, died this adventurous princess, the slave of her imagination and her feelings, whose whole life an old poet has summed up in eight lines, which he puts into her mouth. Although the lines are of little merit, they are worthy of remembrance.

> L'amour par quatre fois me mit en mariaige,
> Et si n'ay sceu pourtant accroistre mon ligniaige,
> Gorrichom i ay conquis, contre Guillaume Arcklois,
> En un iour i ay perdu presques trois mille Anglois.
> Pour avoir mon Mary de sa prison délivre,
> Au duc des Bourguignons tous mes Pays ië livre.
> Dix ans regnay en paine: Ore avec mon Aycul
> Contante ic repose en un même cercueil.

It is a remarkable fact that the memory of Jacqueline of Brabant is still warmly cherished in this part of the country. Many events, some painful ones among the number, have taken place since her time, and are forgotten, while the image of the romantic princess is still popular in Zealand. Her portrait has its place in the poorest dwellings. Relatively recent engravings are to be found, which represent her shooting at the 'papegay;' and near Goes, on the site of an ancient château, which she inhabited at the time of her love affair with Borselen, stands an old tree, still called in the country 'the tree of Jacoba.' It is a chestnut, twisted and marred by old age, propped up in twenty places; but it is said to be that beneath whose shade Jacqueline was wont to sit and think of the generous knight who was then lord of her affections. Since her time the favourite city of the last Countess of Zealand has undergone many vicissitudes.

Twice has Goes narrowly escaped being utterly destroyed: the first time, in 1539, the waters were its enemy; a terrible flood invaded its streets, destroyed its houses, overturned its walls, and drowned its inhabitants. The town had hardly recovered from this disaster when, in 1556, a frightful conflagration laid it waste once more. Meteren reckons the number of houses which were burnt to ashes at six hundred; and Blaeu, who is always correct, though occasionally fond of flourish and mythology, exclaims, 'The two divinities, Neptune and Vulcan, seem to have sworn each in his turn to destroy this city.'[1]

In 1572 war took up the tale; Goes was beset by the people of Flushing. 'The place was well walled, but without ramparts, having only simple gates and ditches of little width.' Its garrison was composed, in addition to the citizens, of six hundred Spaniards

[1] *Theatrum urbium.*

and two hundred Walloons, eight hundred men in all, without artillery, and almost without supplies; and its only hope was in reinforcements from Antwerp. These reinforcements arrived under the conduct of Sancho d'Avila and Mondragon, who effected at low tide, and in the night, a passage similar to that by which the Spaniards afterwards presented themselves before the walls of Zierikzee. Guided by a peasant from Breda, they entered the river at Woensdrecht. 'Mondragon marched first, although he was already aged, and entered the water up to his waist; his soldiers carried each a bag of powder and fuses, and a small supply of biscuit on their heads and shoulders. They had to make two leagues of way, and had but five hours of low tide.' They effected the passage successfully, and on reaching the opposite bank they lighted a great fire to apprise Sancho d'Avila of the happy issue of this daring enterprise. Almost at the same moment the besiegers became aware that reinforcements were on the island. 'That unheard-of feat, and which seemed to be impossible and incredible,' so effectually frightened them that they raised the siege immediately, retired to their works, shipped their guns, with which they had already made a breach in the walls, in all haste; and in the embarkation of the troops such disorder prevailed, each wishing to be the first to get away, that more than two hundred men were taken prisoners or drowned.

This, however, was only an adjournment. In

1577 the army of the States entered Goes, and took possession of the town. The Prince of Orange had it strongly fortified, and thenceforth Goes had thoroughly well-built ramparts, with bastions, glacis, ditches, and a double redoubt protecting a long canal, and ending in two forts, the Ooster and the Wester Schans, which secured its freedom of communication with the Western Scheldt. From that time forth Goes was left at peace, and, with the exception of the tumults which took place in the year 1787, its tranquil existence flowed on without disturbance. The town is no longer walled; its ditches, partly filled up, partly turned into a handsome promenade, have nothing warlike about them, and its quiet streets become animated only on market-days, when the town is very lively, in fact, gay, and even noisy. Crowds assemble in its great square, and overflow into the streets. The pretty and picturesque little market is also full of animation, and one need only count the confectioners', *koek-bakkers'*, clockmakers', and jewellers' shops which occupy the market-place to know that this periodical invasion from the country brings much money into the city.

The Stadhuis stands in the handsome and well-kept market-place. It is a stern-looking building, which formerly had a warlike aspect, with ogival arches, battlements, and machicolations. It was ruthlessly mutilated in the last century, its belfry was decapitated, the shape of its windows was altered to the most commonplace form, and the whole building was transformed into a monument, not indeed devoid of character, but lacking elegance and majesty. At the end of a street, on the right of the Stadhuis, the old church of St. Mary Magdalen rises like a giant among pigmies. Its huge mass, rearing itself far above the surrounding red roofs, produces a very impressive effect. This church is still one of the finest, most elegant in form, and purest in style in the country; and it is, perhaps, the most important. In 1618 it was partly destroyed by fire. In 1621 it was rebuilt, at great cost and in good taste. 'Nothing was spared,' says Blaeu, 'to make it equal to the finest churches of Zealand.'

The little town of Goes boasts of no public edifice of any importance, except these two. For the former dwelling of a sovereign so splendid and luxurious as was the sentimental Jacqueline, this is a small number; but the landscape beyond the town is so beautiful, the country is so rich, that its surroundings make up amply for its architectural poverty.

CHAPTER VIII.

THE ZAND KREEK—A STORM ON A SANDBANK—KATS—THE SCHIPPER KRIJN—KORTGENE—THE APPEARANCE OF VEER.

T is two o'clock. The weather is almost fine again; the atmosphere is still heavy and warm; great white clouds, sloping away from the horizon, come rolling down over our heads. The boat is almost dry; we want to be off, so we give the word to set sail.

'We should do better to stay where we are,' says the *schipper*. 'The wind is coming from the west, and, unless we change our course, we shall make no way to-day.'

'Moderation is wise, even in the best of things, *Schipper*; and we have been long enough at Wormeldingen.'

'Very well, then; let us make the "grand tour," double the point of Colijnsplaat, and pass between Schouwen and Noordbeveland.'

'No, no, *Schipper*; because, by making the

"grand tour," we should sail upon the Western Scheldt, and we know it already.'

'What does that matter?'

'It matters very much, *Schipper*. We are travelling for the purpose of seeing something new, and we want to pass by the Zand Kreek.'

Therefore, the *schipper*, in a very bad humour, left me, and whistled for his *knechts*. While they were raising the anchor, he went down to the saloon to study the large marine chart. He is vexed at having to take this difficult and little-known course in uncertain weather, and with a bad wind.

The Zand Kreek, or Sand Creek, is, as its name indicates, a former gulf, whose sides were rent by a tremendous tide in some terrible night of tempest, and it has since remained open at both ends. Its channel has silted up by degrees, and it is now narrow, of irregular and variable depth, and intersected in three different places by large sand-banks, which still further reduce the navigable space. It is, therefore, easy to conceive that a prudent seaman, for whom the picturesque has no interest, who is not to be tempted by the charms of the unexpected, who is indifferent to the beauties of Nature, and almost entirely ignorant of the navigation of Zealand, should be but moderately pleased at having to set out on a cruise in which a disagreeable surprise may be in store for him.

The grinding noise of the chains—which is an invariable accompaniment of the lifting of the anchor—

has ceased; the *schipper* must make up his mind to the start.

'You positively wish to pass by the Zand Kreek?' once more asks the victim of our arbitrary will, laying his hand solemnly on the chart.

'Yes, *Schipper*.'

'Very well, then; so be it. Let us be off, and may good luck go with us!'

He goes up on deck, and we hear him giving his orders. A few minutes afterwards the glasses and plates rattle, the pots and pans in our floating kitchen clatter, the boat rocks gently, and we are off. We sail swiftly and steadily, steering for Tholen, and presently begin to make long tacks. These zigzags do not advance us much upon our way, for we have to make five hundred yards to gain twenty. For all that we are getting on, and we are seeing the country. A strange country, too; for these singular coasts, probably unique in the world, and almost unexplored, pass before our eyes under all their different aspects. Each time that the boat tacks, the landscape changes, and those arms of the sea, with their flat shores, that seem to be so monotonous, are in reality infinitely various.

It takes us nearly four hours to get well beyond Kattendijk—that is, to make one league. At nightfall we are at the entrance of the Zand Kreek, with the lights of Kats on our right, and the spire of Oostkerke ahead of us. The passage is narrow and difficult, and the danger of our course is increased by the fast-coming darkness. Nevertheless, we advance, trying to distinguish the buoys. Suddenly the *tjalk* receives a shock, and we hear something crack. The *zwaard* has struck! Then come some rapid manœuvres, and a backward movement. We are set free, but this is a warning. We take in sail, heave the anchor, and lie-to for the night.

Where are we? Nobody knows exactly. The night is upon us, thick and black, a sort of warm fog wraps us round like a garment. The water on which we float is phosphorescent; the waves are crested with strange lights, and as they break against the sides of our vessel, they fall back in a sparkling shower: our anchor-chains seem to catch fire from contact with them. Constant lowers a gaff into the water, and stirs it about; it is as though he were stirring a cauldron of molten lead. We let down a bucket, and then empty its contents—myriads of aquatic glow-worms—upon the deck. This amuses us, so we lower the bucket again; and the spectacle is one of the most curious and fantastic I have ever beheld.

The *schipper* follows our proceedings with an anxious gaze. 'That is a sign of bad weather,' he observes; 'may God keep us from ill!' Then he walks away, and we laugh at his fears. It is not long, however, before his gloomy forebodings are realised.

Towards midnight the air becomes oppressively heavy. All of a sudden, in the far distance, the darkness is rent asunder by a blinding flash of lightning; a terrific peal of thunder rolls along the heavens, and reverberates from the watery deeps. In an instant the horizon is blazing; the tempest is loosed upon us in all its sublime horror.

The rain, falling in large heavy drops, obliges us to get under cover. Sea-birds, driven about in the turmoil, pass above our heads uttering shrill, long-drawn screams of distress. The wind whistles in the rigging with a wild and mournful sound; the mast bends to its violence with a harsh grating noise; and the hoarse creaking and straining of the boat alternate with the voice of the *schipper*, as he reads aloud from the Bible to his *knechts*.

Our poor *tjalk* jumps about at its anchorage, like a restive horse tied to a post. Each moment it seems as if everything must give way in one final rent and crash—that the vessel must be torn in two by the violence.

> ' De ce vent sans respect, qui renverse à la fois
> Les bateaux des pêcheurs et les barques des rois.'

It holds its own, however, resisting stoutly; and the storm passes off—not, indeed, without our having suffered, for we are once more inundated, and this time it takes several hours to get rid of the water, which has got in everywhere. But the sun rises radiantly, and with its benignant smile our spirits revive. Everyone sets to work with a will to repair the damages of this memorable night.

We have worked at the pumps, and restored something like order among our household gods, which were half drowned and much knocked about. The rigging and the sails will have to be repaired. We have dragged our anchors during the night, and the storm has carried us on the eastern Scheldt into the Channel of Kats. Let us take advantage of this to go on shore. We will cross the island of Noordbeveland on foot, and the *tjalk* shall come round and take us on board at Kortgene.

At five o'clock in the morning, the boat shoots away from the side of the *tjalk*, and presently we are on the dry land again. The island is sunk in deep repose. We follow the course of the dyke in the first instance, and then we strike across the fields and come to a wide avenue, which leads us to Kats.

Kats is a pretty village of the rustic sort, with the long street, and the two rows of squat houses, shaded by two rows of trees which prevail everywhere in this corner of the country. The long street ends in a church, the only 'monument' in the village, if, indeed, that whimsical construction deserves the name. The church, of entirely original architecture, is something midway between a barn and a boat. Its brick walls are like those of a barn; its adornments, of wood painted green, and picked out with white, are like those of a boat. The whole building has strange curves, odd outlines, unusual shapes— all utterly unclassical, and unlike anything to be found in the drawing-books of the École des Beaux-Arts.

How changeful are human destinies! Who would suppose, seeing this village as it now is, that it was once the capital of a powerful fief; and that the authority of its possessors stretched far and wide? Who would believe that its origin is of venerable antiquity, lost, indeed, in the penumbra of history?

Kats, as the Chroniclers affirm, was founded by a fragment of that great nomad tribe, who, in the first ages of our era, traversed Flanders and Zealand, pursued by the invading Franks. Kats, a village of a hundred hearths, sent out colonies to the neighbouring coasts in the twelfth century. Kattendijk, whose spire we see from afar, was in the beginning called Katsdijk (the dyke of Kats), and long remained a dependency of the neighbouring seigneurie, to which it owed its origin and its name. From that old time, when so many other cities now populous, and long celebrated, hardly existed, dates the decline of Kats—so little known and so humble in the present day.

'In the year 1288,' writes Messire François Le Petit, ' all the isles of Zealand were inundated by tempests; and much of the country was destroyed by that inundation, in the which the seigneurs of Kats suffered great harm.' Thus does everything, and especially greatness, pass away. Nor was this the only evil fortune of the kind that befel the unlucky town. 'In the year 1530,' says Guicciardini, writing of those times as a contemporary, 'on St. Felix's-day the tide was so high that the waters rose above the dykes in many places. Those of Kortgene and Kats undertook to repair the dyke of their quarter, and to divide it into polders; but, two years afterwards, in 1532, the country was again inundated, and the hurricane having come unexpectedly, a vast number of people were drowned in their beds. Those of Kats went out to make an inspection of the dyke, and seeing the bad condition in which it was, they fled towards the heights to save their lives. But the flood destroyed fully one hundred and fifty men, and since then the whole of their country has always remained under the water.'

Kats reposes at present amid waving meadows and fertile fields, careless of bygone dangers, indifferent to former glory, even ignorant of former greatness. All around the town plentiful harvests spring up, and the wide grasslands stretch their green expanse, intersected by great grassy dykes which, from a bird's-eye view, make the island resemble an immense chessboard. On the two sides of those dykes, large fat sheep, suggestive of prime haunches and succulent 'saddles,' busily crop the fine close grass. Lavish abundance, exuberant wealth reign everywhere, and justify the ancient renown of that Noordbeveland, 'so fertile, and so mild and pleasant, that it was held to be the delight of the country of Zealand.'

This fertility, this 'fatness' of the earth—to use the old patriarchal term—continues until we reach Kortgene. Wealth exudes from the land, and on every side are proofs of exceptional prosperity. The pedlars, bending under the weight of their packs, do not deal, as in other countries, in cotton and knitted wares; their bundles contain such tempting futilities as hand-mirrors, silk handkerchiefs and ribbons. We met a shepherd, who carried two umbrellas. The superfluous, you see, displays itself at every step. Even that lonely little tavern—we should call it a *bouchon* in France—perched upon a desolate corner of the dyke, testifies by its signboard to this need for the superfluous. Here we find the fine arts associated with alcohol. Painting, in the form of a bad picture, and poetry, in that of two indifferent lines, recommend the 'drinks' of the establishment to the attention of idle boatmen or solitary travellers in these remote regions:—

> Op Katsche veer, bij schipper Krijn,
> Tapt men genever, bier en wyn.

This pleasing legend, being translated, is as follows:— 'At the passage of Kats, at Krijn the boatman's, gin, beer, and wine are drawn.'

Kortgene, where we arrive after two hours' walking, has a similar aspect of rural wealth. By the waterside, a group of idle men are passing the morning in talking of their neighbours. Village gossip is a proof of leisure. The little town, surrounded with trees, gardens, and orchards, wears a prosperous and smiling aspect, and yet it too has a lugubrious history. Adrian Hoffer, a local poet, who wrote in Latin, has related the sad story in some well-constructed, easy verses, which depict the past condition of the town, and the uncertainty of its existence. The following is a translation:—

> I owe my foundation to the family of Borselen—
> It was that family who caused me to spring up, a little town out of the waters.
> Hardly had I come into existence when flames, consuming my walls,
> Ruined my population and destroyed their goods.
> I raise my head again, my houses, prone to the earth, uplift themselves;
> Already my roofs shine with a new splendour,
> When my father, the Ocean, covering me with his tempestuous waves,
> Destroys me for the second time.
> One tower only remains to bear witness to the past of those unhappy places,
> To show how changeable is destiny, and how uncertain is time.
> Zealanders, learn not to trust yourselves to your natal soil;
> That which the Ocean may respect, it may also annihilate!

Here was no poetical licence; the disciple of Apollo confined himself on this occasion within the strict limits of truth. Kortgene, founded in 1413, by Philip of Borselen, was destroyed the following year by a fire, which originated in a baker's oven. The town was rebuilt, repaired, and restored by its founder, and endowed with a church, only to undergo such terrible devastation by the inundation of 1532, that Guicciardini, who visited Zealand thirty years afterwards, wrote the following melancholy observations among his notes of that journey. 'There was here a goodly walled city, named Kortgene, which was entirely swallowed up by the waters, so there remained of it nothing but the spire of the church as may now be discerned, and here and there in the surrounding waters some other spires and steeples of other goodly villages, which have experienced the fury and the tempests of the ocean, the which give notice to those who sail along that way and also arouse them to wonder and compassion for such disasters and misery.'

Kortgene, more fortunate than Kats, arose a second time from its ruins, repaired the ravages committed by fire and flood, and even became, it seems, a small stronghold; for, in an old engraving which I have seen in the great Atlas at the War Office, the city is represented with ramparts, all bristling with crenelated walls, towers, and ditches. Not a trace of these warlike braveries remain; but the little town has a tidy and well-to-do aspect, very pleasant to look upon. Its streets are wide, well built, and specklessly clean, and the footways are paved with long strips of many-coloured bricks and white stone; these stretch along in front of the houses on either side, like a carpet in marqueterie patterns.

While we were delightedly examining this quaint and uncommon kind of street ornament, a dull sound from afar attracted our attention. We ran to the dyke; the *tjalk* was in front of us, and the *schipper* was making signals. What did they mean? Why was the tricolor flag no longer flying? We advance to the far end of the little jetty, which is about five hundred yards from Kortgene, and forms the landing place. From thence we shout to the *schipper* to bring up the *tjalk*. He, however, makes us understand by signs that the thing is impossible; and, indeed, the wind, without being tempestuous, is blowing pretty hard in gusts, and lashing the water into big waves, which, coming against the current, cause a rough and boiling surf. The boat puts off for us, and, not without difficulty, we approach the *tjalk*, which continues to tack. It is troublesome and even dangerous to get on board; but at length we are safe on deck, and then we learn that the flag-staff has been broken by a gust of wind, and the flag carried away. It would be utterly useless to think of picking it up again, the waves are too rough; and besides, we must double the point of the Wolfaartsdijk before the tide ebbs, and to do this we must describe a long curve in a narrow channel, avoiding four distinct sand-banks. Quick! There is not a minute to lose.

For the first time the wind is almost favourable to us, our tacks are long, we sail rapidly. An hour more, and we shall reach the Veersche Gat. At this moment the horizon suddenly opens out before us, and the view stretches on as far as Roompot, at the river mouth, that is to say, away to the open sea. The vast sheet of foaming water takes a multitude of mother-o'-pearl-like tints, and on the left, Veer appears to us, shining with light and colour, its gigantic church and majestic belfry, its ancient towers, its lofty trees, and red roofs, are all steeped in warm and scintillating radiance.

It would be impossible to give an idea of the lightness, grace, and elegance of the harmonious outlines of that fair city, as it stands out against the silvery sky; it would be impossible to convey the effect of the reds and greens, the greys and blues, which cast their brilliant reflections into this vast sparkling lake.

In the course of my vagabond rambles, from the northern frontiers of Sweden to the southernmost point of Sicily, I have beheld, it is true, grander panoramas, and more imposing spectacles. The fjords of Norway are more sublime of aspect; and Vesuvius, seen from Posilipo, has greater majesty. Any comparison in this sense would be idle and absurd. But I cannot declare too emphatically that never, either in the North or in the South, have my eyes been surprised and rejoiced by equal intensity of colouring, at once bright and delicate, by a blending of tones so fine, harmonious, exquisite, and yet incomparably bold.

Let us, at once and for ever, get rid of the prevalent notion that the skies of the Netherlands are grey, dull, foggy, smoky and opaque. Let certain critics at once and for ever discard the astonishment which they, and their predecessors for the last fifty years, have been in the habit of expressing, that a school of masterly colourists should have existed in a country which is popularly believed to be destitute of both light and colour.

CHAPTER IX.

VEER—A HUGE CHURCH—THE BIRTH OF A TOWN—COMMERCIAL WEALTH AND SPLENDOUR: THEIR SUDDEN MELTING AWAY—A REVERIE.

 HAVE told you how delightful to an artist's eye is the spectacle of Veer, standing out in bright and harmonious colours against the silver background of sky and water. As we approach the town by the Zand Kreek, this charming panorama changes with every tack of the vessel, and, although constantly transformed, is always beautiful.

On landing we receive impressions of a totally different kind, but they are equally vivid and striking. We might not go so far as to sing, with Mignon,—

   'C'est là que je veux vivre,
   Que je veux vivre et puis mourir '—

but we do affirm that the brightly-tinted city is a treasure-trove to the archæologist, the seeker after the unexpected, and the artist. On landing from the boat, we cross the famous dam, descend from the dyke, and find ourselves at the foot of the old ramparts. The slopes are now under cultivation; the warlike fame of the glacis and bastions, whose long grassy lines we have seen from afar, is one of the glories of the past, and their formidable aspect has ceased to exist.

No sooner have we passed these ancient bastions than we arrive at the church, whose vast mass, rising up unexpectedly before our eyes, produces a startling effect. I have already commented upon the dimensions of these Zealand churches, which are almost invariably out of proportion with the towns sanctified by their presence; but never before had I seen such an example as this. It looks as if the whole town, with all its buildings, might be contained within this Cyclopean edifice; and indeed the poor old church—finished in 1448, partly destroyed by fire in 1686, despoiled of its altars and statues by the Reformation, damaged by the bombardment of 1809, transformed into a military hospital at about the same time, and afterwards turned to the purposes of a barrack—could shelter, contain, and lodge twenty times as many persons as the number of the fallen city's inhabitants at this day.

This stone Colossus stands upon the threshold of the little city, an heroic indication of its history. Like an ancient and time-worn bard, it proclaims to the traveller that lofty destinies have been accomplished on the soil he is about to tread. It speaks to him of greatness aspired to, glory hoped for, power won for a while. 'Before you look at me as I am,'

M

it seems to say, 'remember what I have been, and, above all, what I hoped to be!' The story of Veer is, in fact, an epic. The life of the city has been that of a *parvenu*, with such an ending as the Prodigal Son came to, only that there has been no return to the parental dwelling.

The origin of Veer was modest, '*ignobiles*,' says Blaeu. A few fishermen, having settled upon its desert coast, hired out their boats to travellers wanting to cross the water to a little town on the opposite bank, called Kampen, in Noordbeveland. Hence the name of Veer, which means 'passage,' and for centuries the place was called Kamperveer, that is to say, 'the passage to Kampen.'

> 'Het Veer op Kamperland deed my Kampveer benoemen.
> Eer ik een 'stad nog was, ouvringd met muur en gragt.' [1]

An old poet puts this avowal of its humble origin into the mouth of Veer itself, speaking to posterity. In 1280 Count Floris V. sold his territory to the Seigneurs of Borselen, who built several houses, and a castle, erected a monastery, and so established a colony. The second of these seigneurs, Wolfart II., built a church and put up gates. It was not until after 1350 that the town began to flourish. An old charter, bearing date the 30th of March 1350,[2] records that Wolfart, Seigneur of Veer, and Hedwiga his

---

[1] 'The passage into the land of Kampen has procured for me my name of Kampveer. I was of old, and I am still, a town surrounded with walls and ditches.'

[2] See the *Register: Oude Charters en Brieven*, No. 17. This document figures on the Inventory with No. 40.

wife obtained from William V. of Bavaria, in exchange for their castle and residence of Duneboke,[1] situate in the Island of Walcheren, and four acres (*vier gemeten*) of their seigneurie, the free fief of Sandenburg and Veer, and all the rights attached thereto. The results of this emancipation were soon manifest. In 1358 the town was surrounded by ramparts, and at about the same time its trade was extended; the fishing was carried on upon a much larger scale, and the seigneurs obtained from the King of England free entry into the English ports for vessels fitted out at Veer.

After Wolfart V. married Mary, daughter of James I. of Scotland, the trade of Veer made unlooked-for progress. The young Lady of Veer induced Scottish traders, her fellow-countrymen, to come to her city, and there they established the Staple of Scotch wool. In a short time buyers came from every quarter to purchase this valuable raw material. And now, on the great quay alongside the port, the remains of the 'House of the Scottish Merchants' still testify, by their architectural grandeur, to the wealth of those who built it, and to the commercial prosperity of the town.

In the time of Henry of Borselen the prosperity of Veer was again augmented. 'About that same year (1454),' the old annals record that: 'the Seigneur of Veer fitted out several large ships at his own charges,

---

[1] Duneboke is a seignorial residence situated on the territory of Oostkapelle, and almost equidistant between that village and Domburg.

which he sent into the high and low seas with merchandise. From the which there was returned to him very great profit, so that he acquired much land in Zealand.'[1]

Shortly after this time (in 1477), Wolfart VI. purchased for ready money, from Mary of Burgundy, the seigneurie, and, as it was then called, the *Vrijheid*, Franc, or Freedom, of Brouwershaven.[2] Under Anne of Borselen, his daughter, Veer attained the zenith of its commercial prosperity. At that time, if Blaeu's account be correct, as many as sixty ships came into or left its port every day, and its roadstead, which had then taken the name of 'Veersche Gat' (the hole of Veer), was one of the most frequented in the North Sea and the English Channel. Men of many nations met upon its quays. 'The cities of Amsterdam and Antwerp being as yet in their flower,' it was at Veer that Eastern traders disembarked, bringing with them the exotic products of their sunny lands; and to its market, in 1508, sugar was brought from the Canary Isles for the first time by the Spanish ships.[3]

Before this last date, Anne of Borselen, that intelligent and gracious Lady of Veer, whose modesty and prudence Erasmus has so justly lauded, married Philip of Burgundy, a prince born of a left-handed marriage, and entitled by himself 'the great Bastard

---

[1] *Grande Chronique*.
[2] See *Inventaris van het oud archief des Stadt Middelbourg*, No. 470.
[3] Guicciardini, op. cit.

of Burgundy.' Philip was a powerful personage, and of an impatient temper. His device was 'Nul ne s'y frotte,' and his first action was to turn Veer into a warlike fortress, with massive walls, wide ditches, and gates capable of resisting all attacks.

Just then, it seems that Middelburg took fright; and, great city though it was, began to regard the blooming and blossoming of its young neighbour with considerable uneasiness. All of a sudden we find Middelburg thwarting the commercial operations of Veer, and thenceforth regarding her as a dangerous rival. 'No man ought to prefer the place of his own birth to the entire country,' is laid down by the laws of Charondas, and that wise legislator added: 'Such a thought is the beginning of treason.' This great principle, which is so true, and so necessary to observe, was in times past ignored by the people of Zealand and Flanders. The proverbial '*amour du clocher*' has always taken precedence of the love of country with both races. Morose persons pretend that some traces of this sentiment still exist. For my part, I do not believe that they have been perpetuated; and I will not believe, what I have heard stated, that there are Flushing men at this day who would joyfully behold the ruin of Rotterdam, if by that ruin Flushing were to profit. In the fifteenth century, however, such egotistical tendencies found full development: a fact of which Middelburg furnished a striking example.

The presence of the Scotch at Veer had been, so

to speak, the point of departure of the extraordinary prosperity of the town, and to the Scotch Middelburg addressed itself. Great efforts were made to induce them to withdraw from Veer, and to settle at Middelburg; and lastly, to get the famous Wool Staple, that source of so many lucrative transactions, transferred to the latter city. It is exceedingly curious to trace the secret negotiations concerning this transaction in the archives of the Zealand capital.[1] At one time it seemed that the ardently desired object had been attained. James III. died, and on the 20th of March, 1477, the Council of Regency at Edinburgh deputed Jacob Atkinson, Alexander Irving, and John Patonson, to proceed to Middelburg, there to establish the Staple of Scottish merchandise; as the letter of envoy phrases it: *Stapulam nostrorum mercatorum mercanciarumque apud villam de Midilburgo*.[2] The men of Middelburg had, however, a sturdy adversary to deal with, as we shall see. During the whole minority of James IV. they preserved the Staple; and on his majority, they succeeded in getting that privilege confirmed. They even obtained that it should be published 'thoughout all the kingdom and the towns of Scotland, that those of the said nation should be bound, on pain of confiscation of their ships and goods, to come to the said town of Middelburg and its jurisdiction, and to discharge all their goods and

---

[1] See especially the documents in the *Inventaris*, numbered 444, 445, and 464.

[2] This document is also drawn up in French, as is the preceding correspondence which leads up to it.

merchandises in the said town, and not elsewhere.'[1]
But, on the accession of James V. everything was
changed, and that monarch restored to Veer the privilege of which the town had been despoiled. The
Scottish traders were commanded to establish themselves within its walls and in no other place.[2]

The Seigneur of Veer at that period was Maximilian of Burgundy, Seigneur of Beveren, ' Admiral-
captain-general of the sea.' It is interesting to observe
how ardently this powerful patron, an intelligent man,
and thoroughly aware of the importance of such an
advantage, espouses the interests of the new residents.
Some Scottish ships having been stopped, and their
owners detained, he addresses himself on behalf of
the latter to the Burgomaster and the 'Magistrat,'
obtains safe-conducts for them; defrays their expenses,
and causes them to be supplied with ' victuals, and
money in their purse, that they may return to their
hostel.'[3]

Such good treatment attracted traders to Veer.
Shortly afterwards, Middelburg lost not only the
Wool Staple, but was threatened with losing also the
Wine Staple, which was the principal source of its
commercial importance, its wealth and its prosperity.
In order to avert this disaster, the Queen Regent was
obliged to interfere on behalf of Middelburg; to
remind the too ambitious Seigneur of Beveren that
Veer had no rights over the wines of France, and

[1] See *Inventaris*, No. 1,771.
[2] *Ibid.* Nos. 1,854, 1,856, 1,859, and 1,860.
[3] *Ibid.* No. 2,019, dated July 25, 1518.

could only receive at its port, such as came ' of their free will, without being solicited or induced by the said Seigneur of Beveren or others, and without making an advantage, or having any contract, treaty, or understanding whatsoever.' [1]

It appears that the remonstrances of the Queen Regent were less effectual than was expected. Some years later, we find Middelburg demanding an authoritative confirmation of its privileges of the Staple and Standard, and complaining ' that also the towns of Flushing and Veer, belonging to the Seigneur of Beveren, have, by degrees, owing to the favour shown by the said seigneur, as admiral, to the merchants frequenting the said cities, more than to the others, begun to be frequented by foreign nations and traders.'

The Zealand capital reiterates on this occasion that it has always possessed the privilege of receiving ' the wines of Spain, Burgundy, and others coming from the side of the West.' It insists that its position is less favourable than that of the rival towns, ' situated on the same island, which have two arms, and entrance to the sea, and are more propitious for the arrival of boats and ships ; ' while the capital is accessible only by ' a certain long canal, difficult to pass.' Lastly, this remonstrance concludes by pointing out that ' the ruin of the town, to the great prejudice as much of her Majesty as of the other neighbouring countries, is evident.'

The Emperor, Charles V., and afterwards his son

[1] See *Inventaris*, No. 2,172, dated January 9, 1556.

Philip II., being very anxious to settle these differences, endeavoured as far as possible to hold the balance equally between the two cities. To Middelburg they left its privilege of the wines, and they erected its two rivals into marquisates. They also made Veer a port of war, and fixed the residence of the 'Admirals and Councillors of the Admiralty of the Low Countries there.' They established a general arsenal, and 'a house of artillery and other munitions proper for war upon the sea, and things requisite for the fleet.'

All this brings us to the sixteenth century, that is to say, to the zenith of the fortunes of Veer. The town is then famous 'for a good fishery of herrings and other salted fish.' 'The good situation of its roadstead and harbour causes it to be frequented by all foreign traders.' 'Its citizens are very civil and courteous by reason of the frequentation of nobles.' Maximilian of Beveren, its first marquis, 'holds in the town his residence and magnificent court.' It is also in possession of a quantity of 'fair privileges and high prerogatives,' and as many as nine villages are placed under its jurisdiction. 'Among these the seigneurie of Oostkapelle, which properly belongs to it.' Finally, its seigneur, 'by an ancient statute or ordinance enjoys such a pre-eminence that he alone, without any other making competition with him, is entitled to speak for the Estate of the nobility of Zealand'[1] in all deliberations upon affairs.

[1] Guicciardini, Meteren, Le Petit, &c.

It is well to recall such facts in the midst of all these ruins, in the presence of the desolation which now reigns in the solitary streets, on the deserted quays. It is well to recall them also because they had a decisive influence on the great events that mark the end of the sixteenth century.

The antagonism of Middelburg and Veer played an important part in the working out of the destinies of both cities. Veer, with its marquisate, acquired by the Prince of Orange, passing through the hands of William the Taciturn, and becoming a portion of the patrimony of the House of Nassau, had long before this time manifested a love of liberty and a desire for independence. It had been, we say it to its honour, from the first day, almost from the first hour, one of the centres of rebellion against the King of Spain; and Meteren admits that the brave seamen who, under the direction of Admiral Boisot, destroyed the famous armada of Don Luis de Requesens, before Bergen-op-Zoom, came chiefly from the valiant port of Veer.

Middelburg, on the contrary, from a spirit of pride, jealousy and rivalry, much more than from conviction, continued to be the last bulwark of foreign oppression, and from motives of enmity rather than fidelity, exposed itself to all the horrors of that siege, to whose incidents we shall shortly recur.

Animosity between the two rivals had arrived at its highest pitch; and the 'Magistrat' had forbidden the citizens of Middelburg, under pain of arrest and the confiscation of their goods, not only to visit the people of Veer and Flushing, but even to keep up any corrrespondence with them.[1] They were in his eyes what he called them, 'rebellious beggars.' In this struggle it was the capital which was beaten, and nevertheless, by a strange fatality, from that time it made great strides towards supremacy. From the day of its fall it attracted all the living forces of its young antagonist to itself, and from that moment the latter had to date the paling of its brilliant star, soon to suffer total eclipse. The destinies, which, to quote an old writer, ' permitted Veer to develop itself under the ægis of so great and illustrious a prince as William the Silent, seem, having done this, to have exhausted their favours.' Since then, only one brilliant day is recorded upon the pages of the history of Veer.

After having raised the siege of Bergen-op-Zoom on the 1st of September 1588, Prince Maurice repaired to Veer to take possession of his marquisate. The young conqueror received an enthusiastic and splendid welcome. ' He was met with the solemnities and ceremonies customary in such cases, and he distributed money on which were stamped the arms of Nassau and Veer, bound together with a doubly-knotted cord, with the inscription, ' *Nodus indissolubilis.*'[2] The houses were draped, arches of triumph were erected, and the streets were strewn with leaves

---

[1] See *Inventaris van het oud archief der Stadt Middelbourg*, No. 2,573.
[2] *Grande Chronique de Hollande et de Zélande.*

and flowers.' Veer was lovingly bedecked, dressed up for her last triumph, for from that day forth her steady decline was never arrested.

I have before me the original plan of the city, made in 1550 by Jacob van Deventer.[1] This old drawing, alike elegant and simple, shows us the former boundary of the city, much more extensive than it now is, and full of dwelling-houses. There is not a gap, not a bit of waste land, not a trace of decay. The streets are lined with tall and closely built houses, and their lines stretch to the verge of the open country. Overlapping the ramparts, and scattered among gardens and plantations, they form those country habitations in which, as Blaeu says, ' the merchants found the double advantage that they could superintend their affairs, while yielding to the pleasures of the country.'[2]

Even when the old geographer drew the charming picture of the fair city that he has left us, Veer had already lost a portion of its splendour. The girdle formed by its walls fitted it too loosely, and the ruin which was then commencing soon changed into disaster. Entire quarters have disappeared; of the rows of houses which bordered the north side of its harbour there remains nothing. Silence and solitude reign; on every side is a cruel and woeful void. This sudden foundering of a once flourishing city is an extraordinary event. The arms of the town are two towers, from which spring two savages, each holding

---

[1] At the *Zeeuwsch genootschap der wetenschappen.* [2] Blaeu, *Theatrum.*

a cord from which hangs a shield. The two towers represent those which formerly defended the entrance of the port. The way into the city lay between them. One has entirely disappeared; it was suddenly swallowed up by the water.

The little city of Kampen, to which Kamperveer owed, not only its name but its existence, and which figures, with its boundaries, its houses and its streets, upon an old manuscript map of the fifteenth century, to be seen at the Dutch War Office, has also disappeared. Kampen also sank suddenly into the abyss, leaving no more trace than there remained of the tower.

In the presence of such a remorseless destiny, one is oppressed with sadness. Such a succession of catastrophes is too terrible to be recorded without emotion; and, when we compare the brilliant past with the deserted present, we are constrained to pity, and filled with regret.

In the evening, at that solemn hour when all nature seems to reflect, while the setting sun cast a golden light over the dreary scene, I contemplated the dying city. In the midst of the impressive silence of that great solitude, I meditated long on the ruined splendour, the great fortunes which the ruthless hand of fate had wrested from old Veer.

CHAPTER X.

A DISPUTE ON BOARD—AN ANTIQUE FOUNTAIN—A WALK THROUGH RUINS—THE STADHUIS—THE CUP OF VEER—AN HEROIC WOMAN —AN EXCURSION IN NOORDBEVELAND—A 'ZINKSTUK.'

THIS morning a dispute took place on board. While we were taking our coffee, the *knechts* rebelled against the parental authority of the *schipper*. They complained that they had to do too much work, and that instead of going from village to village, we made long, difficult, and even dangerous trips. The discussion, which began by reproaches muttered with half-filled mouths—the men were trying to talk and to eat at the same time—soon took a louder tone, and lastly became abusive.

We pretended not to hear all this. It was no business of ours to interfere in quarrels of this kind. The *schipper* ought to be master of his men, and to know how to make them obey him. The incident, however, puts us out considerably, as we are expecting a visit from some friends, and it would not be pleasant to have discussions of this kind arising just at the hour of their arrival. For this once, however, we mean to ignore everything; and wishing to leave more ample freedom of action to the *schipper*, we have taken our sketch-books and colour-boxes, and set off to the town.

Up to the present we have been occupied in diving into the history of old Kampveer, rather than in a detailed inspection of the town. Let us make up for lost time, and examine this strange place in a leisurely fashion.

Having passed the ramparts, we find ourselves, you will remember, at the foot of the tower of a colossal church. This stone giant, solitary in the midst of the grassy enclosure where it seems to crouch, shaded from the road by grey walls, presents a grim aspect. It has been in turns a sanctuary, a hospital, and a barrack. Its great ogival bays have been closed up, and its many coloured windows replaced by monochrome brick. To meet the necessities of the uses to which it has been put, a number of little openings, which look like the menacing loopholes of old times, have been made in its thick walls. It has preserved the sombre and morose aspect of its two most recent adaptations, something of the hospital and something of the barrack yet linger about it; it has retained the stern and forbidding physiognomy of the latter and the sorrowful appearance of the former; and both these contradict that which has survived of its original aspect and purpose. Let us turn away our gaze from this forbidding object, all the more quickly that, on the other side of the road, is a delightful little building, a beautiful fountain, with the sight of which we may calm our minds and rejoice our eyes. This pretty little edifice, with its straight black roof and its fanciful ogives; with its slender columns and its flaring armorial bearings, hidden like an ancient dryad in a thicket, modestly shaded by great trees like a nymph, is thoroughly Gothic, but nevertheless it seems lost among its morose and dull surroundings, and almost out of place in our age and in this country.

We instinctively look for something else; we fancy that we shall presently see some chattering housewife, in the costume of the Middle Ages, the large Flemish collar and the little cap, coming along the road, with her shining copper pail hanging over her arm. We lend an attentive ear to the sighing of the breeze, thinking that it will bear to us a song of these old days, sweetly warbled by a laughing and still innocent Marguerite, who will presently lean on the margin of the granite basin, and dream of the unknown. But no! echo remains mute, the fountain is deserted; no noise disturbs the stern solitude, no joyous strain comes to enliven it.

Let us go into the avenue, or rather into the street, for such it was formerly. Where trees and glades are now were once handsome and stately houses, and there hardly remains a half-ruined house or a tumble-down cottage here and there, to mark out what was once the line of habitation.

The houses that still remain are not safe from the misdoing of man, almost every year one of them is destroyed, but indeed what would it avail to preserve them? If left empty, they would tumble down of themselves; if occupied, they do not pay for repair. We went one day into a shopkeeper's house upon the port, one of the largest and loftiest of the still remaining dwellings: on all the floors were huge rooms, and there was a spacious court and a garden. Two or three families might easily have lived there, and the rent paid by the only inhabitant does not amount to quite two florins a week.

Let us go on a few steps. At the back of the church there was formerly a great thoroughfare, but now we may regretfully follow the traces of former streets; the lines are there, but of houses none remain. A wide grassy expanse replaces the habitations which were formerly crowded together here; and a post with a large board, on which are inscribed the odd-sounding words, '*Verboden overloop*,'[1] forbids the passer-by to profane the place whence so many peaceful existences have passed away into eternity.

From this spot the view is charming; small houses, harmoniously grouped, mingle their warm tints and their sparkling light with the quieter and softer shades of the beautiful trees, and the rich ver-

---

[1] Literally, 'It is forbidden to cross.' The meaning is 'No trespassers.'

dure of the fields; while the belfry, elegant in form and picturesque of aspect, above the lofty roof of the Stadhuis, is the crown of this fair scene; amid which it has for centuries marked the hours, good or bad, sad or joyous, as they glide away. This belfry is a curious object. It consists of a square tower, cold and bare of outline for three parts of its height, but then comes an elegant spire, terminating in an octagon 'pear,' flanked with pinnacles and pyramids, and so beset with consoles, balustrades, dormer windows, and weathercocks, that it is a sort of architectural porcupine.

The Stadhuis of Veer is one of the finest civic monuments in the country. It is in good style, in good taste, and admirably preserved. Except the belfry, which received much of its ornamentation at the end of the sixteenth century, the whole building has remained in its primitive form, and the façade is just as it came from the hands of the Burgundian architect in 1474. Nobody has harmed it, the years only have set their mark upon it, but the touch of time is the adornment of buildings: far from spoiling the Stadhuis of Veer, the ages have added harmony of colouring to the elegance of its lines. The façade has two storeys, each with six apertures; the windows are surmounted by a surbased and trefoiled arch. A great black roof, flanked by two octagon turrets which rest on corbels, rises to the height of two gables, with redans, and three rows of dormers. Add to this, seven projecting niches, which divide the windows of

THE STADHUIS OF VEER.

the first storey by their open-work canopies and elegant consoles; and in those niches the statues of seven ladies and seigneurs of Veer: Henry, Jacqueline, Adolph, Charlotte, Wilfart, Jan, and Philip.

A double flight of railed steps, modern in form, but not at all inharmonious, leads to the ground floor, while a pillory, placed on the left, and completing the façade, reminds us of the justiciary rights formerly wielded by the 'Magistrat' of this great commercial city.

In the interior of the Stadhuis, we find another and more curious kind of attestation of those rights. Three clenched fists, in bronze, are suspended above the chimney-piece of the former Hall of Justice: they were placed there by three men of Veer who rebelled against the authority of the city, and were condemned to have their hands cut off. By making this present in metal, they obtained the commutation of the sentence into an execution in effigy. It must be admitted that they got off cheaply. The Room of the Three Fists, which is the old Vierschaar, has preserved its primitive form and decoration, and is one of the most curious apartments to be seen in Zealand. The dark brown wood carvings, the great benches with their red cushions, the chair of justice with its desk, back-cushion, and rod, emblem of justiciary authority, are exactly the same as they were when the last sentence was pronounced by the last 'Magistrat.' Even the solitary picture in the room—we cannot say much for its artistic qualities

—adds to the character of this well-preserved Hall. This picture represents the Council of Ten sitting in judgment. I do not know whether mere chance or premeditation presided over the choice of this subject, but I lean towards the former hypothesis. Veer comparing itself to Venice, and its 'Magistrat' to the terrible Council, would be too daring.

In the Stadhuis there is preserved only one curiosity, but that is exquisite in every sense, and justly celebrated. It is that famous cup which was given to the town in 1551, by Maximilian of Burgundy, its first Marquis. Maximilian of Burgundy had it from Maximilian von Buren, whose most famous deeds of arms it records. I have spoken elsewhere of this renowned gem,[1] and I shall now content myself with reminding you that in 1867 the Cup of Veer was exhibited in Paris, in the section of '*l'histoire du Travail*,' and that one of the princes of finance offered the enormous sum of 100,000 francs for it. The Burgomaster and Aldermen of Veer refused the money, preferring to preserve this historical treasure, the glory of their Stadhuis, and I sincerely congratulate them upon so patriotic a decision.

Another *souvenir*, for which they would not be offered the same price, but which is no less creditable to the history of Veer, is a simple record inscribed upon its register of marriages, and which I

---

[1] See *Objets d'art et de curiosité tirés des grandes collections hollandaises*, page 23.

cannot read without a certain emotion. It bears date the 2nd of July, 1608, and I transcribe it here. '*Mynheer Hugo de Groot, advocaat fiscaal van Holland, Zeeland, en West Friesland, Jongman an Delft, wonvende in S'Graven haage, met Jonkvrauw Maria Reygersbergh, Jonge dochter van Veer*,' which being translated is, 'Mr. Hugo Grotius, advocate fiscal of Holland, Zealand, and West Friesland, bachelor, of Delft, dwelling at the Hague, with Miss Maria Reygersbergh, spinster, of Veer.'

You have guessed that the illustrious Grotius, that great, good man of genius who, after having been the friend of Olden-Barnevelt, was to become the Councillor and the Ambassador of Christina of Sweden, is in question. It was indeed to Veer that he came in 1608 to find the devoted partner, to whom he owed first his happiness and afterwards his liberty; for it was Maria Reygersbergh, this proud young Zealander, this daughter of Veer, born in the *Kapellestraat*, consequently quite near the place where we now are, who contrived his escape from the prison of Loevestein, where he was closely guarded, and thus saved him from lifelong incarceration.

'He had,' says Du Maurier, who knew and loved him,[1] 'no other consolation than the society of his wife, and a quantity of books which his friends were allowed to lend him. They sent him a great coffer full, which he sent back after having devoured them. His wife, observing that his guards being tired of

[1] *Mémoires pour servir à l'histoire de Hollande.*

so often inspecting and searching the great coffer full of books and soiled linen—which latter was sent to be washed at Gorcum, a neighbouring city—let it pass without opening it, advised her husband to place himself in the coffer after she had made holes in it with a gimlet, at the spot where his head would come, so that he could breathe, and not be stifled. He took her advice, and was safely carried away to Gorcum, to the house of one of his friends, from whence he went to Antwerp, by the ordinary conveyance, having passed through the public square, disguised as a carpenter, with a footrule in his hand.'

'This clever woman,' adds Du Maurier, 'pretended that her husband was very ill, so as to give him time to get away, but when she thought he was in safety she informed the guards that the bird had flown. At first they were about to proceed against her, and certain judges were of opinion that she ought to be kept in prison in the place of her husband, but she was set at liberty by the majority of votes, and she was praised by everybody.'

After I had inspected the treasures of the Stadhuis, I began to draw the façade, whereupon a native of Veer, who had been observing me from afar, approached, and opened a conversation by a phrase which reminded me of certain classic commencements. 'And I, also—I make drawings.' With this he went away, and presently returning with his sketches, which showed more goodwill than ability, he narrated to me the story of his life, which revealed more fortitude than fortune. He was now employed in the post-office at Veer, but had formerly served in a hussar regiment, and consequently had a small pension; this, added to the emoluments of his post, made his yearly income three hundred and fifty florins, or a little over 700 francs. With a wife and two children such a sum means all but actual starvation. How bravely and resignedly did this poor fellow endure his bitter penury! Some day he hoped there might be a little 'rise' for him, which would give his family sufficient bread. He told me all this as though it were a relief to him to tell it, adding that he loved France, and had worked for a few months in Paris. He asked my name. I gave it. 'Then,' he exclaimed, 'it is you of whom the newspaper speaks,' and again he went away, and returned, bringing me the *Middelburgsche Courant*, in which our expected arrival was, in fact, announced.

This revelation of our 'civil estate' seemed to overwhelm my new acquaintance, and I afterwards learned the source of his profound amazement. Passing by our boat, he had glanced at our little establishment, and observed Constant scraping carrots, while I was attending to the saucepans. These humble occupations were hardly reconcilable, to his mind, with our quality. A baron, a real live baron, of the true old stock, scraping carrots! He could hardly believe his eyes, for would not he, humble *employé* as he was, have thought such an occupation derogatory? There was, however, no doubt about the fact. Henceforward he called myself and my friends 'Those Lords,' speaking to us in the third person. He entreated us to solicit a 'rise' for him, and we promised to interest ourselves in his fate. Van Heemskerk went three times to the Ministry of Finance to recommend him, and they promised him there that the thing should be done. Has it been done? I do not know. It is very difficult to interest a Minister in honest folk who really suffer from hunger. There is so much to be done for those who do not!

Again, while taking the portrait of the Stadhuis, I made the acquaintance of the pastor, as he is called here; and I found he possessed one of my works, '*Amsterdam et Venise.*' I was surprised and delighted at this. You must acknowledge that not to be unknown at Veer is something, especially to us Parisians, for we are but little cosmopolitan, and it is generally enough for us if our fame extends over two hundred yards of Boulevard.

I should have made more progress with my drawing, and also with my two new acquaintances, had it not been for the 'coming out' of a school, which increased our company by about sixty boys and girls. This was too much for me; I gathered up my traps, and took my way to the port.

Poor little port! Once so famous, lively, populous, and noisy, and now so solitary and so still! Traces of its former military and mercantile character are yet to be seen. On the left stands a majestic building, with thick walls and few apertures, terminating on the sea side in a crenelated round tower; this was that naval magazine, that 'general arsenal and house of artillery' which Guicciardini mentions with marked respect. And those elegant houses, with their arched and trefoiled windows, and their decorated gables on the right, quite near us, once formed the ancient *Scotschhuis*, or 'House of the Scots.' Every detail of the building, even to the medallion in the façade, with a ram carved upon it in bas-relief, recalls the great trade in wool done by the city at that period.

Far off, at the entrance of the port, stands a tower, the last remnant of the ramparts, formerly a fortification; and which was defended, even so late as the 18th century, by two pieces of cannon: it is now a tavern.

In vain do we look for the companion tower of old times. As I have already said, it has disappeared with the earth in which its foundations stood deep and strong for ages. If from the summit of the solitary survivor you gaze in search of that mysterious town upon the opposite bank, you will look in vain for it where it formerly stood, and mirrored its houses and its steeples in the limpid waters. Kampen also has been swallowed up for ever, leaving no trace that it ever existed in this world. The land that stretches out before us is all affected by that subtle cancerous disease, the *ral*, of which I have already spoken, and whose ravages are so terrible.

Two centuries ago, this great bay was so filled up with sand, that it was expected the two islands would in a short time be united and thenceforth form but one. Then, on a sudden, the gulf yawned anew. That huge rent, the Veer Gat, opened once again, and more deeply than before, whole towns were buried, their inhabitants were drowned. Then the water retired, the earth arose, shaking off its humid winding sheet, and the old task was resumed; man began once more to dispute the soil with the invading waves. A portion of the land which seemed to be lost for ever was regained; but at the cost of what determined strife, after how many battles, and with what dire alternations!

Within a century, three entire polders, situate on the north coast of Noordbeveland, have again disappeared, and in the place where they once were, there now flows a river forty yards deep. In 1873, the polder of Borselen, thirty-one English acres in extent, sank into the waters. Each year the terrible *val* devours some space or other, carrying away the land in strips. That little dyke before us, jutting out from the opposite bank as if it would come to meet us here, dates no further back than 1835; but it was originally of much greater length. The *val* has already eaten up one-third of it.

It is exceedingly curious to trace the history of this gigantic chess-board, which lies before us, on the map. The grassy plains in the foreground are quite recent conquests. This, which forms a kind of cape, on the right, is called Spiering Polder, and has been in existence since 1856 only. That vast strip of land, stretching away on the left, the Onrust Polder, is but ten years older; while that large strip in the background, the Jacoba Polder, dates from 1769. The Anna Friso Polder, which comes next to the Jacoba, on the sea coast, was reclaimed in 1747; and the Sophia Polder, which follows, in 1775.

The Sophia Polder is now attacked by the terrible *val*. Every possible means is being employed for its defence; no sacrifice is spared; but the hope of saving it is but faint. The game is almost up; already one dyke has been swallowed, and a portion of the conquered ground has had to be abandoned. The dams are being strengthened in the rear, while every effort is being made to fix the soil so as to prevent the slipping away of the reclaimed land. To effect this, not only are the dams reinforced and complicated by an inextricable network of stones and interlaced branches of trees, but *Zinkstukken* are sunk far off in the sea, which, by squeezing down the shifting bottom, avert those sudden displacements which bring about such terrible disasters.

The *Zinkstukken* — enormous constructions in wicker-work — are square rafts, made of reeds and boughs twisted together, and they are sometimes two or three hundred feet long on all sides. They are made on the edge of the coast, and pushed into the sea; and no sooner is one afloat than it is surrounded by a crowd of barges and boats, big and little, all laden with stones and clods of earth.

The boats are then attached to the *Zinkstuk*, and this combined flotilla is so disposed alongside the shore that the current carries it to the spot at which the *Zinkstuk* is to be sunk. When the current begins to make itself felt, the raft is loaded, by the simple process of heaping the contents of the barges upon the middle of it. The men form in line from the four corners to the centre, and the loads of stones and earth are passed on to the centre of the raft, on which they are flung; then the middle of the *Zinkstuk* begins to sink gently, and to disappear under the water. As it goes down the operators withdraw; the stones and clods are then flung upon it from the boats. At this stage of the proceedings, the *Zinkstuk* is so heavy that all the vessels, dragged by its weight, lean over, and their masts bend above it. But now the decisive moment approaches, and the foreman, or director of this great operation, standing on the poop of one of the largest boats, in the middle of the flotilla, on the side farthest from the shore, well in sight of all, his eyes fixed upon the guide-posts set up on the coast, awaits, in excitement which is shared by all, the instant at which the *Zinkstuk* shall come into the precise foreordained position. At that instant he utters a shout, and makes a signal; the ropes are cut, the raft plunges downwards, and disappears for ever, while the boats recover their proper position.

The difficulties of such an operation are easy to

comprehend. It is indispensable that the sea and the sky should be calm, and the director perfectly coolheaded ; for, at the moment when the signal is given, the operation is far from complete, or its success secure. The *Zinkstuk* has yet to reach the bottom, a descent of a hundred or a hundred and fifty feet. Now, if it does not go down quite straight, the current that is felt upon the surface being as strong, sometimes even stronger, below, drags the huge mass, displaces it, and carries it it may be ten, fifteen, or twenty yards farther than it ought to go. Then the whole operation has to be gone over again.

I was present at the placing of one of these *Zinkstukken* in front of the Sophia Polder, and while I live I shall never forget that spectacle. We had embarked at the foot of the old Kampveerschetoren, the last remnant of the ramparts of Veer, the ferryman had deposited us on the top of the dam, and we had walked on to Kamperlandsch Veer, a village which also takes its name from the vanished town of Kampen.

The leader of our little expedition was Mynheer Bruijn, the engineer of the Waterstaat,[1] who had charge of the operation.

[1] Literally 'The Water State.' Thus the wonderful series of works which covers the face of the country and protects it against inundation, is designated in the Netherlands, and this appellation is also applied to the corps of engineers charged with the management of those works. The organisation of this corps bears a considerable resemblance to that of the 'Corps des Ponts et Chaussées.' The expedition was composed, besides, of a young statesman of great talent and with a brilliant career before him, then a member of the States-General, now Minister of Public Works, Industry, and Commerce, a provincial deputy for Gueldres, my friend Constant, and myself.

After having roamed for a long half-hour about this pretty village of Kamperlandsch Veer, we packed ourselves into a local carriage, more picturesque than commodious, and very much shut up indeed, for it was impossible to let down the glasses, and thus, by sandy roads, full of ruts, where Macadam had never been heard of, we reached our destination.

There we were well rewarded; never was a more delightful combination of colours offered to the eyes of artists and lovers of nature.

Under an azure sky stretched a sparkling sea, its waters shading from green to blue, and from yellow to violet, all the delicately graduated tones harmoniously blended together.

In the distance, as though marking the horizon, stretched a long green strip of land; this was the Island of Schouwen; and the massive spire of Zierikzee stood out in strong relief against the sombre black background of the sky.

At our feet was the *Zinkstuk*, surrounded by its flotilla. The great red sails, furled upon the masts, the green poops, the rudders adorned with burnished copper, the red streaks, which abound in the painting of these boats, the coloured shirts, the brown vests, the blue girdles, all touched by the bright rays of the sun, form a medley of brilliant colours, and compose a striking picture.

But we were not allowed a lengthy contemplation of this fair spectacle from afar. We were soon seen and summoned. A sloop put off and came to take us on board, and we speedily found ourselves in a great *koff*, laden with stones. The signal was given, and a general commotion at once set in.

On all sides men were in motion, and five hundred brawny arms were flinging the contents of the boats upon the great raft; a truly Titanic stoning. Projectiles rained from all sides without an instant's pause, until the half-empty boats were bending over upon the vanishing *Zinkstuk*, and the moment came when the decisive command was to be given. Then silence, absolute and impressive, fell upon the multitude. Suddenly the signal was given, a creaking noise was heard; the fifty boats righted themselves at the same moment, and turned towards the point at which the great raft that had separated them had just disappeared.

Never shall I forget the strange spectacle presented by all these boats, bumping one against the other, getting entangled, and grouping themselves in a hundred different fashions. The swarming men, stooping and raising themselves up again, the uplifted arms, the flying stones, the spurting water covering the boats with foam; and in the midst of the confusion, the *Polderjongens* armed with their tridents flinging the clods of earth with great strength and rapidity on the raft. Now for the first time, I had an exact and precise idea of what a naval encounter in the old times must have been.

The tumult declines at certain points; flags are hoisted from the tops of the masts, the large sails are shaken out, and, with the aid of a gentle breeze some vessels get loose, sail out and desert the field of battle. These are the boats whose task is done, and which are empty. They retire one by one, and the great expanse of water, which, save on one spot, was a little while ago deserted and solitary, is now furrowed by the vessels making their way towards the horizon.

During this scene, I stood side by side with a man attired in true Zealand costume, tall narrow hat, buttoned vest, and velvet breeches. This was the chief of the menaced polder, the *dijkgraaf* or 'Count of the dyke.' This man was a thorough Zealander, who had never seen anything but his own spire of Wiesenkerk and that of the neighbouring town, and he was a little upset by meeting with a stranger. He could hardly understand how anyone could belong to another country, and not at all how anyone could speak another language than his own. Nevertheless, he was a most excellent man. His name was Van Leeuwen. I made a note of his name, and he afterwards sent me his portrait.

This worthy Zealander was as deeply moved as I was by the impressive and curious spectacle ; and the sight of emotion in such a man would make you understand better than all I can say, how grand and impressive was the scene that had just taken place before our eyes.

THE DIJKGRAAF VAN LEEUWEN.
(From a Photograph.)

CHAPTER XI.

THE COUNTRY —THE 'DIME' — COUNTRY MORALS AND MANNERS —THE 'TOL'—WESTHOVEN AND DUINBEEK.

F we were to follow exactly and methodically the order of our voyage, it would be necessary for me to take you to Middelburg, to come back afterwards to Veer, and from thence to recommence our excursions in the north of the island. But it is easier and more simple to condense into one narrative our various sojourns in the Zealand capital, and to go immediately through the northern portion of the Island of Walcheren.

I take your consent for granted ; and passing by Gapinge and Scrooskerke, visit Oost kapelle, West kapelle, and Domburg.

Here we are, with staffs in our hands, stepping along the high road.

First, let us wave a farewell salute to that pretty villa, set in flowers, shaded by great trees, and whose spacious verandah looks so hospitable. It is the dwelling of the Burgomaster of Veer, an amiable and learned person of very dignified manners, concerning whom I shall have something to say hereafter.

And now, turning to the right, we pass by that prosperous farm, with its orchards and dependencies, above whose portal, like a diadem upon a princely brow, we behold the somewhat pretentious inscription, 'La Maison de la haute Montagne.' This French appellation is a contradiction to the surrounding landscape, which is essentially Dutch. Whence this fine title was derived I cannot tell, I have only been able to learn that in 1694 it was not new.[1]

Now we are in the midst of the fields: they are all rich with crops, and the fruit trees are heavily laden; while in the vicinity of the villages, flourishing kitchen gardens display their long rows of highly cultivated vegetables, set out like regiments in order of battle. The kitchen garden and the orchard are to be seen everywhere in Zealand, and they mean abundance in the household, variety in the family fare, and are, together with the grazing land, the only sources of industry which are not obliged to pay the dime (or tenth), for throughout the whole island, that remnant of feudal rights, still exists; and, if I am to believe what those interested in its maintenance tell me, it is not likely to be abolished.

This is a custom peculiar to the country, and curious

---

[1] This is not the only French inscription decorating a rustic habitation in the island. On the road from Middelburg to Flushing my excellent friend, Monsieur Loup, of the Royal Archives, beheld the following: '*Rien sans peine.*'

enough to deserve mention. Besides, as we are in the fields, we may as well talk of cultivation as of anything else. The dîme then, exists in Zealand, and every property is liable to a double tax; the ferme, which, as in France, is paid to the proprietor of the soil, and the dîme, for which the tenant is accountable to another proprietor; for, strange to say, the greater number of the Zealand landlords, though proprietors of dîmes, seldom possess a claim to those which are raised on their own harvests. The ferme, unless it be otherwise specially provided, is paid in money.

The soil is officially divided into hectares (a hectare is $2\frac{1}{2}$ English acres), for the metrical system prevails in the Low Countries. But in Zealand, old things are not yet entirely put away, and the people count by 'gemet,' that is to say, by the acre. In the north of the island, the gemet measures a space of 34 ares 39 centiares.[1] In the south, I am told, the gemet measures less, having been reduced to the exact third of the hectare. This difference in measurement brings about certain complications, but the gemet has the great advantage of ancientness. In searching the old papers existing since the end of the thirteenth century, we find that it was employed as the agrarian measure, and in a country of traditions the possession of such antiquity goes for much.[2]

The average rent paid for the gemet varies

---

[1] The 'are' is a little more than 119 square yards English; a 'centiare' is a hundredth part of the 'are.'

[2] See the Archives of Middelburg. *Priviligie Boek*, No. 4, page 8. Titles of the year 1304, in which this word is employed.

between twenty and thirty florins, according to the quality of the ground and the other charges upon it. These charges, to which we shall have to recur, consist chiefly in the maintenance of the dams and in works of irrigation. The charge of thirty florins represents only the actual soil with the farm buildings. The farmer must have his own cattle, his own draught animals, and the agricultural materials indispensable for his farming operations.

Besides, he is not quite free to farm the land as he chooses; his hands are tied by certain customs. Thus in the country which we are now crossing, the whole system of culture is spread over a period of eight years.

In the first year colza is grown and the land is manured. In the second, wheat is produced; in the third, beans, which, being cut and dried or ground, are afterwards used as food for the cattle. In the fourth year, wheat is again sown. In the fifth, haricot beans. In the sixth, wheat once more. In the seventh, potatoes; and in the eighth, the land is let to lie fallow, and manured. In a country so marvellously fertile as Zealand, the farmer, by taking care that all his fields are not brought to the same point, has a very complete method of culture, which permits him to provide abundantly for all the necessities of his industry, and to make a good profit by his excess of production.

The dime is paid in kind, except for the first or 'colza' year, when it is counted at twenty-five cents—

which is about fifty-two centimes—the hectare. When the harvest is ready, the farmer makes his sheaves up into stacks, generally composed of four or six, and arranges them in his field in rows equidistant one from the other. The proprietor of the dime then comes, chooses the first stack which pleases him, places a bough of a tree upon it, and starting from it, counts to the thirteenth, on the top of which he places another bough, and so the enumeration goes on. When every stack in the field has been counted, the dime is fixed, and the farmer may then take away all his own stacks, but he is forbidden to touch those on which a branch is laid; and it happens very often that these remain exposed to the depredations of the birds, while the rest of the harvest is safely stored at the farm.[1] This happens frequently, when the proprietor of the dime lives far off, and in order to take possession of his goods, has a long journey to make and considerable expenses to incur; then he naturally prefers to wait for a good opportunity. The proprietors of the dimes have therefore recourse in some places to a mutual understanding in order to avoid a costly removal every year at a fixed epoch. They meet at Middelburg and proceed to what may be called the dime exchange. On meeting, they exchange mutual informations. It is known what the year will produce; a fixed price for each district is decided

---

[1] This thirteen is not a fixed number, it varies in the different cantons. In certain communes the master has the right to one sheaf in ten, in others to one in twelve.

upon, and the dime being brought under tariff, the farmer is able to buy back that arising from his own crop; or, if he does not care to do so, the proprietor may exchange the dimes which are too far from his own dwelling for others in his neighbourhood.

While we have been talking of taxes, potatoes, wheat, and colza, we have arrived at Wiesenkerke: a large and handsome village, well built, admirably clean, and with the remains of an old church, very venerable of aspect. Formerly there was a castle here, and the lords of Wiesenkerke were great personages. Several among them held high office in Zealand; but the castle itself is deserted, and the family now lives in Guelderland, where, faithful to its old traditions, it has gained the respect and affection of all.

There is a festival air about the place to-day, although it is still very early; the peasants' carts are being harnessed everywhere. The heavy, handsome mares, with harness ornamented with burnished copper, are already between the shafts. The long, green vehicles, streaked with bright colours, are taking up their joyous cargoes of boys and girls, and when they set out laughter and kisses will be the order of the day. Here come the pretty peasant girls, with bare arms, straw hats pulled down upon their foreheads, and bright blue ribbons floating from their shoulders: jewels glitter on their foreheads, on their necks, and on their fingers. How daintily attired they are with their showy petticoats and their pretty handkerchiefs! One detail of their dress reveals the religion of these gay damsels. Blue and violet are their reigning colours, and from that we may conclude that they are certainly Calvinists; if the handkerchiefs were red and yellow, we should be equally sure that they were Catholics. But to-day, whether Catholics or Protestants, they have but one religion—amusement.

Everything indeed gives way to that, even strict propriety, which has always been held indispensable to Christian maidens. You must know in fact that these gay and rosy lasses, with their innocent smiles, their placid air, and their candid eyes, have notions of their own respecting female virtue, which do not pass current elsewhere. Chastity is almost unknown among them. In our country this would be considered a great scandal, but here it is held of no consequence.

With this exception, the population of Zealand is fairly honest and upright; theft is almost unknown in the country. The peasant is indeed, as he is everywhere, somewhat keen and sharp about his own interests; that is his nature, but he is singularly less artful, overreaching, and unscrupulous than in many other countries which I might mention. His word is much more to be relied upon than that of the Flemish peasant. He does not lie for the pleasure of deceiving. He is trustworthy, sincere, not covetous, and, moreover, benevolent. 'There are few departments which contain so great a number of charitable establishments as the Mouth of the Scheldt,' we read in an official statement in 1813.[1] These asylums for indigence and misery bear witness to the charity of the inhabitants of Zealand. If the French writer who wrote these words could return to-day, he would have nothing to change in his record.

Added to this, they are a peculiarly religious people. Many of these farmers, whom you would suppose to be illiterate, will talk to you about Luther and Melancthon, and especially of Zwinglius and Calvin, with a perfect knowledge of their subject. They will reason upon original sin and saving grace like a doctor of old, quote texts to you, and explain the Synod of Dort, of which you probably know very little. All these questions are thoroughly familiar to them, and they will discuss them unweariedly to any extent. But every other subject is a dead letter.

If we are to believe an old author, this was not always the case. An annalist of the sixteenth century, who records the habits and customs of the Zealand women, tells us that 'their gowns were cut out behind down to the shoulders, and in front left the whole of the breast uncovered, although there was amongst them great modesty.' And he adds afterwards: 'The girls, who were well favoured beyond those of all other countries, did not enter into the state of marriage unless they were of spotless virtue, and if any girl had fallen from that estate, whether

---

[1] *Annuaires Statisques du departement des Bouches-de-L'Escant, pour l'Année* 1813.

secretly or as a known thing, however young, handsome, or rich she was, she could find no man to marry her.' At the present day, if this old annalist were to return to the world, he would find it necessary largely to modify his description. The young girls of Zealand are far more decently dressed, but they are less scrupulous, and the social code would inflict no such penalty as that which he describes. The morals of the people of the province are extremely licentious, and customs prevail amongst them which we find it difficult to explain when we consider the honesty, uprightness, and strictness of their conduct in other respects.

It would seem that every effort to reform their morals would be entirely useless; it is, indeed, vain to think of it. All the exertions of the clergy are rendered useless by the obstinacy of the peasant nature. 'Who is this person who comes here wanting to teach us?' they will say, 'does he think we are going to learn from him how to live? The customs of our forefathers are good customs, we will not change them for him: if he thinks ill of them, let him go back whence he came, and wait until we come to fetch him!' Long experience has obliged the pastors, on pain of seeing their churches deserted, to shut their eyes to the facts of life in the villages.

But enough on this unpleasant subject. Let me add that a profligate husband or a faithless wife is almost unknown in Zealand.

Here come the carts ; just listen to the shouts, the laughter, and the songs. They are all singing the 'Maddolinata,' on their way to the kermesse. ' Oh, Harmony ! what crimes are committed in thy name !' Happily, the ' passage ' paid, the gate is opened, and the long line of rustic equipages take the road to the town at a heavy trot. On this day, the receiver of the ' *tol* ' has a great deal to do.'

The 'tolhouse' stands beside the gate, which crosses the road. On the left is a small house ; on the right a huge post, surmounted with the arms of the Netherlands. Every vehicle has to pay a toll, and the money goes to the repairs of the road. This indirect tax is very costly to collect, for the fifty *tollen* in the island of Walcheren require fifty houses, inhabited by fifty families, who have to live upon the product of the impost, before a stiver goes into the funds of the State, or the pockets of private individuals, according to whether the State or a private individual be charged with the keeping of the highway.

In certain portions of the province, for example, in the Island of Zuidbeveland, the inhabitants have reformed this old tax, and replaced it by a fixed duty, paid by all the proprietors in the island. This modification is a very sensible one, for each possessor of a field is interested in having easy access to it, and consequently the roads should be in good condition. The Beveland proprietors have abolished all the *tollen*, and founded a sort of syndicate, which undertakes the keeping of the roads, and, under the title of '*Middelen van Straaten en Wegen*,[1]' provides for the distribution of this special tax.

In Walcheren, things are a little behind the time; and the whole system, which I acknowledge is more picturesque than practical, especially when one is in a hurry, is adhered to.

The *tollen* were formerly much more numerous than they are at present. The high roads and canals were encumbered with them, they constituted a sort of custom-house placed on the frontier of each seigneurie, and the duty charged there extended to every kind of product. At that time the authorisation to establish a *tol*, or a *tolrecht*, as it was called, was a coveted privilege, whose possession constituted a feudal right. Thus we find in all the ancient contracts these singular rights granted with 'their franchises, rights, roads, and *tols*.'

At present, on the contrary, the *tol* produces but small returns. In most cases the Commune assesses the houses, the gate, and the revenues which it produces at a few hundred florins; and on payment of this sum, and the strict observance of the tariff, the farmer of the *tol* has to give no account of his collections to anybody. I was told that one of these farmers, a very strict Calvinist, who regarded the collection of *tol* as an occupation incompatible with the observance of the Sabbath, prefers to renounce the exercise of his right on that day, rather than infringe

---

[1] 'Means for the streets and roads.' The tax is fifteen centimes the hectare in Zuidbeveland.

his religious convictions. I leave you to imagine how brisk is the Sunday circulation on that road!

Notwithstanding the meagre returns of the *tol*, the roads are very well kept in Zealand. They are generally divided in two throughout their whole length. One of these halves is paved, generally with bricks, while on the other the earth is simply trodden down, without macadam, paving stones, or bricks. This second side of the way, which is much the easiest and least uneven, is called the *Zomerpad*, or Summer road, The other is specially reserved for winter.

But we have passed through the *tol* long since, and here we are talking still. Let us get on.

Oost kapelle, where that long string of vehicles stopped us, is a gay little village, trim and well kept, very ancient, nevertheless, for a letter of Floris V., dated 1273, mentions its name. This territory formerly enclosed 2,500 acres, and contained two seignorial residences, one at Duinbeek and the other at Westhoven. That of Westhoven is the largest, and the most considerable. It was built at the commencement of the twelfth century, and fortified by the Knights Templars, to whom it belonged. In 1314, two years after the suppression of the Order of the Templars, by Clement V., the Counts of Holland and Friesland laid hands on this seignorial territory, and on its castle, taking the latter for their own dwelling in the island. Afterwards, Westhoven came again in fief to the Abbots of Middelburg. In 1540, Abbot Floris received there a visitor illustrious above all others, the Emperor Charles V. From the Abbots of Middelburg Westhoven passed into the possession of the bishops; and in 1572, at the time of the anti-Spanish and Reform movements, the castle was burnt, and the fief abolished.

Duinbeek is less well known to history. Nevertheless, it is of no small antiquity, for you will remember that it was in exchange for their residence and castle of Duinbeek, with four acres of their seigneurie, that Wolfart van Borselen[1] and his wife obtained the free fief of the city of Veer, from William V., in 1350.

From that time forth Duinbeek was a pleasant and enviable residence. It is not, however, thitherwards that we are going, nor is it towards Westhoven. We reserve the latter for another time, when we shall admire its deep moat, and its old machicolated towers; at present we are going to see another residence, no less picturesque, and no less agreeable, but quite modern.

This is the fine domain of Overduyn, and we shall reach it in half an hour.

[1] Hunne veste en noning te Dunebeke in Walcheren met vier gemeten ambachts. See *Inventaris* &c. No. 40

CHAPTER XII.

OVERDUYN—THE 'BIBLIOTHECA CATSIANA'—DOMBURG—NEHALENNIA—WESTKAPELLE—A FAMOUS BATTLE—THE DAM—THE POLDERJONGENS—THE SPANISH TYPE.

O have an exact idea of the extraordinary fertility of this fair province of Zealand, one must see the Castle of Overduyn. But is Overduyn a castle in the feudal and warlike sense of the word? Certainly not; it is what we should call in France a country house, one of those rustic abodes to which the Romans gave that pretty name of 'villa,' as often wrongly as rightly applied by us. In a word, Overduyn is a very handsome and comfortable house, with a wide, green sward before it, on which does and their fawns gambol. It is surrounded by a fine park and a luxuriant garden; in the background are stables, outhouses, an extensive kitchen garden, and a large orchard. Hard by is the farm, with its great granaries, cattle sheds, piggeries, and rustic habitations. A wide verandah opens upon the lawn; there are cascades in the park, benches in the corners of the

alleys; there are no gates, no barriers of any kind, in a word, all is easy access and cordial welcome.

Such is this hospitable dwelling, very different from our French châteaux, surrounded with high walls, closed in with lofty gates, sojourns of luxury, giving the lie to Chénier's lines in *Les Gracques*:

> Où l'on vit sans luxe on est hospitalier.'

Let us go in boldly, with head erect; we have nothing to fear. The master of this Zealand Eden is in exact harmony with his fine dwelling and this delightful landscape. He is as charming as they are, as cordial and as open-handed.

Several times have I seated myself under those green branches, taken my place at the table in the house, in the company of charming ladies, opposite to the most indulgent, kindest, and best of grandmothers, whose kindly smile has reminded me of another smile far away; and each time I have left the place with a feeling of repose, my spirits tranquillised, and my brain replenished, for the owner of Overduyn is not only a wealthy and amiable man, he is a scholar in the best sense of the word.

You remember that when we were at Brouwershaven we told you you must look elsewhere for a monument to the memory of Cats.[1] Here, at Overduyn, we find it, not in an edifice of marble or of bronze, but in the materials left by the poet himself; in his works, collected with pious care, and in

[1] See Appendix.

all the remembrances of his long career that it has been possible to discover.

Mynheer de Jonge van Ellemeet has collected the 217 different editions or fragments of editions of the weighty and compact works of the poet of the 'Sinne en Minne Beelden' in a specially constructed bookcase, plated with iron and impervious to fire, as well as safe from sacrilegious hands. And he has also preserved in special portfolios the originals of the drawings which have served to illustrate these various editions, and collected in a fireproof casket all the documents that throw any light on the biography of the great patriot to whose memory he has devoted so much care. His title-deeds, all the documents concerning his 'civil status,' the patents of his various decorations, his order of knighthood, as well as the armorial bearings which were granted him by Charles the First, are there, together with his private correspondence, his account books, and the letters of his daughters. A pious hand has collected these treasures; and they form a whole which enables us to resuscitate to some extent that great figure of a former age, that Dutchman of the golden time, who on more than one side of him is perhaps the most typical and the truest personification of the ideas of his time and the temperament of his country.

What I admire most in the owner of Overduyn is not, however, his devotion to one great historical figure. His patriotic resolution to let nothing be lost which can recall the most illustrious of the poets of

Zealand is certainly deserving of all our gratitude; but it appears to me still more remarkable that Mynheer van Ellemeet has not allowed himself to be absorbed by the great man upon whose memory he has lavished his fortune and his time. He has not been carried away, in fact, by passing his daily life in the company of the memories that the vanished poet has left in this world. He has not raised the pedestal so high as to falsify the proportions; and his judgment remains as clear, as correct, as calm, and even as severe as if he had always regarded Cats with indifference.

In addition to the valuable books and unique documents which compose what has been called the *Bibliotheca Catsianna*, Mynheer de Jonge van Ellemeet possesses a very remarkable collection of water-colours. We must not pause to do more than glance at his portfolios; they are well worth looking over, but it is not for that purpose we have come to Overduyn.

That we may gain an idea of the extraordinary fertility of this fair province of Zealand, let us make a tour of the place, and study attentively the charming points of view which offer themselves in rapid succession. And, first, let me remark that everything here is the creation of the master. All those luxuriant shrubberies, those fine trees, those plantations where rare exotics reflect their bright green foliage in the little lake on whose breast black swans are sailing. 'There is not a tree here,' said he,

P

with legitimate pride, 'which I have not planted; and that little wood, which in any other place would have required a lapse of time exceeding that of the lives of several men for such a development, has grown up to what it is within forty years. Is it not wonderful?' And then he reminded me that this is not even the most fertile part of Walcheren. Remember that we are almost on the brink of the sea. Overduyn signifies 'opposite the dunes,' and, as its name indicates, the house stands at a few hundred yards from those little hills of white sand.

In spite of the sand that mixes with this prolific soil, in spite of the winds which blow from the Ocean and the North Sea, not only do the trees take root and grow, but plants from hot countries live in the open air, flourish there, and brave the winters; for winter here is mild and clement. Even in the days when Guicciardini visited Zealand it was so, and the Florentine was quite astonished to find an Italian vegetation in these latitudes. 'The Isles of Zealand,' he says, 'approach nearer to the Arctic Pole than does any other region of the Low Countries, except the countries of Holland and Friesland, and for this cause it seems to me that those islands ought to be colder, and consequently less capable of producing flowers and herbage. Notwithstanding this, all the region grows oranges and other trees, and divers sort of herbage and flowers in every season of the year.' At that epoch of rudimentary geography, when the mystery of submarine tides had not been penetrated, such a phenomenon must indeed have appeared extraordinary. Winters without great cold, summers without torrid heat, rendered the country an object of wonder; a sort of rural paradise, whose climate everybody praised, without trying to explain it.

Having made the tour of the park, let us glance at the farm, at those superb outhouses in which are stowed rustic equipages and machines, the indispensable arsenal of modern farming. As we pass we see the empty stables—for the animals are in the fields—and the double house of the farmer. Every well-to-do peasant, in fact, possesses a double dwelling, one house for winter and another house for summer. The two are separated by a courtyard, and each is adapted to the requirements of its special season for use; but both are clean, neat, admirably kept, with the rustic luxury of shining furniture, great dishes of blue delft arranged in perfect order over the chimney-piece, and utensils of copper as bright as gold.

Our visit is over; let us resume our way, and now, as we step out briskly, let us cast a glance at those warlike towers, lofty crenelations, and ancient trees which overshadow a feudal court. There, safe from surprise behind its deep moats, stands that warlike castle of Westhoven, of which we have already spoken. But we must hasten on, a little more walking along a road which lies between picturesque and orderly country houses, and we shall have reached Domburg.

Domburg is the Scheveningen of Zealand, the favourite watering-place of Walcheren, simple notwithstanding its aristocratic pretensions, and thinly peopled notwithstanding its old renown. In the fifteenth century it was almost the same as it is to-day. The inhabitants of Middelburg and the castles on the other islands had constructed some elegant cottages on the sands, and came thither to pass the hot months of the year in the shelter of its woods. 'It was,' say the old chroniclers, 'a sort of small terrestrial paradise;' exalted destinies were foreseen for it; the same are hoped for in this day, but they do not realise themselves. Nevertheless, more than other places this had a right to hope. Was it not the most ancient situation on the sea-coast? Was it in vain that the Romans had chosen it to establish therein one of their posts, to build that 'burg,' which being constructed in the midst of the Dunes was to give it its name Duneburg, corrupted in the Middle Ages into Domburg? With such an origin was it to remain insignificant? That glorious past nobody contested; and now, even if it were contested, would not the antique coins of Trajan and Antoninus, of Vitellius and Posthumius, which have been found in its soil, protest against such a denial? Better than that, would not the very stones resent the affront? And what stones? The most eloquent and the most respectable of witnesses, for they are the altars of the ancient gods.

The Romans indeed, as if they desired to thank

the tutelary divinities who had guided them to land in so propitious a spot, under so serene a sky, in the midst of such fertile fields, covered these shores with temples and consecrated stones. 'The god Neptune, the goddess Nehalennia, and the other gods and goddesses presiding over these provinces' (*Diis deabusque præsidibus provinciarum*), received their praises, and the smoke of their sacrifices rose towards the heavens.

These altars, erected by the piety of the ancients, have been found. After many vicissitudes, they now form a portion of the Museum of Leyden, and interesting reproductions of them may be seen at Middelburg at the 'Zeeuwsch Genootschap.'[1]

The statues of that strange goddess, Nehalennia, a Scandinavian adaptation of the Greek Σελήνη, are the most numerous. They represent the kindly goddess, under a graceful canopy, sometimes standing, but more frequently sitting, with a basket of fruit, the emblem of the benefits which she lavishes on mortals, in her hand. Sometimes a dog, significant of her unfailing vigilance, lies at her feet. She always wears the same costume: a cap, with wide strings, is placed upon her head, a long robe covers her body, and a pelerine hangs from her shoulders; and from this simple and modest drapery her fine calm face looks out with charming expression, full of grace, beauty

---

[1] These altars, which were either used as materials, or placed in the church, were partially destroyed in a fire which almost annihilated the church of Domburg in the last century.

and goodness. Torrents of ink were shed in the last century in discussion of this gentle, sympathetic and charming Nehalennia. The seigneur of Domburg (then the rich Mynheer van Dieshoek, alderman of Middelburg and director of the East India Company in Zealand) had the various sides of the altars engraved in a series of plates. These plates were distributed throughout the world of antiquaries, and gave rise to many disputes; some holding for that Scandinavian incarnation of the Moon, of which we have just spoken, others recalling the fact that Homer designates Neptune Θεὸς Νεάλαμνος, and claiming the gracious Nehalennia as Queen of the Sea and Mistress of the Waves.

Since then other altars erected to the gentle goddess, and tombs which bear her name, have been found, but no final settlement of the question has been made. The epoch at which the Dutch tombs and altars were erected upon the shore is one so distant from ours as to render its obscurity almost impenetrable, and many other events have happened since, which demand our attention. Let us then leave these ancient memories, and advance a little in the succession of the ages.

During the whole of the mediæval period Domburg was, as it is to-day, a pleasant place, upon which it pleased the Counts of Zealand to lavish privileges. In 1300 its name appears on the audits of the accountants of the province; and in 1327 there is a question of the rights of its citizens, together with those of Westkapelle and Middelburg: '*de rechten der poorters van Middelburg, Westkapelle en Domburg.*' It was strange that the citizens should be called '*poorters,*' which means 'gate-keepers' to a city without gates, for Domburg was never fortified, the town never possessed either ramparts or walls, and consequently had no gates. This secondary position did not, however, prevent its being one of the most favoured resorts in the island; and if it be true, as Blaeu says, in his majestic Latin, and apropos of Domburg, that 'a city is not constituted by its walls, nor its ditches, but by the laws, the rights, and the assembling of its citizens,' Domburg must be regarded as a city, and no insignificant one. In the second half of the fifteenth century it was conceded by Mary of Burgundy to that Henry of Borselen who, by means of the 'great profit' which he made upon sea, acquired 'great lands in Zealand,' and it was endowed, in 1535, with a weekly market, and afterwards with a horse-market, which rapidly became of importance, and achieved a well-merited reputation.

At the present day Domburg is a bathing-place, and a small agricultural town; but being ambitious, it desires to develop itself and to grow, and it is not without envy that it looks on the one side towards Scheveningen, and on the other towards its Belgian rivals, Ostend and Blankenberghe. Unhappily, there are serious obstacles to its progress, and the difficulty of communication is not the least among them. It takes an hour and a half to go from Domburg to quiet Middelburg, the capital of the island, and Middelburg itself lies out of the way of the ordinary routes of travel.

For my part I am not anxious to behold the transformation of Domburg. The simplicity of this modest bathing-place pleases me. I picture it to myself as a place of repose for the body, and of relaxation for the mind; as a refuge for those, who, wearied of the strife of existence, want for a few weeks to escape from the whirlwind that is always sweeping them about, or as a shelter for those adepts in family life who desire to pursue, by the side of the ocean, those happy and wholesome habits and peaceful traditions which form an essential portion of their well-doing. But to picture Domburg overrun by a motley and mundane crowd of powdered faces and trailing petticoats, resounding to the noise of a tempestuous Wagnerian orchestra, with Aspasias lounging under its shady trees, and a swarm of rickety Alcibiades on its sand hills, I frankly acknowledge does not enchant me. Nevertheless, that is just the dream that it cherishes, and perhaps the fate that awaits it.

While everything is still quiet, honest, and calm, let us walk through its rural streets, smile at its tiny Stadhuis, climb its highest sandhill, from whence we can look over the entire island, like a gigantic nest amid flowers and foliage; and after having traversed its little wood, with its tangle of underwood and its impenetrable thickets, its boughs interlaced and huddled together by the action of the wind from the sea, let us strike out into that long bare road, dusty, sandy, unpleasant and sunburnt on all sides, along which we must journey to reach Westkapelle.

I am going to describe Westkapelle to you, 'not such as you see it to-day, the most unfortunate of cities, bereft of its walls, its houses, and its inhabitants, a waif thrown up by the sea and the sport of the elements; but such as it formerly was, the neighbour of the ocean, situated upon a fertile coast, having a commodious and frequented port, a prosperous trade, and a name whose reputation spread afar.' Thus says old Blaeu, and old Blaeu might now, if he could return to this world, utter in absolutely identical terms the same dolorous and vain regret.

This once flourishing town, whose origin goes back to the Roman occupation,[1] which was so largely endowed with those two great sources of the wealth of maritime cities—fisheries and commercial navigation—whose privileges, contemporary with those of Middelburg,[2] were so considerable and so enviable that a residence of three years was obligatory on any person desiring the honour of being admitted to the number of its citizens; that city, relations with which were so much sought after, that it was interdicted to

---

[1] Vestiges of villas and tombs have been found at Westkapelle, and in its environs an antique altar bearing a dedication to Hercules has also been discovered.

[2] The *Keure* of the city of Westkapelle was granted in 1223 by Floris IV., that of Middelburg in 1217. These two documents are the most ancient in the archives of Middelburg.

any stranger to reside on its soil or traffic within its walls without having purchased the right to do so; is now shorn of its greatness. That city, to which in 1223 Floris V. granted unequalled rights; that seigneurie which, in 1377, Count Albert included in the dowry of his daughter, and gave it precedence of Flushing and Rommerswaal, that rich port and commercial centre is now a small and humble village. Its inhabitants, pressed by poverty, harried by want, have not only renounced commerce, but almost entirely abandoned their fishery. They who formerly permitted no one to have 'hearthright' in their city who did not own a ship on the sea, now reckon half a dozen fishing boats as their whole wealth, and almost all earn a precarious livelihood by working at the dam which protects their shore.

All the inhabitants are occupied on that immense work of art which defends the entire island against the ravages of the ocean. The land formerly formed a sort of cape, and was besides defended by a line of dykes, as it still is higher up in the environs of Domburg, and lower down in the environs of Zoutelande. At what epoch the cataclysm which swept away the natural rampart occurred history does not record, but it was certainly after 1253, for on St. Martin's Day in that year, in summer, a great and terrible battle took place among these very sandhills, in which the then existing disposition of the soil played a decisive part.

'The Countess Margaret of Flanders, who claimed

the right of suzerainty over Walcheren, had sent her son Guy, at the head of a formidable army—no less than 150,000 men as the chroniclers assert—to effect a descent on the island. The young Count had promised his mother to reduce Walcheren to obedience, or to die in the attempt. Margaret's son arrived with his fleet before Westkapelle, where he did not expect to meet with any serious resistance; but Floris, brother of William the Second, King of the Romans, and generalissimo of his army, had been informed by his brother of the departure of the Flemings and of the direction which they had taken. Hastening to concentrate all the troops that he had in Zealand, he took them by forced marches to Westkapelle, and there he concealed them among the sandhills by which the city was surrounded, so that their presence could not be suspected from the sea side. Count Guy, quite unsuspicious, commenced his disembarkation. He had already landed with his advanced guard, when the Dutchmen suddenly rose as if by magic, and their general, seeing that it was time, showed himself, with his troops in good order of battle, and went courageously to meet the Flemings at the charge. The combat was great and lasted for long,' relates the old chronicler from whom we borrow the recital of this sanguinary affair, 'for as fast as they disembarked and put their foot on the ground they were despatched, and the more they hastened to disembark that they might succour the first landed the more were slain of them, and there was so much blood spilt in that quarter, of those Flemings who were killed by the Dutch, that it rose above the shoes of them that walked in it.'

'There died of the men 50,000 on the spot, besides those who were drowned, and a great number of persons who were chased like a poor flock of sheep: these perceiving the King, cried to him for mercy. The King, remembering the favour of God which had been shown him in this victory, gave them their lives, and permitted them to return to their own country, after that the Zealand peasants and soldiery had despoiled them, and left them naked, and being on the territory of Flanders they gathered the green leaves of trees and other herbage and foliage, with which they covered their nakedness, until they came into a sure place, where they might find better.'

The great dam that has replaced these sandhills, rendered famous by dear-bought victory, is one of the most important and costly of those wonderful works which have been executed by the engineers of Zealand as a defence against the sea. It was after the visit of Charles the Fifth to Westkapelle that this gigantic work, until then incomplete, was brought to perfection. Since that time the sums which it has cost to keep it in repair are so considerable that it is a saying in the country that for the same price the dam might have been made of silver.

Nevertheless, notwithstanding the conquered difficulty and the immense expenditure which this work represents, it is far from producing so great an impression upon the mind of the beholder as might be anticipated.

This great dam is no less than 2,800 yards in length, it rises from eight to ten yards above the level of the low tide, and at its greatest extent is 100 yards in width. These proportions are gigantic; but in order to enable such a mountain, thus constructed by the hands of man, to resist the fury of the waves, it was necessary to reduce that fury and to diminish as far as possible its violence and effect. Therefore the dam has been given a very gentle inclination on the sea side, and a very long slope, so that the tide, broken, diminished, and lessened in force in ascending, reaches almost to the summit without having encountered a single obstacle upon which it may vent its fury. Now it is exactly this long slope, this unbroken inclination, that prevents the magnitude of the work being discerned at first sight; and in order to comprehend its colossal proportions and to feel all its beauty one must study it with attention, reflection, and calculation. The materials employed do not lend themselves to great architectural effects. On this uncertain and little known soil it is impossible to lay very heavy loads, and it is indispensable that the whole of the work should present a considerable cohesion, with a specific weight relatively small.

The first operation is the formation of ballast with very solid, compact earth, of a clayey and sticky kind. This is jammed between poles, enclosed in a sort of case, and studded with large-headed nails. On this bed of earth is laid an enormous pad of plaited straw, which extends the whole length of the dyke. Upon this pad is placed a wickerwork construction, somewhat resembling the *Zinkstuk*, which I have already described, and over that a layer of basaltic stones, if they are to be procured, or of Vilvorden stone.

The immense labour of keeping a construction of this nature, two English miles in length, and constantly exposed to the violence of the raging sea, in repair, is self-evident. A whole village is fully occupied in watching over its preservation and incessantly repairing it, and thus it is that the entire population of Westkapelle, absorbed by this one anxiety, is now organised, and, so to speak, enrolled and trained for the purposes of this labour only.

With the exception of some honest folk at the other end of the district, who live by agriculture, and are disdainfully designated as 'peasants' in consequence, the whole village may be said to be employed upon the dam. The inhabitants are formed into special corps; the pile-drivers or carpenters, the makers of fascines, or navvies, are divided into gangs, with a responsible chief and a paymaster. Every man in the place undergoes a long training—indeed it begins in his childhood—in the methods of the work.

This somewhat adventurous existence, with its alternations of excessive toil and complete rest, with its spells of danger and of *dolce far niente*, seems to possess a special charm for these people, resembling that of the sea for the sailor. They regard the keeping of these works in repair as a sort of privilege reserved to themselves; admit very reluctantly the aid of strange workmen, and treat as interlopers any who come from another part of the country in the hopes of being employed on the dam. This is an exceptional fact, and the more noteworthy, that in every other part of the Netherlands the labourers engaged in the service of the Waterstaat are almost always strangers, not only to the locality, but also to the country, and belong to that special class of navvies who are called, in Holland, *polderjongens*, or 'polderboys.'

These *polderjongens* are, for the most part, natives of Brabant, and even of Belgian Brabant, which is a curious fact, for Belgian Brabant is not, like Zealand, a country of dykes and polders. They work in gangs of twelve, under a headman, who rules them, leads them, and makes contracts for them by the job, for they adopt the 'piece-work' system. A woman is attached to each gang; to cook, wash, and attend to the lodgings of the men. She is the wife of one of them in virtue of that strange rite known as 'a puthaak marriage;' a ceremony with no great solemnity about it, although it involves consequences which are serious enough.

When a *polderjongen* has accumulated the small sum that will suffice for the basis of his capital as a ganger, and has found a woman bold enough to undertake to associate with him and his future gangsmen, he goes in search of an older ganger, and requests him to consecrate the projected union.

The sage thus consulted generally delivers a brief sermon to the two neophytes; explaining to the woman the duties about to devolve upon her, and the bearing of the engagements into which she is entering; and then, when he has made sure of the mutual consent of the contracting parties, he takes a *puthaak* (or hook of a certain shape, which the *polderjongens* use for drawing the planks together), and places it on the ground. The contracting parties jump over this implement, and the marriage is concluded.

The 'ancient' presiding over these primitive espousals then takes up the *puthaak*, and presents it to the bridegroom, who lays hold of it as a sceptre-matrimonial, with which he may henceforth either remind his wife of the obligations which she has contracted, or punish the breach of them, in case of need.

These *puthaak* marriages have an indefinite duration; as, however, they are not recognised by the law, they may be dissolved by the free will of either party. When the unfortunate woman who has married after this fashion has had enough of her life of privation, labour, and suffering, she generally runs away. When on the contrary it is the husband who wishes to put an end to the union, he assembles his comrades, commences by 'treating' them to *klare*, so as to incline the balance of opinion towards his own side, then details his grievances, and finally breaks the famous *puthaak* in two. The unhappy repudiated woman is, whether she be guilty or not, obliged to go out into the desert like a modern Hagar, or in other words to take her courageous self-abnegation, her usefulness, and her industry to some other market, unless indeed one of the same gang should be sufficiently gallant to propose a new union to her.

The dwellings of the *polderjongens* must be seen in order to make such a life of wretchedness and toil comprehensible. The meanest wayside cabin is like a palace in comparison with the straw huts and the crazy boats in which those stalwart labourers sleep. There is not a bedstead nor an article of furniture in the whole camp, a few mattresses and some chests comprise the entire plenishing. The comfort, cleanliness, and well-being which are so dear to the rustic Dutch, seem to be a dead letter to these people. They have one master who rules them, one tyrant who makes them forget all. His name is Gin. This is the god for whom they work; it is for this that you may see them standing in the water up to their waists, raking and carting away the earth with marvellous industry and without an instant's respite. Their employers will tell you that they are good workmen, but only on the condition that they are allowed to drink. A special temperament is indeed necessary to enable them to endure such an existence, and it seems that they are inclined to this kind of life from their earliest youth. Among the number of these *polderjongens* are the sons of fathers who worked in this way all their lives, but there are also unclassed folk, waifs and strays from a superior order of society, whom vice or adverse fortunes have brought down to these depths. An engineer who had frequently employed gangs of these poor people told me one day the following story:—

'A *polderjongen*,' he said, ' died upon my works. He had been crushed by a falling beam, internal mischief was done, and he was carried off in two days. No one knew his name, and before dividing his belongings among them, his fellow-workmen, who had constituted themselves his legitimate heirs, wished to make out the inventory in the presence of a superior authority. His bag was brought to me and was solemnly opened in my presence. It contained only some valueless clothing, a silver spoon, and a book. The spoon was handed over to the woman of the gang, the clothes were divided among the men, and as for the book, which was dirty, greasy, dog-eared, and mouldy, nobody cared for it. "Oh! it is his prayer-book," said the chief of the gang to me, " he must have had something heavy on his mind, for he was always poking his nose into that book, and muttering some prayer or other." With this, he gave the despised volume a kick. 'I had the curiosity to take it up,' continued my friend, ' and to look at it that I might ascertain to what religion this prayer book belonged. To my great astonishment I perceived that I had a Horace in my hands.' Horace!

can you imagine the poor wretch reading and rereading that book? Can you see him, in rags, at the end of his day's work, reciting the Hymn to Bacchus, and repeating the poet's strophe:—

> 'Quamquam, choreis aptior et jocis
> Ludoque dictus, non satis idoneus,
> Pugnæ ferebaris.'

By what great misfortune, through what impure ways had he come to this terrible pass, what vices, what crimes had flung him down into the abyss! "Did he drink?" I asked the chief of the *polderjongens*. "Oh! like all the rest," said he; then, much surprised by my interest in the dead toiler, he said, "If you care for the book you may keep it." I paid a florin for it,' added the engineer, ' and I have carefully preserved it.'

At Westkapelle it would, I am sure, be impossible to find a hidden Latin scholar, or a stray *savant*, among the toilers on the dams. Here the recruiting goes on among the people only, and everybody knows everybody else. Besides, apart from a very pronounced taste for *klare*, and a relative indifference to all comfort, which betrays itself in the shabby houses so much less cared for than in other parts of the country, there are few points of resemblance between the labourers on the dam and the ordinary *polderjongens*. Like them, they are, it is true, industrious, good workmen, and somewhat quarrelsome in their drink, but the family exercises all its rights here; the home, that object of fascination to every true Zealander, makes its salutary influence felt; each workman inhabits his own house, takes a wife when he is rich enough to do so, and rears his numerous offspring as well as his precarious position permits.

In the rest of the island it is said that the population of Westkapelle is a race apart, with brown eyes and black hair; the last trace, we are assured, of the Spanish occupation of the country. As I had been told to observe this singularity, I looked attentively at all the faces I saw, and I did not find in any the smallest indication of an infusion of foreign blood. But even had such signs been numerous and striking, surely no student of the history of the country would conclude from thence that the population had been renovated by the conquering race? The Spaniards in fact occupied the country only politically, never effectively; the few troops whom they maintained in the island of Walcheren were cantoned in the great cities, at Middelburg, Flushing, and Veer, and did not live in the country places or in the villages. These troops, besides, were Walloon or German companies, commanded by Spanish officers it is true, but in too small a number to count in the implied sense.

The real Spanish troops, composed exclusively of Spanish soldiers, did not come into the Low Countries until 1566. It was the Duke of Alva, who, after having chosen them from among the heroic companies who had occupied Piedmont, brought them into Flanders. They were composed of 10,000 men in all, and their general was so afraid lest they should become corrupted by contact with the people of the country, and lest their discipline should be relaxed by association with the population, that he sedulously kept them apart from the natives. If we remember that Walcheren was relieved from the Spanish yoke in 1672, that the troops of the Duke of Alva never occupied it effectively, and that, besides, 10,000 men, speedily decimated by a merciless war, could not have had a great influence on a population of five millions of inhabitants, we shall see at once that the foreign type attributed to Westkapelle could not, supposing even that it existed, be placed to the account of the former masters of the Low Countries.

We have travelled through the villages and inspected the people; we now want to get a good look over the whole of the district; and this is easily to be had, by ascending the tower at the far end of the old town. Formerly, this tower belonged to a church, which, having been for a long time in a ruinous condition, was pulled down in 1831. I am told that it contained several curious objects which were not preserved. We found remnants of them, in the form of some delft tiles, which had formerly belonged to one of the old tombs, and represented a seigneur and dame in all their 'bravery.' We found these tiles, which were broken and incomplete, on the wall of a local *tapperij*. The tavern-keeper had seen the two tiles as he called them, entire, but a portion of them had since been destroyed. These are the sole artistic remains in the district.

The church tower, now converted into a lighthouse, is ascended by one hundred and seventy-eight steps. From its summit there is an almost boundless view in every direction; nothing arrests the eye; there is no limit except the horizon formed by the sea, or the neighbouring islands, whose outlines are lost in the mist, and blend with the pearl grey tints of the firmament.

We look down on the island which forms a base for our pedestal. It is surrounded by sandhills, intersected by canals and roads, enamelled with fields and groves, and adorned by the steeples of the towns and the village spires, which rise on every side. At our feet lies the whitening harvest, and, a hundred yards away, the village with its red roofs thrown out against the sombre green of the trees and the tender green of the fields. The view from this rural Belvidere is beautiful.

At the top of the lighthouse we encountered quite a numerous company: the keeper, delighted to show off the mechanism of his gigantic lantern, a member of the States-General, a deputy for the State of Guelderland, and a formidable number of winged ants. The member of the States-General, a great proprietor in the country, and thoroughly acquainted with his province, was explaining its division and its peculiarities to the member for the State of Guelderland. The latter seemed to take an extreme pleasure in the conversation. The keeper, as I have already said, was there in the fulfilment of his duty. As for the ants, I have never been able to understand how they came to perch themselves so high up; perhaps it was to justify the Spanish proverb, 'For its misfortune wings have grown upon the ant.'

We finished our inspection, cast a last glance upon the wide, bright, sunny scene, descended our one hundred and seventy-eight steps, resumed our road, and passing through Meliskerke and Pappendamme reached Middelburg.

CHAPTER XIII.

MIDDELBURG—ITS ORIGIN—ITS FIRST 'KEURE'—ITS HIGH COMMERCIAL FORTUNES—FOREIGNERS AT MIDDELBURG—ITS RELATIONS WITH FRANCE—THE 'ABBEY OF GOOD WILL'—THE WIJNHEEREN—ARNEMUIDEN AND VEER—A LONG SIEGE—REVIVAL AND DECLINE.

IDDELBURG! There are few cities whose history I should better like to write, not only on account of my admiration of that charming town, which, like a stately old dowager, is adorned as in its best days, exquisitely clean and coquettish; and which, notwithstanding its uncommon prosperity, has preserved the manners of its good old times and the monuments of its good old tastes; but also because few cities have had an existence so full of incident. The clash of arms has indeed resounded there but seldom, the glories of war hold but a moderate and secondary place in its annals, just enough to prove that it was capable of heroism when heroism was required; but the struggles of industry and of commerce, and their great results, form part of its daily history.

The results of progress are to be traced in it from hour to hour; on its market-place, and in its exchange—the resort of all the trading peoples of Europe—business of such importance was transacted as to spread prosperity and plenty throughout the whole country.

Middelburg is of very ancient origin. I will not trouble you with the almost fabulous birth that has been ascribed to the city. Its name, which means the 'City in the Midst,' comes, as Guicciardini tells us, from the fact that it is situated almost in the centre of the island. A more complicated etymology and more pompous explanation has been given of this appellation. Reygersbergh, in the first chapter of his 'Cronyk van Zeelandt' (1644), invokes Tacitus, evokes the Emperor Claudius, and calls in the Romans. Then comes a certain Hugo Floriacenis, who gives the town Metellus for a father, and baptises it 'Mitelburgh.' Now who was this Metellus? A Roman, says Hugo. Not at all, answers Monsieur François Le Petit, he was the father or stepfather of Matio, who built a castle, then called a burgh, in memory of King Metellus, and this burgh he named Metelliburgum, which is the famous city of Middelburg.

In the sixteenth century this latter explanation, which has very little plausibility, was, it seems, accepted to some extent, for we find it adopted by certain erudite pens, and the learned Erasmus does not hesitate to give our town the majestic name of Metelliburgum in his letters. But after all, of what avail are that pompous birth and that princely baptism, if both one and the other were destined to lead to several centuries of utter obscurity? Now this is precisely what happened.

History says nothing, or next to nothing, of Middelburg during the first ten centuries of our era. We only know that in 836 it was taken and occupied by the Normans, and certainly their occupation did not greatly aid in its development. The Normans having taken their departure, monks replaced them, and those monks so conducted themselves that they were expelled in their turn.

All this time Middelburg was not a large city by any means. 'In the year 1131, when the Regulars of Middelburg were driven out of their convent in consequence of their profligate life, by Gombault, Bishop of Utrecht, the said city of Middelburg was yet only a village.' These may justly be called small beginnings.

The active patronage of William II., King of the Romans, was required to enable Middelburg even to begin to be a town. 'That prince laid the foundation of the Munster, which became the present great church; enlarged the cloister, granted privileges to the monks from Antwerp, who had replaced the expelled religious, and having secured the gratitude of those whom he afterwards constituted his depositaries and guardians of his mortal remains, he beautified the surrounding town, enclosed it within walls and endowed it with public establishments.'

But, before that time, his ancestor, William the

First, had already granted it the famous charter, that precious *keure* which had become the law of the city, and was afterwards to become that of the country. The text of the *keure* has been preserved; it commences in a lofty strain: 'In the name of the Father, the Son, and of the Holy Ghost, Amen. This is the Law that is called *keure* by the burghers of Middelburg, affirmed by the oath of those whose names and seals are placed below.'

'In what place soever the inhabitants of Middelburg transport their persons and their goods, they remain under the protection of their Counts, as well as under the protection of the officers of justice instituted by them, and these latter shall, on their side, aid and do justice to all those who, whether natives or foreigners, shall come peacefully to establish themselves at Middelburg.'[1]

This deed, which inaugurated a new era of hospitality and protection in these districts, constituted the 'Magistrat' of Middelburg grand justiciary of all the flat country. It instituted a court in the town, before which all crimes and misdemeanours committed in the province were to be tried, and it completed that institution by fifty clauses or paragraphs, forming a sort of penal code. This privilege, confirmed by oath by the Counts of Holland, the Countess Joan of Flanders, and by their officers and governors, was renewed and extended, on the

---

[1] Van Merris Groot, *Privilegie Boek*, No. 1, folio 170.

11th of March 1254, by William the Second, King of the Romans.[1]

On the 1st of June 1274, the merchants of the town obtained from Count Floris V. faculties for constituting themselves into a corporation; and eleven years afterwards, on the 19th of June 1285, they obtained the right of establishing looms for weaving wool (*wolwercke te makene*.[2]) This was the dawn of the cloth manufacture, an industry so important throughout the Flemish and Saxon countries, that it seems to be the point of departure of all great commercial prosperity. At Middelburg this manufacture was to take such a development that less than a century later, William V. of Bavaria thought proper to proscribe the sale of foreign cloth fabrics throughout the entire island. 'It is forbidden,' wrote he on the 31st of May 1355, 'throughout the whole of Holland to sell woollen cloths, with the exception of those which are called *scaerlaken*, and which are manufactured at Middelburg, or in another portion of the Island.'[3]

Observe, that while they ensured its industrial fortunes, the Counts did not neglect the security of the inhabitants of the city. In 1290, it was so well fortified, that the Flemish troops found every attempt upon its ramparts vain, and its citizens were so brave that they did not only stand on the defensive; they

---

[1] This document is the most ancient charter written in Dutch, in existence. It forms a portion of the archives of Middelburg.
[2] See *Inventaris van het oud archief*, No. 5.
[3] *Privilegie Boek*, No. 4, folio 9.

repulsed their enemies in two bloody battles, 'in which 4,700 were killed,' and drove them away in the direction of Borselen.

In 1302 the fortune of war was less favourable to Middelburg; Guy of Dampierre had twice beaten the Dutch troops, and the good town yielded rather under the pressure of famine than before its assailants.

At that moment the city was already rich and lacked only one other element of prosperity—the presence of foreigners. A privilege accorded on the 1st of May 1323, supplied this deficiency. A free fair summoned the English, Scotch, and Flemish merchants to the town twice a year, and from that time forth Middelburg rose rapidly to greatness. The English were the first to flock to the town. The archives do not record at what period they began to frequent it in great numbers, and the historians are equally silent on that point, but it is likely that it was soon after the institution of the biennial fair. They afterwards established the Staple of their Wool at Middelburg, demanding a guarantee for it which was accorded to them, and annually renewed, no doubt on condition of a tolerably heavy payment. A charter on parchment, dated on the Sunday after St. Agatha's day, 1383, and signed by Albert of Bavaria, casts some light upon this institution, which was already ancient. It grants the renewal, for the duration of a year, of all the rights and franchises possessed by the English and other merchants for their Staple of

Wool in this country, and assures them of official protection.[1]

After the English came the Italians from Lombardy, who settled at Middelburg. Smallegange, in his careful chronicle,[2] records their appearance in this same year, 1383, and a charter granted on the 9th of February, 1384, by Albert of Bavaria, authorises them to create those 'tables of exchange,' which then did such important service to all traders.

Commerce in gold and jewels was speedily added. These goods were displayed in a special building constructed on the model of the 'Lombard,' of Bruges, and which bore the name of 'het huus te Lombaerden,' or the 'House of the Lombards.'[3] This house, situated in the Lange Noord Straat, in the western quarter of the city, contained rich treasures. A document bearing date 1458 informs us of the fortunes which were made there; it is the 'act of cession and of transfer,' signed 'Raphael de Drua, Lombard, of the House of Lombards at Middelburg,' by which the said Raphael de Drua 'cedes and transfers to his two sons his houses, capital, and moveable goods, such as jewels, chains, gems, money, gold and silver, either coined or in ingots, and balance of all credits still to be recovered.'

Almost simultaneously with the Italians, the Spaniards make their appearance; then a few years

---

[1] Charter deposited in the archives. *Inventaris*, No. 74.
[2] *Nieuwe-Cronyck van Zeeland*, 1696.
[3] April 2, 1390. See *Inventaris*, No. 80.

later come the Portuguese and the Algarves. In proportion as the circle enlarges itself the amount of transactions is augmented, and the variety of imported products creates new outlets for local industry.

From the earliest years of the fifteenth century the influx of foreigners becomes so great that the 'Magistrat' is obliged to take measures of order and supervision to prevent the disturbances which might result from such an assemblage of men from various countries.

Thus, in 1405, we find the burgomaster and aldermen directing that no inn or tavern shall henceforward be kept by a foreigner. Any person claiming the right to keep one of these houses of entertainment must be a citizen of the town, and further, to prevent disputes, sellers must not lodge with buyers, but must have their separate and particular dwelling, and must, on no account, either buy or sell any merchandise outside of their own commerce. Buyers and sellers are also subjected to a strict tariff.[1] I also recommend to the attention of the curious the ordinances of the 6th of May, 1460, where fines to be paid in bricks are specified.

Thus we see that foreigners had every sort of guarantee and inducement to settle and trade in a city which offered them such perfect security. After this the aldermen forbid, in the interest of their coasts, 'Orientals, Spaniards, Portuguese, Dutch, Frenchmen, or others, to come forth out of their ships

[1] See *Inventaris*, No. 108.

either night or day, armed with axes, rapiers, poniards, or other weapons,' and to secure the health of this foreign multitude they took prudent measures against epidemics, while at the same time they regulated that debauchery which in maritime cities the strictest magistrates are obliged to tolerate.[1] So wise an organisation was indeed the indispensable corollary of the edict issued at the Hague on December 5, 1405, by William IV. of Bavaria, by which all merchants introducing their products into the island of Walcheren were obliged to present them in the first instance upon the market-place of Middelburg.[2]

It would be very pleasant to follow step by step the development of this industrial prosperity, to dwell upon the commercial expansion that was so fruitful in good results, and to study its smallest details. At first this great foreign development did not operate directly; connections were made through the counting-houses at Bruges. The corporations of foreign merchants, then called the 'nations,' having an organisation at once administrative and financial, governed by consuls, and presenting such cohesion that they attained to political influence, served as intermediaries. They it was who established the first stores and set the first agencies going. We constantly find their names in the handwritings of the municipal scribes or the legislators of Middelburg.

---

[1] *Register Publicatien van Middelburg* 1562, *tot* 1603, No. 2,410 of the Inventory.
[2] *Gulden Register*, folio 148. *Inventaris*, No. 103.

The councillors and traders of the 'nation' of Lucca, those of the 'nation of the coast of Biscay and province of Quipuscua,' those of the 'nation of Venetia,' of the 'nation of the seacoast of Spain,' of the 'Portuguese nation,' of the 'nation of Andalusia,' are all enumerated in their turn. To these the merchants of the Hanseatic towns are to be added.

By degrees the 'prestige' of Bruges declines, while that of Middelburg increases, and in a short time the latter city no longer requires a negotiator between itself and the other peoples of Europe. The greatest, the most eminent among the foreign Powers do not hesitate to hold direct communication with the 'Magistrat' of Middelburg. In 1439 we find Francesco Foscari, the Doge of Venice,[1] addressing himself to the authorities of the city, and his example was followed by the administrators of more neighbouring territories, and the governors of less distant cities.

In 1482, the Mayor and Aldermen of Calais,[2] in the following year the Lord Mayor and aldermen of London,[3] in 1489 the prefect, the baillie, the councillors, and traders of Edinburgh,[4] took up their pens by turns to exchange courteous words and profitable bargains with the 'Magistrat' of Middelburg. After governors, baillies, ministers, and mayors, come kings themselves, who do not disdain to enter into direct com-

---

[1] Charter on parchment, *Inventaris*, No. 202.
[2] See *Inventaris*, No. 530.
[3] Ibid. No. 549.
[4] Ibid. No. 602.

munication with the capital of Zealand :—James IV. of Scotland, Henry VII. of England, and others; and this continues until in due time 'Lycorne Herald' of the ' most noble and puissant prince having the rule and governance of the kingdom of Scotland,'[1] and ' Bretagne, king-at-arms to the most Christian Queen, Duchess of Brittany and Milan,'[2] present themselves before the burgomasters, aldermen, and councillors of Middelburg.

At this point the history of the city becomes especially and doubly interesting to us, for we arrive at its connection with old France, at the close and intimate relations which existed between Middelburg and our former compatriots. This portion of its history is little known either in Holland or among us French people, and I will take leave to lift a corner of the veil that hides it.

At what epoch did our ancestral compatriots enter into the commercial relation with the Middelburg merchants that afterwards attained so great a development? It is very difficult, if not indeed impossible, to answer this question. By adopting certain more or less imaginary dates, we may assign a venerable antiquity to the transaction, but as I am desirous to advance nothing except grave and proven facts, I shall limit myself to the data afforded by the archives of Middelburg and the statements of certain trustworthy authors. With the assistance of these

[1] *Brieven van der Stadt*, 1500-1529, No. 50, *Inventaris*, No. 104.
[2] In 1521; Charter 258; *Inventaris*, No. 1,161.

authorities we may assign, if not a certain, at least a probable date to the beginnings of the great commerce between Middelburg and the French towns.

The first document in the archives in which we find mention of French merchants bears date May 12, 1440. This is an act of seizure. On the demand of certain traders of Rouen, the law officers (*taalieden*) of Middelburg place an embargo upon a ship in the roadstead before Arnemuiden, laden with wines on her voyage to Amsterdam. As you will perceive, this document reveals a great deal. As a matter of course, any measure of such a nature, taken by lawyers, in the name of injured parties, indicates previous contracts, and consequently relations of old date. In 1440, then, the Staple of French wines already existed at Middelburg, and that Staple was itself only the result of a much more ancient connection.

Why, indeed, should it have been thought desirable to establish a Staple unless those wines came thither in great abundance, and unless their consumption had long before been included among the needs of daily life? If such were not the case, to establish the Staple would have been to strangle a new trade in its birth without any advantage whatever accruing from the deed.

Therefore, as the Staple existed in 1440, we may confidently reckon that our compatriots had been in the habit of frequenting the market of Middelburg and the port of Arnemuiden for at least half a century before that date; that they had not come thither in great numbers at first is evident, because otherwise their presence would have led to the granting of privileges analogous to those which were granted, as we have seen, to other 'nations.' And, besides, Smallegange, who mentions in his excellent Chronicle[1] the arrival of the Lombards and the Spaniards in 1383, and that of the Portuguese in 1390, makes no allusion to the French. Let us see, then, whether there does not exist between the two dates, 1390 and 1440, a record of any fact which brought about a considerable extension of the connection between the French and the Zealanders.

On the 6th of August, 1415, the marriage of Jacqueline of Bavaria, daughter of Count William VI., with Duke John of Lorraine, son of Charles VI., King of France, took place, and, as it seems to me, this incident, occurring within the half-century in question, had a great and special influence upon the mutual relations of the two nations.

Jacqueline was the princess-heiress of the two great countships of Holland and Zealand. On the death of her father she proceeded to assume the government of them, and her young husband, who already looked forward to the time when he should unite under his own rule the two fairest fiefs of Europe, would naturally do all in his power to further the union of his future subjects, and promote commercial exchange between them. Unhappily, death and madness traversed these wise and hopeful projects.

[1] *Nieuwe-Cronyk van Zeeland*, 1096.

In 1417 Duke John of Lorraine died, and the insanity of Charles VI. enabled the English to invade our territory, and permitted them to occupy Normandy. Thus we lose the traces of our compatriots, for the traders of Bordeaux and Rouen were from thenceforth numbered among English merchants.

We must, therefore, not be surprised to find that the presence of the French at Middelburg did not become a prominent fact in the history of the city until after the victories of Charles VII. had set France free from the yoke of the foreigner; and especially until after Philip the Good had seized upon the inheritance of Jacqueline of Bavaria.

In 1456, we find rules laid down for trade in the 'white wines of France and the red wines of Gascony,'[1] and we discover that our compatriots are settled in the country, where they exercise functions of various kinds. Guillaume de Poupet is Receiver of Finances;[2] Jean Lanternier, barber and valet to the Count de Charolais, obtains the office of ballast-master in the port of Arnemuiden;[3] Jean Hewet, of Troyes, in Champagne, sets up at Middelburg as a surgeon, 'meester van surgie,'[4] and Jehan Clementsot gets a license to keep a gaming-house.[5] At length, in 1406, their number has increased so much that Maximilian makes special mention in his edicts of the places 'where those of the nation of France are ac-

---

[1] *Inventaris van het oud Archief van Middelburg*, No. 300.
[2] Ibid. No. 298.   [3] Ibid. No. 324.
[4] Ibid. No. 368.   [5] Ibid. No. 441.

customed to lodge,' and grants to all of that nationality a franchise of nine months for their ships, vehicles, provisions, and merchandise, consisting of wines, cereals, &c.[1]

The French merchants did not reside at Middelburg from preference. Their ships put in at Arnemuiden, because there the wines were gauged, and the counting-houses were established; and although at Middelburg itself a special landing-place was reserved for them, which is to this day called the Quay of Rouen (Rouansche Kade), all those who were not obliged by local trades, or by holding some special office, to reside in the city, lived at the waterside. In this respect indeed they did but follow the fashion of the time, for Guicciardini says that 'at Arnemuiden more than elsewhere the merchants dwelt for the most part of their time.' There we shall find the Bretons, the 'nation of Brittany,' as they were then called, and in the roadsteads, alongside of ships from Rouen, others from St. Malo.[2] It is in order that she might 'found and build a chapel for the said Bretons in the new Church of Saint Martin, in the said Arnemuiden, that the Most Christian Maude of France, Queen Duchess of Brittany and Milan,' she who was then called 'the good Queen,' sent her king-at-arms and her 'procurer' or attorney, Johann Leden, to the 'Magistrat' of Middelburg.[3]

Even then the intercourse between the two

---

[1] *Inventaris*, No. 639.   [2] Ibid. No. 526.
[3] Ibid. Nos. 1,149 and 1,150.

countries was of long standing. In another letter, dated from Cognac on the 9th of March, 1520, the good Queen invokes 'the former amity and continuation of merchandise between one and the others.' These good relations, confirmed by mutual confidence (for in 1507 the magistrates of Middelburg paid a sum of nine thousand florins on the account and 'in acquittal' of the Breton merchants),[1] were not destined to remain uninterrupted. The almost incessant struggle between Francis I. and Charles V. were about to put many hindrances in their way. The young Emperor did, however, confirm the right to the Staple on the 25th of June, 1524, and although, in consequence of the hazards of the war, a good many ships, laden with French wines, were about that time obliged to abandon the port of Arnemuiden, and to put in at Veer, the privilege remained none the less a source of large profit to the town, and prosperity to the inhabitants.[2]

No more convincing proof of the latter fact is needed than the earnestness of the protest of the people of Middelburg against a proclamation by the Regent in 1546, which seemed to threaten Arnemuiden with the loss of its lucrative monopoly by the extension of the privilege of the Staple to the city of Zierikzee.

For the rest, having secured the co-operation of a certain number of French towns, the merchants of

---

[1] *Inventaris*, Nos. 1,165 and 1,166.
[2] Ibid. No. 1,316.

Middelburg did not sleep upon their laurels, but made great efforts to obtain the confidence and friendship of the whole country. In 1538, they sent deputies to La Rochelle to plead in favour of their city, and to endeavour to divert certain wine-growers who dealt habitually with Bergen-op-Zoom from their customary market. The deputies produced such an impression, that the mayor and aldermen declared their proceedings ' to be right and equitable, and the occasion of continuing more and more the ancient friendship and frequentation of their town.'[1]

Better still, a few days later ' the said mayor of La Rochelle declared, in the presence of Joost Doversteghe, Burgomaster of Bergen-op-Zoom, that none should henceforth be obliged to go to the market of Bergen.'[2]

This, however, did not prevent Joost Doversteghe from making an agreement with certain individuals, and about the same time the ships of Middelburg arrested upon the Roompot some boats laden with French wines, which were on their way to Bergen. This would seem to prove that competition from that quarter was not at an end.[3]

From that time forth, however, it may be said that the commercial relations between the two cities were not only cordial, but active. This is proved by the bitterness with which, in 1550, ' the mayor, aldermen, and councillors of the town of La Rochelle

---

[1] *Inventaris*, Nos. 1,958, 1,960, 1,961, 1,964, 1,965, and 1,966.
[2] Ibid. No. 1,696.   [3] Ibid. No. 1,690.

complained to their Zealand colleagues' of the subsidy of five sols which it pleased his Majesty the Emperor to put upon wines coming into the city of Middelburg, and of 'the prejudice which the two towns sustained thereby.' Thus, notwithstanding the tax, the disagreements between the monarchs, the risks of war and violence which were the inevitable result of the royal discord, the mutual relations of the two countries became daily more intimate, closer, and more confidential.

Nor was this the case with respect to the Breton coasts only. In an edict of 1558, which enumerates the French wines at that time most in demand at Middelburg, I find the following names :—' Anseroiche (no doubt, Auxerre), Orleansche, Petauwe (no doubt, Poitou), Paillette, Cognasche, Anjosche,' &c. The consequence of this daily extending connection speedily made itself felt. Commerce between the two places grew so rapidly, that the prosperity of both was great.

The French colony at Middelburg became not only very numerous, but very rich, and I may add that it was also distinguished for charity and benevolence, a large portion of its wealth being employed to relieve poverty and prevent misfortune. Evidence of this benevolence has been preserved from the ancient date of 1580, which denotes such lofty and delicate feeling, that I cannot resist the temptation to quote it at length. The document refers to the inauguration of what our compatriots of those days called by the euphonious name of '*Liber bonæ voluntatis*,' or the 'Book of Accounts of the Abbey of Good Will.'[1] The founders of this association, the abbot and brethren of Good Will, state their request to the magistrate, accompanied by the following considerations, which sufficiently indicate the aim and bearing of this charitable institution :—'As it is thus that the Eternal One, our good God, commands us all to hold in consideration His poor members, and to minister to their poverty, calamity, and misery, the merchants and traders of the French nation, bearing this in mind, have in time past, for the relief and subvention of the said poor, introduced a very praiseworthy and most holy custom among them, for several years faithfully observed, as well in this city of Middelburg as in the city of Antwerp, by which the excessive expenses that formerly were made on banquets given by the French merchants the first time they arrived at the said towns, have been by common accord converted into works of charity and alms, so that, in place of the said useless expenses, it was ordered and consented that the French new-comers should give to the almoner's box, ordained for the said purpose, a certain sum in money, according to their quality, the inventory of their goods, and the taxation of the said French, in order that the said sum should be distributed to the poor, the unfortunate, and the unhappy of their nation, arriving by

---

[1] See *Register ten Rade*, April 18, 1566, page 442. *Inventaris*, No. 2,871.

land or by sea in the city, so that, without begging, they may be enabled to return to the place of their birth. In the said almoner's box were also to be placed for the same purpose the earnest money which the said merchants received from the sale of their merchandise, together with the fines paid by those who contravened the ordinances and statutes which had been constituted among them, that they might live in peace, tranquillity, and union; and in order that the collection and distribution of the said moneys be made duly and without reproach, there shall be elected, by plurality of votes, a superintendent, to be called the "Abbot of Goodwill," with certain of his assistants who shall take order that the whole be faithfully administered.'

This venerable document inspires us with such a good opinion of our compatriots, that we cannot select a more favourable moment for taking leave of them, and we must not allow them to induce us to lose sight of Middelburg and its history.

The valuable privilege of the Staple of the wines of France was, as I have said, one of the most important sources of wealth to the old city. The greatest commercial fortunes of that epoch had no other origin. The wine merchants—'Wijnheeren,' or 'lords of the wines,' as they were called—formed with the coopers the two richest branches of industry, and the united trades composed the most influential and powerful corporation of the town. They carried things with a high hand in the Town Council, and had authority in all the affairs of the city. When by-and-by we visit the Stadhuis, we shall see large paintings representing imposing groups of grave and majestic personages, of austere mien and air so noble that they might be taken for a bench of magistrates; but they are simply the members of the corporation of the 'Kuypers'—the master coopers and wine merchants of that time.

The other trades were likewise formed into corporations. In 1430 the most important among them —such as butchers, bakers, oil merchants, chandlers, ironmongers, barbers, cloth-cutters and workers, &c. —received their rules and were invested with their privileges. Their general organisation bore considerable resemblance to what we know of the corporations of the Middle Ages. They were subject to certain conditions of capacity and to certain public services. Their members were bound to acquire the rights of citizenship, to pay a fee on entry, and to have served a previous apprenticeship. In certain trades the candidate had to execute a piece of work or undergo an examination. Besides this, in time of peace members of these corporations were bound to do military service for a year, and were afterwards enrolled in the various companies which composed the 'trades.'

In exchange for these obligations and for this service, the corporations possessed several privileges and enjoyed prerogatives which in some cases were the source of large profits. Thus, the members of the corporation of butchers had not only the sole right of slaughtering cattle of all kinds, but the inhabitants were forbidden to purchase meat out of the town. The inn-keepers and tavern-keepers had to take their necessary supplies from the public market, the Vleesch-huis, or 'house of meat.'[1] Every individual was permitted to knead or bake his own bread, or to have it kneaded with his own flour and baked by the baker; but no one was allowed to sell bread unless he belonged to the corporation of bakers.[2] None except members of the corporation of the oil merchants could sell butter, cheese, eggs, mustard, salt, vinegar, soap, pottery, brooms, wooden spoons, forks, sieves, &c.[3]

Barbers were permitted to practise surgery (*syrurgie*) on payment of a small supplementary tax. Their rule also extended over the jaws of their fellow-citizens, for foreign dentists were tolerated in the town only during the kermesse.[4]

The cloth-workers and tailors ('sewers and makers of coats') had the exclusive privilege of supplying the 'trade of the boatmen' of Arnemuiden. As for the cloth mercers, not only did they make their brethren of Arnemuiden pay a tax, and oblige them to share the expense of the annual trade procession, but they reserved to themselves the sole right of displaying their goods. The other traders were obliged

---

[1] *Ordonnancie voor de Vleeschhouvres. Inventaris*, No. 164.
[2] *Register Diverse Gildens*, No. 60. *Inventaris*, No. 165.
[3] *Inventaris*, No. 166.
[4] *Diverse Gildens*, No. 44. *Inventaris*, No. 169.

to confine themselves to their houses or cellars. The only exception made was in favour of the English and Scotch, who twice a week were permitted to set up their booths upon the market-place.[1] And finally, almost all these regulations were accompanied with this curious restriction, 'It is forbidden to married men to live with any woman except their own wives.' And it seems that such a recommendation was by no means superfluous, for in 1411 we find the 'Magistrat' obliged to occupy itself with the question of bastardy, which was becoming serious.

None of these corporations, however great their privileges, approached in importance to that of the Kuypers and the Wijnheeren. Thus, whenever this predominant association thought proper to complain of any encroachment on its rights, all the others made common cause with it. This was only just; for it was to the interest of the tailors, who possessed the right of making clothes for the sailors, that the number of ships coming into the port of Arnemuiden should be considerable; and the same was the case with the drapers, who furnished the cloth to the tailors; with the innkeepers, whose houses were frequented by masters, traders, and seamen; and also with the butchers and bakers, who furnished provisions for all.

Therefore, no sooner was Arnemuiden—the port in which all this traffic was carried on—menaced with serious competition by any maritime city of Zealand

---

[1] *Diverse Gildens*, No. 25. *Inventaris*, 170.

or any neighbouring port, than a chorus of complaints and remonstrances made itself heard in the Great Council of Malines, and frequently echoed as far as the Court of Spain. You remember what a storm of protest arose when Veer attempted to usurp the famous Staple of Wines. That Middelburg should rise like one man 'to prevent its neighbours from proceeding further in their efforts to secure for themselves that which it regarded as the fairest jewel of its crown,' is easy to understand; but that it should contend with the elements, that it should endeavour, by force, and contrary to the decisions of nature, to retain certain advantages, was to exhibit an ill-regulated love of monopoly, and to put forward exorbitant pretensions. This is precisely what Middelburg did. In our days, there seems to be something almost silly in its complaint of the desertion of the fishermen who abandoned Arnemuiden, 'which by the action of Flushing has lost the traffic of herrings.'[1] It seems absurd when we say, in reference to Middelburg, that 'the citizens and inhabitants of that town had no other purpose than to transport themselves into wholesomer, more pleasant, and more frequented places than is the same city, the air of which is reputed by all to be unhealthy and hurtful to the human body.'[2] Nevertheless, such were the protests which were put forward and the reasons which were assigned.

---

[1] *Register Differenten tusschen de stad Midd ende steden van Vlessinge, Veer, &c. Inventaris*, No. 1,924. [2] *Inventaris*, No. 2,172.

To preserve its own leonine privilege, and to prevent the fishermen and ship-owners from using other ports more commodious and easier of access, Middelburg did not hesitate to 'foul its own nest,' to exaggerate the defects of its climate and the insalubrity of its air. This must have been hard upon its astute corporations; but they knew well what they were about. To threaten Charles V. or Philip II. with the ruin of Middelburg was to threaten the Court of Spain with the loss of a large revenue, and that Court, being always needy, was willing to connive at any extortion and to sanction much more exorbitant pretensions, if only it might thereby secure itself from such a loss.

We must not, however, conclude, from the sacrifice of its pride, to which the Zealand capital submitted in order to preserve the prosperity of its port, that it was invariably on good terms with the latter. It was by no means the case that a perfect understanding always subsisted between Arnemuiden and Middelburg, and that their union was a cloudless one. Arnemuiden, overtaxed, and exhausted by the exactions of its powerful neighbour, more than once made bitter complaint, raising its lamentable voice and making known its grievances to the Sovereign Council. It is very curious to observe with what disdain the 'Magistrat' of Middelburg treats these complaints, which it qualifies as 'frivolous, impertinent, and other than true facts,' and with what haughtiness it replies that the inhabitants of

Arnemuiden 'are not the cause of the arrival of ships, but the good and secure depth of the water, and the due control and police kept by those of Middelburg over the place of Arnemuiden.' The 'Magistrat' invokes, in support of its uncontrolled domination, the example of Delft, 'none having ever thought of questioning or limiting the empire of that town over Delftshaven, which is two leagues away from it, while hardly half a league lies between Middelburg and Arnemuiden.' And, when the ill-treated port revolts, and retorts that, 'to make a true comparison and similitude, the city of Middelburg is like a sack, the belly representing the town, and the mouth of the sack the place of Arnemuiden; the mouth of the sack being cut off, the rest will be useless and of no good,' Middelburg promptly replies that, although the business is done at Arnemuiden, 'the moneys are at Middelburg, and so are the traders,' for there are 'such merchants in Middelburg, that two of them do more trade with their own money than all the men of Arnemuiden in general.'[1]

I have thought it worth while to bring to light a few items of this dispute between two cities linked together by such complex interests, having so many points in common, and identically the same sources of revenue to protect. These acrimonious utterances enable us to judge of the spirit of antagonism which then existed between all those cities; for they were

[1] *Register Differenten tusschen de stad Midd ende steden van Middelbury en Arnemuiden*, No. 14. *Inventaris*, No. 1,461.

rivals, and always jealous of one another, notwithstanding their community of interests. Nature, which had created these intimate relations, was now about to terminate them. The port of Arnemuiden shortly began to silt up with sand, and Middelburg was placed in direct communication with the sea by a fine canal, which served as a harbour. This was an inestimable advantage, 'so that,' says an old author,[1] 'the largest ships come so commodiously, and in such great numbers, that its commerce yields to no other city in Holland.'

Dissensions of far greater gravity broke out before long. The great movement of emancipation was progressing. In 1572 the taking of Brill brought things to a crisis. Veer and Flushing flung themselves into the movement, while wealthy Middelburg which had just been reinstated in the plenitude of its privileges, remained faithful to the house of Spain, to which it owed the momentary overthrow of its rivals and the restitution of its precious prerogatives. For a long time the contest was waged at a distance, and with varying fortunes, but, towards the end of 1572, the Zealanders resolved to strike a great blow, and to overthrow by force of arms the last remaining bulwark of Spanish oppression in Walcheren. On both sides great works were constructed, the dykes were fortified, and the bombardment began. But the people of Veer and Flushing had a great advantage over their adversaries—they were masters of

[1] *Les Délices des Pays Bas.*

the sea; while poor Middelburg, having no means of getting supplies, notwithstanding the courage and self-denial of its inhabitants, was forced to yield to the pressure of famine, that implacable enemy of all besieged places. A first convoy of provisions, led by Sancho d'Avila, was beaten back to the point of Borselen, by Jan le More, Admiral of Flushing, but succeeded after a second effort in getting through the lines, and relieving Arnemuiden.

'The fight was very cruel,' says a contemporary, 'for none were spared; all were either killed or drowned. On board the great ship "the Elephant,"[1] all the human limbs, arms, legs, heads, &c., were collected in baskets, so that it seemed to be rather a slaughter-house than a ship.'

A second convoy, led by Admiral de Beauvays and Colonel Mondragon, was to have passed by Westkapelle, disembarked there, and gained Middelburg by the inland route. A portion of the provisions reached the town safely, and Mondragon remained there to take the command. It was then June, and in November a fresh attempt by Admiral de Beauvays failed completely, and from the roofs of their churches the besieged could see the Spanish ships chased by the fleet of Admiral Boisot, and flying in the direction of Bergen-op-Zoom.

At last, in January, 1574, when the town was re-

---

[1] The 'Elephant' was one of the largest ships of the Spanish fleet, which was captured in the course of the action by the people of Flushing.

duced to the last extremity, the Spanish commander resolved to make a final effort, and this time he neglected no precaution to secure victory for his fleet, that great armada which we have seen sail out from Bergen-op-Zoom, under the command of Romaro, and whose disastrous fate we have witnessed under the walls of Rommerswaal. 'At this moment famine pressed so hard upon those of Middelburg, that they had already eaten all the horses they had, the dogs, the cats, and the rats. They made bread of linseed and other seeds, and ate the husks from which the oil had been extracted.' Between the last Christmas day and the surrender, more than fifteen hundred and fifty persons died of starvation.

A manuscript note of that time, communicated to me by my friend, Mynheer van Stoppelaar, will awaken terrible recollections, hardly seven years old, among ourselves. 'I, Andries Mathieusz,' says this note, 'I married my wife on the 21st of February, 1574, on the very same day when this town of Middelburg was given over into the hands of the Prince of Orange, and to celebrate our wedding we had cakes of linseed (*lysnet wafelen*), and horse's flesh at two schillings the pound, a pound of bread costing six schillings, and at this price it is not easy to have any; likewise a pound of butter at four schillings.'

It was in fact at that date that Mondragon was forced to yield. Some days before he had despatched Captain Trenchart to endeavour to hurry up the reserves, and had ordered him 'to represent the weakness of the soldiers: that there died of them more than twenty each day, and that they would no longer eat the husks of linseed, and were reduced to despair.[1]

Succour was not to come; on the 19th of September, Middelburg capitulated; Mondragon obtained permission to retire with his troops on the most honourable conditions, and three hundred citizens of Veer and Flushing were placed as guards over their rival, now humiliated, vanquished, and prostrated by famine.

The result which was expected from this victory did not, however, come to pass. Instead of allowing this rich and important city to be ruined by the jealousy of its neighbours, instead of permitting Veer and Flushing to take possession of its commerce, and to deck themselves in its spoils, the States took the commercial prosperity of their new conquest under their safeguard, and the event turned out quite other than had been anticipated. Veer, forsaken by commerce and abandoned by foreigners, declined from day to day, and although Flushing made rapid progress, which was, indeed, only due to its admirable position at the entrance of the Scheldt, it never attained the first rank. As for Middelburg, its attachment to the Spaniards, a matter of mingled interest and gratitude, did not survive the sufferings it had endured in their cause. The city held that its

[1] Meteren.

debt was paid; henceforth all its sympathies turned towards the common country, and it proved itself as well disposed to the States as it had ever been to its first masters. It was well recompensed: all its privileges were confirmed, and on several occasions the Stadtholder took up his residence within its walls. A great number of letters and documents, written by the hand of William the Silent himself, are dated from Middelburg.

A fresh impulse was given to the already well-developed commercial instincts of the town, and it speedily became more powerful than ever. Many establishments of public utility, together with institutions of credit, which were of great benefit to its distant transactions, were founded. In 1600 a bank of exchange, which not only replaced the Lombards and their 'tables of exchange,' but undertook the negotiation of bonds, and the payment of letters of credit, was established; and in the same year the *Assurantie Kamer* or ' Chamber of Assurances,' the first which existed in the United Provinces, was opened. In 1636 the *Leen Bank* or ' bank of loans,' which facilitated loans and regulated exchanges, was instituted, to be succeeded in 1661 by the *Kamer van de desolate Boedels* (literally, the 'Chamber of hopeless credits'), which provided, as far as possible, by means of curators, administrators, and sequestrators, for the defence of the interest of creditors, by keeping a watch on insolvents and fugitive bankrupts.

Besides this, when the constitution of the famous

East India Company took place, the Zealand capital was not forgotten. Middelburg had a fourth share in that enterprise, and the benefit reaped by its whole population was enormous. A single example will suffice to indicate the wealth of the Company. At the beginning of the seventeenth century we find the two principal fiefs of the island in the possession of its chief agents; the Seigneurie of Westkapelle, in that of Mynheer Veth, Burgomaster of Middelburg; and the Seigneurie of Domburg in those of Mynheer van Dieshoek, Alderman of the same city. Both these personages were directors of the East India Company, and it was with the profits of that Company that they purchased these princely domains. Its new source of prosperity did not lead Middelburg to overlook its privilege of the Staple, and that feudal prerogative continued to place the town in obligatory and constant relations with the whole world. 'Our capital,' says Smallegange, who wrote in 1696, 'is, at this moment, in continual correspondence and constant communication with the East and West Indies, with Brazil, the coast of Guinea, Angola, the Levant, Italy, Spain, England, &c.; all merchandise coming from the East is subject to our Right of Staple (*Stapel recht*). Wines, oils, essences, and other liquids coming from the Eastern Countries, from Italy, France, and Spain, were obliged to put into port, before the Crane of Middelburg, and there be verified, measured, and gauged.'

Now that all feudal privileges have vanished before the modern spirit, and that the principles of commercial liberty have swept away these extortionate prerogatives, the great commercial fortune of Middelburg has ceased to exist, and its prodigious activity has given place to tranquil leisure. If the Zealand capital should sometimes regret its high and palmy days, which were so fertile in great institutions, if it should cast a sorrowful retrospective glance upon its vanished commercial prosperity, who could blame it? More sensible, more intelligent, more reasonable than other eminent places which have fallen into decay; Middelburg comprehends the causes that led to its industrial decline, and does not rebel against progress; the wise city is not like its Flemish rivals, who, being also deprived of their former splendour, revolt against God and man, and would fain turn back the course of the ages, that they might recover their primitive state. Middelburg has preserved relics of its past sufficiently great and sufficiently beautiful to console it; and few cities are better deserving of a visit, such as we now propose to make to the ancient capital.

CHAPTER XIV.

A BREAKFAST ON BOARD—THE ABDY HOTEL—THE ABBEY AND THE STADHUIS—'LANGE JAN' AND 'GEKKE BETJE'—THE TREASURE-HOUSE OF THE TOWN—THE ZEALAND SOCIETY—THE TAPESTRIES—THE KERMESSE.

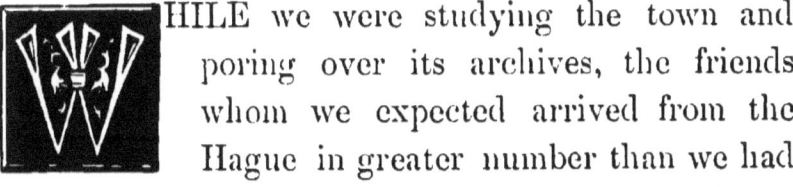HILE we were studying the town and poring over its archives, the friends whom we expected arrived from the Hague in greater number than we had counted on, but we were not likely to complain of that. On the other hand, those whom we expected from Brussels have unfortunately not arrived at all. We have two ladies with us, Madame de Stolipine, whom you already know, and the Princess Naritschkin, and there are four men, Nicholas de Stolipine, the young Prince Gagarine, Count Goubatstow, and a young Russian tutor. You may imagine how our guests were welcomed. We did the honours of Middelburg, and then we set out in our boat and went down the canal to Veer; there we gave them a breakfast prepared entirely by ourselves, and by a lucky accident I have found the *menu* amongst my notes:—

Le potage Parmentier.
Les hors-d'œuvre.
Les bouchées aux crevettes.
L'omelette au jambon de Zélande.
Les tournedos en tortue.
Les pommes parisiennes.
Les poulets de grain rôtis.
La salade.
Les haricots verts à la maître d'hôtel.
La flamusse charolaise.
Le gâteau de Middelbourg.
Dessert.
Vins : scherry doré, saint-julien, rudesheimer et Rœderer.

Our cooking was pronounced excellent, and we were also complimented upon the style in which we served up the repast. True, the two best sauces, appetite and good humour, came to hand on the occasion, and they no doubt contributed largely to our success.

After breakfast we visited Veer and its Stadhuis. The Burgomaster, who was waiting for the ladies at the Stadhuis, constituted himself our guide, and showed us all the curiosities of the place in the kindest manner. Then we returned in a carriage by the road along which I have taken you on foot. We stopped at Overduyn, and we dined at Domburg. Now we are once more at Middelburg, and we are going out for a fresh inspection of the Zealand capital.

The sun is bright, and the city is full of life and bustle. The kermesse is going on, and from morning until night, as well as from night until morning, everybody is astir. Let us go and fetch our friends; they are at the Abdy Hotel.

The Abdy Hotel is not a vulgar caravanserai; it deserves more than a passing glance. Let me take you into the house; perhaps you may hereafter be glad that I have done so. Who can say what destiny has in store for him? If some day, weary of the joys of this world, and wishing to renounce the fuss and bother of existence, you would like to bury yourself in a half-solitude, while still residing in a city, you had better come to the Abdy Hotel. Calm and peacefulness seem to have taken up their abode in this place, and never was there a dwelling so conducive to meditation.

It seems, indeed, as if the fates had combined to make of this renowned, frequented, and busy hotel a silent and solitary retreat. In order to reach it one has to thread a perfect maze of streets, cross a labyrinth of places like courtyards, and pass under a whole series of feudal arches. It is like penetrating into some fortress; which done, one finds oneself in a wide space, shaded by fine trees, and surrounded by venerable Gothic buildings. On the right and left are ogives, turrets, dormer windows, ancient gateways, venerable arcades, and archaic gables, the whole surmounted by a spire, partly of wood and partly of stone, called *lange Jan*, or 'long John,' which terminates in a gilded weathercock. This space is the courtyard of the ancient Abbey, which was built by Bishop Gondebault, enlarged and decorated by William II., King of the Romans, and, after the expulsion of the abbots and the departure of the monks, secularised and transformed into the Court of Zealand.

We ought to be thankful to those who, while they have adapted these ancient religious edifices to civil purposes, have scrupulously respected their character. They might have entirely done away with these constructions of a former age, and substituted something utterly commonplace for them. They have not done this, and they ought to be emphatically praised; for although two modern buildings occupy the extremities of the square—the Governor's palace on the one side, and the Abdy Hotel on the other—and injure to a certain extent the venerable effect of the whole, the discord is not to be imputed to the carelessness or the bad taste of the authorities. The enemy who has done this was fire.

Let us hear what the old authors—those who continued the work of Guicciardini—say:[1]—'The said Abbey was a beautiful structure, which, by a dreadful fire that arose in that city (Middelburg), was almost entirely burned. Among other parts, the roof of the church; the spire of the tower, which was lofty, fair, and straight; the refectory; the circuit of the cloisters; the kitchen; the chapter-room, with also the large and ample library, exquisite pictures of great price, and altar-tables; likewise several rich vestments and jewels of the church.'

Blaeu estimates that more than two hundred houses were destroyed in this terrible conflagration.[2]

[1] Edition of 1625. [2] Blaeu, *Theatrum urbicum Belgicæ Fæderatæ*.

The houses were rebuilt; but the library, which included precious illuminated manuscripts of the great school of the Burgundian miniaturists, and the 'exquisite paintings,' among which there must have been masterpieces of Jean Grossart—the great Jean de Mabuse, as he already wrote his name at that period—for he was then living at Middelburg, and he worked for the abbots, were gone for ever.

The great clock-tower rose like a phœnix from its ashes, springing again from the soil with which it had been levelled, grander, more lofty than before. 'They have put a new cap upon the tower,' writes Meteren, a contemporary of this resurrection, 'which has cost—together with the large new bell and so great and beautiful a horologe, that nowhere can the like of it be seen—near to one hundred and fifty thousand florins, according to the calculation that they have made who understand the matter.'[1] And now the great and beautiful horologe squeaks out the hours, and at intervals of seven minutes drones a fragment of a chant so Wagnerian in character, that it makes the hearer keenly regret the wasteful expenditure of good money, so long, long ago.

But we have lingered long enough in this historic square. Its portrait has been taken twenty times,

---

[1] In the works of the poet Cats, folio edition. The drawing is by Van de Venne, who lived at Middelburg at that period, and not only did the illustration to this edition of Cats, but a number of other plates from Pietersz van der Venne, then a bookseller in the town. See the register of deeds, grants, pensions, &c. of the States General, at the date of July 22, 1620.

and you will find an original sketch of it in the Kenderspeelen, and two or three curious views in the Zealand Chronicles. The sketches and engravings of the last century represent the square occupied by a regiment of citizens in warlike array. Let us go into the hotel and join our friends.

The Abdy Hotel, as I have already said, is not an inn of an ordinary kind. It has no flaunting signboard; there is nothing about it to attract the eye; one has to divine it, so to speak, behind the screen of trees that hides its façade, and its name is written up in letters so small that the inscription is hardly legible. The house is clean, the rooms are simply furnished, luxury is conspicuous by its absence. The Abdy Hotel is highly esteemed in Middelburg, much frequented by people from the country, and it is said to be the favourite resort of commercial travellers, a noisy and talkative class of persons in all lands.[1] And yet, notwithstanding this, all is calm and silent in the Abdy Hotel. It might almost be a deserted house. Life within its walls is as regular as in a cloister. In the morning people take their coffee; in the afternoon they dine; in the evening they sup on boiled eggs. Breakfast, dinner, and supper take place at fixed and immutable hours; and nobody ever thinks of disputing them. If you were to ask for a cup of tea at noon, it would be proposed that you should wait until nine o'clock in the evening. If you

---

[1] Especially in the *Cronyk van Zeelandd*, by Smallegange, 1696.

were to ask for a cup of coffee, you would be put off until the next morning.

Observe, that the grave and dignified Mynheer Bulterys is absolutely convinced that in acting thus he fulfils all the laws of hospitality according to their most liberal interpretation. Stern of countenance and majestic of bearing, he belongs to that class of Zealand hotel-keepers who consider that they exercise a priesthood rather than a profession. They would be astonished if they heard themselves described as dealers in soup and lodgings. They regard themselves as members of an order of superior beings, to whom Providence has assigned the beneficent office of housing travellers and feeding the hungry. If they accept compensation, it is merely that they may not offend their customers, and if they fix the scale of that compensation somewhat high, it is to show that they take those customers to be both rich and generous.

Observe also that, individually, I have nothing but praise to bestow on Mynheer Bulterys. In my favour he departed in many respects from rules which his numerous customers regarded as utterly irrevocable. On several occasions he made an exception in my favour of which I am justly proud, and which I esteem all the more highly, that other persons, much more distinguished, and especially more powerful, than myself, have not been treated with the like consideration. The following anecdote will satisfactorily illustrate my meaning :—

One day, while the Governor of the province was still residing at the Abdy Hotel (the Government House was not yet quite ready for him), Mynheer Bulterys was announced, and addressed his Excellency as follows:—'Governor, you have a palace, and you lodge at my inn. Many unfortunate travellers, not so well off as your Excellency, knock at my door every night, and I am obliged to deny them admittance. Is this just? I venture to put the question to your Excellency.'

The Governor, taken aback, could only ask, 'What do you want me to do?'

'I desire,' replied Mynheer Bulterys, respectfully, but firmly, 'that your Excellency should go and live at your palace.'

Here come our friends! Let us leave the old Hof van Zeeland, not without saluting from afar the hospitable mansion of the Governor, where his charming family reside. I have a great affection for them all, and hope it is to some extent reciprocal. And now let us set out on our exploration of the old city.

Middelburg, or 'the city of the centre,' is a handsome town, circular in shape, with a round space in the middle of it, and winding streets outside of this round space. The people we see in the streets are round, affable, and kindly-looking. If you examine the plan of the city, you will see that not a street, a lane, a passage, or an alley in it forms a straight line. If you look at the people, you will not see one who has an ill-tempered expression or in any way a disagreeable aspect. An old writer says of Middelburg, 'It is a round-faced city'; and this description applies as well to the people as to the place. I like to dwell upon the curious analogy between the curvilinear character of the city and the affability of its inhabitants. Right lines are sometimes impressive, but they are always somewhat cold of aspect, severe, and rigid. Curves, on the contrary, are never so. Is it a mere matter of coincidence between these two facts of a different order, which can only be expressed in the French language by the same word (*ronde*), or is there interdependence in it? Does the roundness of the inhabitants proceed from the roundness of the city, or, on the contrary, did its architects desire that the capital of Zealand should justify the old saying of the country, '*Goed rond, goed Zeeuwsch*'; or, 'Very round, very Zealandish'? I cannot decide this question, and I think it best to leave it in doubt, especially as the roundness of both city and citizens may be otherwise explained.

If we study the map of the city, as Smallgange shows it in the fifteenth century, we shall see that the Abbey forms a sort of nucleus in the centre, that around this the streets are built in a circular fashion, and lead to a rampart which describes an almost perfect circle. Let us, then, take the map published by Blaeu, which is exact and complete in all its details. The primitive moat in the former has become the *lange delft*[1]—that is to say, the principal road through the city—and the streets have been made in parallels with this high road, and also in curvilinear fashion. Even the canals partake of this character, and the ramparts which enclose the city complete the system of concentric curves.

The Abbey, with its rounded form, was, then, the point of departure of the whole construction.

As for the roundness of the inhabitants, I think they inherit it from their ancestors—astute traders, who, being perfectly well aware that 'flies are not to be caught with vinegar'—that is to say, with a forbidding air and pinched faces—contracted habits of sociability from associating with the foreigners who frequented their city. Besides, we must not forget that Middelburg possessed for four centuries the Staple of the wines of France, and the '*purée septembrale*,' as the curé of Meudon called it, has never disposed anybody to melancholy and moroseness, but, on the contrary, makes them frank, amiable, and jolly companions.

Now the Staple exists no longer; and the Wijnheeren, having come down from their pedestal, have ceded the place to mere wine-sellers; but the former good humour remains, and the custom of hearty welcome also.

We are going now to look for the Burgomaster, Mynheer Schorer, at the Stadhuis, and for the Secre-

---

[1] Literally 'the long ditch.' The word *delft*, which is no longer used, was originally derived from the verb *delven*, to dig or hollow out.

tary of the town, Mynheer van Stoppelaar. I am certain that both one and the other will receive us with a cordial shake of the hand, a pleasant smile, and courteous words; no affectation, no reserve, no uncalled-for ceremonial, and that from the first we shall feel ourselves on familiar ground and perfectly at our ease. It is a pleasure to be welcomed after such a fashion. And observe, this is not the rule in the case of the chief magistrates only.

I remember one day that Constant and I, being caught in a very heavy shower of rain, took refuge on the threshold of a shop. We made ourselves as small as possible (which was rather difficult), so as to avoid being wet through, when presently the mistress of the house sent her daughter, a pretty girl of sixteen years old, whose blushes I can still see, to open wide the door behind us. Was not this a charming way of offering us a comfortable shelter and saying, 'Gentlemen, you are at home'?

We go by the *lange delft* to the Stadhuis, and on our way we do not omit to admire several beautiful façades which still remain of old Middelburg. We pass on the right an ancient but well-preserved, or rather well-restored, wooden house; also one of stone, terribly mutilated. Both are deeply interesting, but for different reasons. The former is a specimen of the ancient wooden dwellings that formerly adorned the whole of the city, the other is historical. It was formerly the 'tol' of the Counts of Zealand.

On the left we come to a glittering façade, decorated with carvings and curiously mingled brick and stone. This is called 'The House of the Sun,' on account of a shining star which adorns it, and it was formerly the dwelling of a great shipowner. The star is a reminiscence of the bas-relief which adorned the poop of one of his ships. I should rather have taken it for the house of an architect, judging by the two medallions on the front; the first representing an individual holding a compass, and the second the same personage holding the capital of a column in his hand. This house is a fine specimen of Zealand architecture in the commencement of the seventeenth century.

Also on the left stands the old French church, and beside it the 'Bank of Loans,' originally 'The House of the English and Scotch.' The ancient 'Scotischhuis' was illustrious in the commercial history of the old city, and still retains the characteristics of its famous past. We cannot, however, dwell on the architecture of all these dwellings, however interesting, for in a few minutes we shall be contemplating the beautiful Stadhuis of Middelburg.

This Stadhuis is a real gem. It, is, indeed one of the most graceful and elegant buildings in existence, not only in the Low Countries, but in the whole of Europe. It is not of very great size; it has neither the majestic dimensions of the Halle at Ypres, nor the grandeur of the Hôtel de Ville at Brussels; but, with its two storeys and its elegant belfry, it is the model of what was called in the Middle Ages in France a *parloir aux bourgeois*.

The foundations of the Stadhuis were laid in 1468, and, if I remember aright, it took twenty years to build. It belongs to what is commonly called Burgundian architecture—*i.e.* to the florid style—somewhat tempered by the approach of the Renaissance. In its façade there are twenty-two apertures, ten on the ground floor, ten in the first storey, and two in a projecting gable which ornaments the left side of the edifice. All these openings have ogives, and are surrounded by a simple ornamentation. Those of the first storey are divided by double niches, each containing two statues, placed back to back, and standing under a canopy which, being prolonged in the form of a counterfort, rises to the roof. These statues are twenty-five in number; they represent the Counts of Holland and Zealand. Above the windows of the first storey are elegant ornaments, imitating panels, and extending upwards to the edge of the roof. The latter, which has twenty-four small dormers, terminates on the left in the gable, enriched with niches and pinnacles, which I have already mentioned, and which faces the square; and on the other side by a gable surmounting the lateral façade, which opens into a side-street. The external angle on this side is masked by a tower, with a balcony, niches, and a pierced pinnacle, constituting what was formerly called the 'Brétèque.' This beautiful façade, in perfect preservation, and in which there is not an ungraceful line, is surmounted by an elegant belfry, square and massive throughout two-thirds of its height, afterwards octagon-shaped, pierced, and flanked by four slender turrets, resting on corbels. Were it not for its bulbous roof, which was added after the building of the tower, this belfry would be a model perfect at all points. Even as it is it produces an excellent effect, and is to be reckoned among the finest buildings in the country. In the interior is enclosed the old bell of the city—the bell that called the citizens to arms and the magistrates to council; the bell that rang for festivals, and gave lugubrious warning when fire deepened with its baleful tints the colour of the red roofs of old Middelburg, or when the watchers caught sight of a marauding enemy from afar.

The belfry also rejoices in a clock—always five minutes in advance of the hour marked by *lange Jan*. This peculiarity, which is well known to the public, has procured for it the nickname of *gekke Betje*, or 'Foolish Betsy,' on account of its habit of preceding its long and majestic rival in the march of time. I need not trouble you with the recital of the adventures that illustrate this nickname: it is clear that 'Long John' has not been able to regard 'Foolish Betsy' during so many centuries with total indifference. On her side 'Betsy' has not remained insensible to his incessant contemplation. You may guess that a municipal romance forms itself around these two stone puppets—an inexhaustible romance, whose last chapter cannot be written until one of the two lovers has fallen for ever. It is said that 'Betsy' is threatened with destruction. One of the magistrates told me with profound regret that for a long time the municipal tower has been in an unsafe condition. 'We shall be obliged,' he said, 'to put new foundations under it, or to pull it down.' This latter hypothesis made me wince. 'Pull it down! Could you think of such a thing? Cut the head off one of the most beautiful buildings in the whole of the Netherlands!' 'It is very true,' he said; 'but it would cost a large sum to restore it; and who knows whether we should obtain the necessary credit?' 'You will obtain it— I am sure of it,' said I. 'I could not suspect the city of Middelburg of refusing such a thing; the very doubt does it a gratuitous injury.'

The interior of the Stadhuis has been completely restored. Pure and intact on the outside, throughout all that portion which faces the square, it has undergone sundry alterations in the interior, which coincide in date with its partial reconstruction and enlargement in the last century.

Only one portion of the interior has remained almost intact; the *Vierschaere*, formerly the Justice Room, whose rich dark wood carvings have a truly venerable and imposing effect.

On the first landing is a Museum, or rather a treasure-house, composed of two spacious halls and a long gallery. In its halls every object of art or of value belonging to the past of the ancient and flourishing city has been collected. We feel that the whole municipal life of Middelburg is represented and, so to speak, embalmed in these religiously preserved works of art. The pompous name 'Museum' has not been given to this collection of interesting objects; it is simply called *Oudheids Kamer*, 'The Chamber of Antiquities.'

The first hall is entirely hung with portraits. Here we find the old corporation of the Kuypers and Wijnheeren which I mentioned in the preceding chapter, excellently represented on panels, very well and solidly painted. Look at those stern faces, those venerable figures, those personages all attired in black, so grave and dignified, so proud and lofty of aspect, in their huge wide collars, and you will acknowledge that I do not exaggerate when I say that it is difficult to believe ourselves in the presence of a guild of mere merchants. They are much more like an assembly of royal councillors deliberating upon the fate of a great empire.

Opposite to these imposing personages, who enjoyed all the privileges of the Staple, hang the portraits of the brothers Evertsen, the victorious admirals of Zealand, the naval heroes of Middelburg. There are the brothers Cornelius and Jan, both sons of the soil, 'born of a Zealand family devoted to the sea,' as an old inscription says. They raised the supremacy of their country to its highest point; and after their death Middelburg erected a superb monument to their memory in token of its gratitude. This monument was at first placed in the Church of St. Peter, but after the destruction of the ancient sanctuary it was transferred to the Church of the Abbey.[1] Presently we shall see the chains which were given them, the gold medals which were struck in their honour, their insignia, their speaking-trumpets, and many other souvenirs piously preserved by their descendants. But before we leave this hall, which is eloquent of their renown, let us glance at their illustrious relative, the son of Cornelius Evertsen, who was also a famous admiral, and surnamed 'Keesje the Devil.'[2] The gallery which we now enter is full of curious and interesting documents, carefully preserved relics of old Middelburg, models of monuments (among which is that of '*lange Jan*'), and statues of carved wood of great artistic value.

At last we reach the inner sanctuary, where the books of the Guilds, the badges of the officers of justice, the keys of the city, and the famous bell of the Guild of the Kuypers are arranged in handsome glass cases. Here also are goblets in precious metals, each having its local interest or historical value as well as its fine artistic form. Articles of furniture, too — huge chairs, benches, credence tables and doors; among the latter is a portico, in three parts, covered with fine carvings, and belonging to that transitional period which preceded the Renaissance, and which was so rich in significant and harmonious

---

[1] The history of the Evertsens was written in 1820 by Mynheer J. C. de Jonge, assistant archivist of Middelburg.
[2] Keesje is a familiar abbreviation of Cornelius.

ornamentation. I should never come to an end if I were to enumerate the various and interesting objects in this collection. I think it better to refer all who care for such things to the excellent guide-book drawn up by Mynheer van Stoppelaar, in 1876.

Beyond this treasure-chamber is another room, as yet unknown to the public, but which, I hope, will soon be accessible to them : in it the business of the Orphanage was formerly transacted, and at the beginning of the seventeenth century it was handsomely decorated with old wood-carvings. Since then it has been the depository of the archives, and the carvings have disappeared behind bundles of useless documents.[1] Mynheer van Stoppelaar hopes to instal the archives in another place, and, after having restored the 'Chamber of the Orphans,' to use it as a supplementary hall in the Museum. This excellent and highly to be applauded project is to be accomplished by dispossessing the butchers of their present quarters—a long vaulted hall, with ogival windows, on the ground-floor of the Stadhuis, in which the 'Vleeschhal' was installed in the fifteenth century, and where it has ever since remained. The hall has preserved its ancient aspect, and is highly picturesque, though few notice it, because of the ignoble

[1] These archives are admirably kept. They have been catalogued with extraordinary care and erudition by Mynheer van Stoppelaar, archivist to the city. The inventory has been published, and, as may have been remarked, I have borrowed very largely from it. It is an almost inexhaustible source of curious and interesting information, which I recommend to those who do not shrink from reading, somewhat dry and difficult, on account of the old Dutch.

purpose to which it has been turned. It is to be hoped that the transformation will speedily take place, that raw meat will be dispossessed by the archives of the city, and that a vast and beautiful hall will be added to the Museum.

The collection in the Stadhuis is not the only one of the sort in Middelburg. The Zealand capital boasts of a learned society, a sort of provisional Academy, which bears the harsh-sounding name of 'Zeeuwsch genootschap den Wetenschappen,' or 'Zealand Society of Science.' This society, of which I am an honorary member, has also formed a very interesting museum, less distinctly local than that of the city, for it extends to the whole of the province, and comprises documents of the highest value. I need not dwell upon the importance of this excellent society, upon the services which it renders to literature and art, upon the qualities and reputation of its members, but shall merely say a word about its Museum and its Library, which are both very rich in objects of interest relating to the history of Zealand.

The Museum is rather eclectic: a little of everything is to be found there, from the altars of Nehalennia, discovered at Domburg, to the Congreve rockets with which the English fleet set fire to Flushing; from the first microscope, invented in 1590, at Middelburg, by Zacharias Jansen, to the ropemaker's wheel which van Ruyter used when he was apprenticed to the trade of rope-making. There are, besides the objects of art, some good pictures, a number of medals, and a collection of conchology and natural history.

The library includes, in addition to a great number of solid works, every book, great or small, ancient or modern, good or bad, written for the young or written for the old, which treats of Zealand, and these form a very curious collection of all that concerns the province, either nearly or remotely. The greater part of these books are Dutch, but there are a good many Latin, French, English, and Spanish works. Among the ancient manuscripts there are only two written in French; one is entitled, 'Toutes les notables histoires en brief qui sont advenues durant le temps du viel Testament jusques à l'aventement de nostre Sauveur Jesu Christ,' and the other is called 'Les Harangues proposées par devant les électeurs de l'Empire en 1519.'

The visitor interested in the past of Zealand, its history and its variations, both physical and commercial, will be particularly pleased with an immense atlas, divided into twenty gigantic parts, and containing all the charts, plans, sketches, engravings, and pictures of every kind which have ever been made of Zealand and the Zealanders. You must know that there is, probably, not a country in the world which has had its portrait taken so often as this province, and there is hardly a country which has given birth to a greater number of little-known great men and local celebrities. Not a town, a village, a residence, a castle, a fortress, a dyke, or a monument could be mentioned which has not been reproduced many times; and there is not a burgomaster, an official, an alderman, a baillie, and especially a pastor, who has not had his portrait taken, in full face and in profile, in half and full length. You may imagine what a formidable collection all these portraits make.

The documents they illustrate are counted by thousands; and the catalogue, a work which would do credit to a Benedictine monk, contains more than eight hundred pages of small text.[1]

I turned over the whole of this collection with infinite pleasure; but you need not be frightened: I am not going to give you a detailed account, nor even a superficial sketch of it.

From this collection of plates one curious and satisfactory fact is to be derived. From the year 1750 down it seems that taste became completely corrupt, and skilful treatment ceased to exist. Up to that time the engravings, water-colours, and drawings are all, or almost all, marked by a certain artistic treatment, and they are really valuable both in conception and execution. After that date they become foolish, vulgar, and rough, and display neither taste nor art. What is the cause of this? I can only state the fact, but without attempting to explain it. It is also curious to observe, and cannot fail to strike anyone who makes a close inspection of the streets of Middelburg, that, with the exception of this well-preserved Stadhuis, the town possesses a

[1] This catalogue was drawn up by Mynheer R. T. Lantsheer.

very small number of works of art in proportion to those which it must have possessed formerly. As Blaeu remarked, its dwelling-houses, so early as the seventeenth century, with half-a-dozen truly artistic exceptions, were simply elegant, spacious, and commodious.

In addition to the Stadhuis, which is a gem, as I have already mentioned, and the buildings of the Abdy, or Abbey, Middelburg contains only one edifice which is of real interest from an architectural point of view. This is a two-storeyed house, well known under the name of 'Inde Steenrotse' (or 'to the Rock'), which was no doubt built by a master stonemason, for the bas-reliefs which adorn it represent all the different processes by which stones are converted into edifices. The house belongs to the halcyon days of the Renaissance in this country. It was built in 1590. Although its mutilated gable has been clumsily repaired by the substitution of a frieze a century or two later in date, it is grand and impressive. With the exception of this habitation, which is perfectly pure in style, and the above-mentioned edifices, few buildings in Middelburg can be called artistic.

The Exchange is curious, but its carvings are clumsy. I have studied the church called the Dôme, or Cathedral, in all its details, and under every aspect, and I cannot see anything to admire in it. In any other city one would be less exacting, would be content with the existing monuments, and delighted with the charming points of view, the clean streets, and the shady quays, which have only one defect—they are ill-paved. But from this city, once so rich, so powerful, so highly privileged, more is expected.

A similar observation applies to the art history of Middelburg. No great school of painters, such as Haarlem, Leyden, or even Delft can boast, exists here. By making diligent search you will find that three or four meritorious painters were born at Middelburg, where their names are no longer known. Jean Grossaert sojourned there for a while; Van de Venne lived and Bieseling died there; but all these were foreigners.

The only claim of the city to artistic fame of an original kind rests upon the tapestry works which existed within its walls at the commencement of the seventeenth century. Judging by the specimens which have come down to us, this was a great and noble industry.[1] The designers from whose drawings the work was done were not to be deterred by any obstacles, or conquered by any difficulty. Their patriotic genius associated the labours of their art with the glory of their country, and extended to the representation of naval encounters. They even portrayed whole squadrons. It is, however, for the magnificence of its borders that the Middelburg school of

---

[1] The handsomest of these tapestries, of which there exists a very interesting monograph, are preserved at Middelburg, and in the Nedelandsch Museum, at the Hague.

tapestry chiefly merits praise; it would be difficult to find anything more beautiful in this kind of art-fabric.

Specimens of these tapestries are to be seen at Middelburg, in the Palace of the Government only. The 'Hall of the States' is hung with some of those heroic designs which I have just mentioned, and never were works of art more fitly placed. The Zealand Deputies, while providing for the welfare of their province, have before their eyes a memorial of the glory of their ancestors and a sample of the industry of their fathers.

There are some other tapestries in the old Zealand capital, products of another country and another age, but none the less precious and beautiful, and these it would be unjust to leave unnoticed. I allude to the marvellous 'Gobelins,' with which one of the walls of the old Palace of Justice is hung, and which are among the finest specimens of French manufacture that have ever been produced.

They represent 'The Triumph of Alexander,' by Lebrun, and were given by Louis XV. to the individual who erected the building in which we see them at the present day, and who had been ambassador at the Court of France. The extraordinary state of preservation in which they remain is due to their not having undergone any change of place.

Evening has come, and the town is full of animation. The kermesse is in full swing—we must not forget that; and, if those horrid paving-stones which I mentioned a while ago have not deprived you of all inclination to take a walk, we will turn our steps towards the Stadhuis.

The paving-stones are indeed cruel, and we may righteously anathematise those who placed them there, for they were culprits in a double sense. The ædiles of the present age are not to be held responsible for the martyrdom we have to suffer. If they were accused they would gravely reply that the instruments of torture in question date from the fifteenth century, and that the respect in which they are held forbids their removal. And if you were to object that their great age is not a sufficient excuse for their defects, you would be informed that these historic paving-stones were supplied in the good old times by husbands who had failed to observe that curious injunction which we found, to our amusement, in the Acts of the old corporations. When the delinquents were detected the magistrates sentenced them to provide a certain number of paving-stones for the town. After such an explanation we must not complain—

> Nos pères ont péchés, nos pères ne sont plus,
> Et c'est nous qui portons la peine de leurs crimes.

Let us, however, forget these cruel paving-stones awhile and observe the peasant women who are flocking into the streets. They are all arrayed in their best clothes; and the pretty girls, with bare arms, tall hats, and gaudy handkerchiefs, are adorned with a profusion of jewellery. The young men wear

U

shoe-buckles, waist-clasps, and large buttons in their collars. The buckles and clasps are silver, and worth from ten to fifteen florins apiece; the neck-buttons are gold, and worth fifty florins. You may judge from this how well off these country-people are, and why it is that there are so many jewellers in Middelburg.

As we advance into the town the crowd becomes more dense; penetrating odours from the *poffertjeskramen* pervade the air, and joyous shouts mingle with the groans of barrel-organs and the discord of open-air orchestras, all performing with horrible persistency, but without the slightest agreement among themselves, the deafening and eternal 'Mandolinata.' Never was there an air squeaked, piped, shrieked, bellowed with such fury and obstinacy. All the 'carrousels,'—so merry-go-rounds are called in Holland and Zealand—the humble wooden coursers of our fairs replaced by heraldic lions and hippogriffs, under spangled canopies, and the revolving machines gorgeous with pictures, lanterns, and looking-glasses—are provided with a gigantic barrel-organ; and it grinds out this inevitable 'Mandolinata' without mercy or intermission. Then, as though this maddening music were not enough, the human voice comes to its aid. We reckoned seven children in one of these merry-go-rounds all screaming the wretched song, translated into growling gutturals, at the utmost pitch of their hoarse voices.

The scene is one of noisy gaiety; and it would

MIDDELBURG, DURING THE KERMESSE.

seem that the deafening music, the constant repetition of the same tune, excites the placid Zealanders, acts upon their nerves, and leads to a sort of intoxication, which is largely assisted by wine and gin.

There is, however, nothing violent in this intoxication. In the whole of the great throng no fighting, no quarrelling ever arise; and if the young men and the girls lay hold of one another it is merely for the peaceful purpose of a kiss or many kisses. Those groups of laughing peasant-girls who rush by us, holding hands, are not in the least shy, and advances would have to be very marked indeed to offend their modesty.

Let us away! This deafening music, the shouts, the riot, the laughter, the buzz of voices, the proclamations of the conjurors and acrobats, the challenges of the cheap-jacks, the whirling 'carrousels,' with their crowds of riders mounted on mythological animals, and spinning round amid lamps and lanterns, all reflected in the mirrors; the glittering of the spangles and the gilding; the whole vast whirligig, in short, begins to produce its effect upon the visitors. The popular intoxication is catching: we begin to feel inclined to make fools of ourselves also. Quick! let us begone; or presently we shall be found astride a lion or a panther, whirling round and shouting the 'Mandolinata.'

CHAPTER XV.

ARNEMUIDEN—THE COUNTRY—THE ZEALAND 'POLDERS'—SOUBURG
AND THE EMPEROR CHARLES V.

E will now resume our journey across the island. After all that I have said of the connection between Middelburg and Arnemuiden it is natural that we should direct our steps towards the latter place, which is, indeed, only half an hour's walk, through a beautiful bit of country, from our starting-point.

There is much that is strange and mysterious in the existence of Arnemuiden. That once powerful, busy, crowded seaport, which was destroyed by the waters and rebuilt at the rear of its former position, is now a mere inland village, equidistant from the Sloe Channel (the arm of the sea which in former times bathed its shore) and Middelburg. Even the little river Arne, to which Arnemuiden owes its name, has disappeared amid the various transformations of the soil, and so thoroughly that any trace of it would now be sought in vain. The Arne was not without importance in its day, for it was the medium of the commercial transactions of Middelburg in the dawn of its history; and these transactions speedily became so considerable that the Counts established a 'tol' at the junction of the Arne with the trenches of the infant city. We have seen the remains of that tol. Do you remember the famous house of stone—that 'steen' which we remarked in the centre of the town, situated in the most frequented street, and now, oh, vanity of vanities! occupied by a draper?

At the extremity of the Arne a few dwellings were erected. By degrees a fishing population grew up there, and after a while the settlement became important. 'It was a fair village, with a castle, having many rich inhabitants, both traders and others.' The first Arnemuiden was not destined to a long term of life. 'By the violence of the course of the waters and the impetuous waves of the sea it was buried in the deep. The place whereon it stood, according to all histories and all authors of maps, cannot be otherwise seen or pointed out except between the port of Middelburg and the new Arnemuiden, on a sandbank, the which now lies between the country of Sankt-Joos and the canal of Arnemuiden.' Thus, in simple, but exact language does a witness of the first overthrow and ruin of the place tell the story.

It was in 1438 that the 'fair and prosperous village' foundered in the sea. The seigneur of the country, Gilles of Arnemuiden, succeeded in saving a great many of the inhabitants. He made them abandon the submerged district, which was shortly to be nothing more than a dangerous sandbank, and establish themselves on the dam. Thereupon the new Arnemuiden that we behold to-day was founded; but how changed from that which had been! In the sixteenth century Guicciardini visited the place. We will let him tell us what it was like at that time.

'Ramue,' he says, 'is called in Flemish Arnemuiden. It is the last town in the State of Walacria (Walcheren). It is small, and not enclosed within walls; but its port is very famous throughout all Europe, because of the great number of ships of all nations which it receives every day, and also sends out to all parts; so that, many times in the year, fleets may be seen coming and going from Spain, Portugal, France, and England, to the number of thirty, forty, fifty, and more ships.'

He also tells us that the little town is 'situated marvellously well for the commodity of the sea.' Around it there is a constant stir of life and labour, for a dockyard has been set up, 'and they are always employed there in building ships.' At length the navigation of the port was so regularly established, and its relations with the principal towns of Europe became so frequent, that, in order to prevent disputes between shipowners and sea captains, the distance between the port of Arnemuiden and those ports with which it was in what might almost be called daily communication was geographically determined.

From Arnemuiden to London was reckoned at forty-two leagues; to Dieppe, fifty-four; to Rouen, seventy-five; to Brest, 125; to La Rochelle, 172; to Bordeaux, 211; to Bilbao, 226; to Lisbon, 380; to the Island of Madeira, 480; to the Canary Isles, 580; and to go to Leghorn, in Tuscany, was reckoned a sea voyage of 780 leagues.

The successor of Guicciardini (who continued his work) visited Arnemuiden in 1625, and speaks with no less admiration and enthusiasm of the town than does the Florentine traveller. It is 'much celebrated,' he says, 'and recognised as a city by foreign countries, such as Spain, Portugal, Italy, France, and others, that is to say, by all Christendom, on account of the great traffic which is done there, and the great navigation from all places. Because of which, and especially for its good situation on the sea, the Count of Zealand formerly erected there the toll-house of his county. This is the house that figures in the arms of Arnemuiden.' The writer adds, further on: 'It is also well built and very populous, and rich in citizens and inhabitants.' What has become of all this splendour? Alas! we must once more quote old Villon:

> Mais où sont les neiges d'antan?

Destiny was implacable towards this unhappy town. No sooner had it reached the zenith of its prosperity than its port began to silt up. Sand and mud banks heaved themselves across its channel, and could only have been cleared away at the cost of immense labour and vast expense. Middelburg, with which city, it will be remembered, Arnemuiden had ventured to contend on several occasions, first tried to drive a hard bargain. As the price of its aid it refused to co-operate with its unfortunate neighbour, and at last laid claim to its communications with the sea. A canal was dug out which established direct communication with the Sloe Channel, and thenceforth poor Arnemuiden was doomed to extinction.

From that day forward, in fact, its commerce died out; navigation ceased, the merchants departed, and only the fishing population remained faithful to the forsaken port. Its inhabitants, deprived of their former employment, took to making salt; then by degrees agriculture claimed them, and now they either work on the land and are called somewhat disdainfully 'peasants,' or such of them as have remained fishermen visit the coasts of England and Scotland in their flyboats. They do not bring the harvest of the North Sea into Arnemuiden; they unload their boats at the mouth of the Maas or that of the Scheldt; faster sailing vessels carry the fish to Antwerp or Rotterdam, or it is despatched by railway to Brussels, Cologne, or sometimes even to Paris.

It is strange and sad to contemplate the town, which was once an important seaport, in its present condition of an inland village. The impression is, however, lessened by the interest with which we follow the course of the dams, the onward march of those indefatigable pioneers, which have created a new soil by their successive victories over the sea. The gulf that once washed the coast of Arnemuiden is, in fact, completely filled up at the present time. Golden harvests are reaped on the spot where formerly a forest of masts was to be seen. *Seges ubi mare fuit.* In 1644 an immense polder already stretched itself out in front of Arnemuiden and took as if in defiance the name of the 'Polder of Middelburg' (Middelburgsche polder); and seventeen years later the Nieuwerkerk polder completed the isolation of the poor town, which since that year (1661) has been connected with the Sloe only by a long canal. In 1681 the polder of Sankt Joosland added its fertile extent to the land reclaimed from the waters; and its prolific fields, replacing the sandbank of Sankt Joos, formerly so much dreaded by seamen, opposed a fresh barrier to the encroachments of the ocean. Lastly, quite recently (in 1857), the Rijlevelds polder, hitching itself on to the point of Sankt Joos, has formed a sort of cape, which, by stretching out into the Sloe, has narrowed that ancient arm of the sea on which the formidable fleets mentioned by Guicciardini once sailed, and reduced it to the condition of a sandy river.

We may easily understand what a community of interests exists between all these strips of reclaimed land. They depend in some degree upon each other. If the latest spoils of ocean were to founder under the violence of the tempest, those which are immediately behind would have to stand anew the shock of a raging sea, and might, perhaps, be unable to resist its terrible force. For the safety of the entire island it is, therefore, necessary that the dykes which protect the polders, that series of ramparts erected by the hand of man, should not be damaged at any one point of their whole extent, and hence the necessity for incessant watchfulness and the intervention of the State, both as regards the new works to be undertaken and the maintenance and repair of those which have long been in existence. This superintendence and intervention form one of the most important branches of that water service which is called in Holland 'Waterstaat.' Like the French administration of the 'Ponts et Chaussées,' the Dutch Waterstaat recruits its superior staff from among the most distinguished engineers elected from special schools; and, as among us also, these engineers, who are distributed over the provinces and districts, have a hierarchical organisation, and are placed under the authority of a superior administration, which takes care that equal attention is paid to all portions of this great public duty, and creates the necessary unity and an indispensable correlation between the works at all points of the territory. The engineers of the Waterstaat, like the engineers of the Ponts et Chaussées, have the direction of the great works of the State, the construction of roads, gates, viaducts, and jetties; but, in addition, as I have just said, they are obliged to exercise a constant and strict supervision over the dykes, and also over the management of the polders. Nobody is permitted, in fact, to create a polder or to execute the works necessary for its preservation without having previously submitted the plans for the approbation of the Waterstaat ; and in order to render the intervention of this superior court really efficacious the law requires that the Administration of the Polders should be subjected to a great variety of obligations, which makes of that Administration a general public service. From the President of the Polders, or Dijkgraaf (Count of the Dykes), as he is called, down to the miller whose business it is to raise the waters by the aid of his mill, every member of the staff having the direction or superintendence of the polders is sworn, every member of the Council, every *employé* under their orders —all, even to the lowest of the superintendents, have fixed and precise duties which are imposed upon them by the law, and which they are obliged faithfully to perform. In the same way the Waterstaat may interfere when it thinks proper by prescribing works of consolidation and by ordering indispensable repairs ; this, too, with the certainty of being implicitly obeyed. Thus, from one end of the kingdom to the other, the central Administration, holding in its hand all the threads which move its multiplied interests, ensures the tranquillity of the inhabitants, and preserves, so far as it is possible, the integrity of the territory. In Zealand the intervention of the Waterstaat and the Administration of the Polders is more active than in any other province ; and this is explained by the nature of the soil, by the geographical situation of its scattered islands, subjected on so many sides to the devastating action of the waves. The story of the past is there to demonstrate the necessity for this perpetual supervision. Those strips of land, won and lost, then reconquered, and this over and over again, imperatively demand the special attention of the legislator. Thus we find in Zealand a classification of polders which does not exist in any other province. They are divided into two categories, the 'Free' polders and the 'Distressed' polders. The 'free' polders are those which yield a return from each over and above the cost of the works of defence against inundation. The greater part of the inland polders belong to this category. Agriculture derives considerable revenues from them; and the Administration, or 'Polders bestuur,' as it is called, is obliged only to keep up the dykes, which separate these from the neighbouring polders. Now, these dykes, never being exposed to contact with water, and not having to sustain the shocks of the sea, are easy to preserve, and can be kept in repair at little cost. The interior polders, therefore, generally return large profits and occasion but small expense; and are called 'free,' because, under the surveillance of the Waterstaat, they provide freely for the defence of their soil. The 'distressed' polders are in a totally different case. Generally speaking, the keeping up of their dykes is so costly that they can make no return, and in some instances the defence of the soil costs more than the soil produces. In the latter difficult case the proprietors, as we can see at once, would be obliged to renounce their property and to relinquish to the ocean that fragment of the earth which it has cost them so dear to dispute with it. This costly territory is, however, absolutely necessary to the preservation of the neighbouring lands, to which it acts as a kind of rampart. Without it the district which lies behind the polders would be difficult to preserve, being threatened by the waves in their turn, and would produce such small returns that they would hardly cover the expense of defence and repair. Then the Waterstaat intervenes; classes the polder thus circumstanced among the 'distressed' polders, levies a tax upon the products of the soil, which absorbs almost the entire revenue, and undertakes, in the place of its legitimate proprietors, the task of its preservation.

I have endeavoured thus to explain as briefly and as clearly as possible the complicated question of the polders of Zealand. It is, however, hampered with a crowd of prescriptions, exceptions, and rules, which render it very difficult of comprehension; and besides it is far from being admitted to be of absolute necessity in the other provinces. The proprietors of the Dutch polders and the engineers of Noord-Holland assert that the situation of the Zealand islands is infinitely preferable to that of the districts which extend from the extremity of the Zaan to the point of the Helder; and even the grass lands of Delftsland and Westland, 'in these latter countries,' they say, 'are really below the level of the low tides; so that we require a whole series of elevating apparatus, mills, and canals to raise our waters and to give them, in an artificial river, at a level above that of our meadows, an inclination strong enough to send them directly to the sea. In Zealand, on the contrary, the level of the soil is above the sea at low water, so that it is only necessary to open the sluice-gates at certain hours of the day, and the tide flows out directly and without cost.' These arguments are not, in appearance at least, devoid of foundation; but, on the other hand, the Zealand engineers assert that the division is just, and that the intervention of the Government is absolutely necessary. Now, as they are paid for being better informed than anybody else upon the merits of the question, it would be rash to conclude that they are in the wrong. I do not pretend to decide between conflicting opinions, still less to bring the parties to an agreement; I leave that to others who are more experienced than I.

The keeping up of the means of defence of the 'free' polders is, as I have said, entirely at the charge of those persons who are interested. The Polders bestuur divides the cost among the proprietors in proportion to the extent of land held by each. It is not always, however, the proprietor who pays the money, for it may happen that by certain clauses of his lease he has transferred the burden of these obligations to his tenant. This occurs frequently when the proprietor is a foreigner in the country, and certain wealthy Belgians who possess land in Zealand always take that precaution. The relegation of these charges to the farmers has more than one drawback, among others that of rendering the proprietor indifferent to the security of the polder, and also of preventing the great works of defence being carried out with as much care and efficiency as they require. It is evident that a tenant whose lease has a limited duration does not care to incur expenses which are meant to secure the existence of the property far beyond the limits of his own contract. He will naturally use all his influence to limit the extent of the works, and will frequently confine himself to mere repairs, when a thorough renovation is absolutely indispensable.

While contemplating the charming country beyond Arnemuiden which forms the polders I mentioned to you just now, it is difficult to believe that one is standing on land whose precarious existence is at the mercy of a damaged dyke or a broken sluice-gate. Nothing can exceed the beauty of the road, shaded by great trees, which winds its picturesque course from Middelburg to Flushing. It is no less eccentric than the roads in the northern island, which, being all perched up on the dykes and overshadowed with leafy trees, seem like roads in the air.

About half-way between the two towns, perhaps a little nearer to Flushing, we come upon a very pretty village, thoroughly countrified, very Zealand-like, with an old church and a sumptuous summer residence. The village is called Oost Souburg, and was formerly celebrated for its castle. This was 'the house of the old Admiral, Maximilian of Burgundy, Seigneur of Veer,' as the annalist Meteren calls it. Guicciardini describes this castle as a 'magnificent dwelling.'

In 1556 the Emperor Charles V., worn out by pain, sorrow, and who knows what emotions?—perhaps by remorse as much as anything else—dwelt here for some time. He was waiting at Oost Souburg for a propitious wind to enable him to embark at Flushing for Spain, whither he was going to bury himself in the cloisters of St. Just. Who shall tell what were the bitter thoughts of this scourge of the Low Countries as he walked in the shade of the cool and leafy trees? No doubt he remembered the sanguinary 'informations' which he had had drawn up in 1542 at Middelburg and Arnemuiden 'against the people of the Judaic sect.' Perhaps he also remembered that he had countersigned that famous document addressed by Ghyslain Zegers to the Council, a document in which the terrible persecution of the Anabaptists was prescribed. That was indeed a sanguinary production; neither sex nor age was to be respected; the child and the old man, the mother and the son were to be dragged together to the same stake: a horrible production, in which it is seriously discussed 'whether, for the multitude, it would not be better to execute the said obstinate persons by the sack or to have them put in a ship and let them be drowned, than to decapitate or burn them all?'

The inexorable old monarch must indeed have been in haste to fly for ever from those Low Countries, whose soil was red with the blood he had spilt, to get away for ever from those Provinces which were about, through him and his implacable son, to be exposed to all the horrors of civil war.

Nothing can be more repulsive than the portrait which Marillac, the Ambassador of France, painted of Charles V. in his decline, when a few days previously, he renounced the royal authority, in favour of his fierce and gloomy son. 'The Emperor,' says Marillac, 'has sunken eyes, colourless lips, a face more dead than alive; his neck is shrunken, and his speech is feeble. He is short of breath, his back is bent, and his legs are so weak he can hardly move out of his room.'

On that solemn occasion he was unable to speak; so it was Philibert of Brussels who explained the condition of illness and suffering to which the unfortunate monarch was reduced, and announced the unexpected resolution that was to surprise Europe and astonish history. The Emperor himself speaks in similar language, in that memorable 'Act' which he dictated during his sojourn at Souburg, 'feeling ourselves moved by many pressing and just reasons, and finding ourselves too heavily laden with the burden of old age and continual maladies, which have lately brought us low, and deprived us of all necessary strength for the management of affairs.'

What a shipwreck was this! What annihilation!

X

May we not say with Seneca, '*Non est illa magnitudo, tumor est?*' The document which contains these terrible avowals, 'given at Zuythbourg, in Zealand, on the 17th of September 1556,'—a document which was afterwards to render the name of the little village of Walcheren illustrious—is the Act of abdication in favour of his 'most dear and beloved brother Ferdinand, King of the Romans, of Hungary, and of Bohemia,' who inherited the Imperial purple, while the crown of Spain, to which the Low Countries was attached, was placed upon the head of Philip II. And yet, not all these woful acknowledgments, nor this unexampled renunciation, availed to mollify fate. The Castle of Souburg, where the last act of the Imperial tragedy was accomplished, was not destined to survive the struggle in which this pitiless policy plunged the country. Being occupied, in 1573, by the Spanish troops, it was attacked by the people of Flushing. 'This,' said old Meteren, 'was one of those eminent places which was disputed by all, as to which should have it.' Being unable to preserve the Castle, the people of Flushing burnt it; and the inhabitants of Middelburg beheld, from their rampants, the lurid light issuing from that great brazier, which reddened the distant horizon.

CHAPTER XVI.

FLUSHING—MUTINY ON BOARD—IN SEARCH OF A DINNER—THE BEGINNINGS OF A GREAT PORT—PHILIP II. AND WILLIAM THE SILENT—SPANIARDS AND ZEALANDERS—'THE BEGGARS OF THE SEA'—THE BOMBARDMENT—GOOD WISHES.

THE land route from Middelburg to Flushing is as pleasant and varied as the sea-voyage between those two towns is monotonous and dreary. Imagine a great canal, sixty yards wide, bordered by two stone dykes of such a height that the tops of a few trees can barely be seen above them, and this wide waterway extending, before and behind, far beyond one's view, unenlivened by any object. Such is the 'Kanal door Walckeren.' You may suppose that there is not much to amuse the traveller by this route.

The canal ought to be alive with a hundred vessels, bristling with masts, gay with expanding sails, and the floating wreaths of smoke from swift steamers, full of stir and animation, but there is nothing of the sort to be seen on it. Occasionally a heavy *tjalk*, and six times a day a little steamboat, which plies between Flushing and the Zealand capital, are the things of life that walk these waters.

It makes one sad to think of the vast sums that have been swallowed up in these works, and to contemplate the labour that has been expended, without producing any apparent effect on commerce. Gigantic sluices have been constructed at the two extremities of the immense canal that leads to Veer, and a vessel of any considerable tonnage passes on that side about three times a year!

In addition to the dreariness of the passage through this melancholy canal, we had our full share of the wet and wretched weather that distinguished the summer of 1877 ; and, to crown our misfortunes, our boat was in a bad condition, and our crew were in a bad humour. Ever since our great sail to Bergen-op-Zoom, the *tjalk* had been letting in water both above and below; eight nights out of ten we slept in damp beds, and frequently found a couple of inches of water in our cabin in the morning.

The insubordination, which at Veer had begun to manifest itself in sharp words, steadily increased.

We ought to have used our authority and threatened the crew with penalties, but as they believed themselves to be indispensable, they opposed us with that *vis inertiæ*, against which the strongest authority and the sternest resolves avail nothing. Our chief anxiety on arriving at Flushing was to ascertain whether, with a boat in such a condition, and a crew in such a temper, we could possibly get on to Antwerp. It was our intention to be present at the celebration of the Rubens' fête. As we knew hardly anything of the navigation of that arm of the Scheldt called the Hond (or western Scheldt), and which was our proposed route, we thought it well to consult a competent authority, and we applied to the Consular Agent for France, who took us to see the official head of the Dutch pilot-service.

The latter personage came down to our boat, and, having made a careful inspection of it, informed us that it would be highly imprudent to attempt the voyage we had projected, even in fine weather. 'As for setting out in rough weather,' he added, 'that would be worse than an imprudence, it would be madness; with a bad crew, you would never get to Antwerp.'

As for the last month, rough weather has been the rule, fine weather the rare exception, we were greatly perplexed, and held a consultation as to what we should do, and how we should act with respect to getting rid of the *tjalk* and the crew. Heemskerk had just offered to turn back and take the whole concern to Rotterdam, when the evil genius of the crew incited them to a proceeding which got us out of our difficulty. The sailors deliberately struck, absolutely refusing to do their work, and as we had made no written contract with them, but trusted to a verbal agreement, they summoned us to quit the *tjalk* within twenty-four hours. The honest fellows fully believed that we were at their mercy, and were rejoiced to think that they were putting us into a difficult position, whereas they were, in reality, rendering us a signal service.

Our plan was formed in a moment. We had the boat taken into the dock, and we hired, from the Company of the State Roads, an empty van. Into this we packed everything on board the *tjalk* that belonged to us, and, having given orders for the despatch of the van to the Hague with all our heavy baggage, while we kept only some indispensable articles as portable luggage, we bade a courteous farewell to our quondam crew, who were greatly astounded at this unforeseen result of their conduct. Thus we found ourselves perfectly free from every care and anxiety.

The question now was where to bestow ourselves. A magnificent signboard induced us to seek hospitality from the landlord of the Grand International Hotel. The Grand Hotel was a very small one; the rooms were, however, clean, and that was the chief point. The beds were of a humble description, but there again we were not disposed to be exacting; and the people of the hotel were polite and attentive. On two points only there was a sensible deficiency, but those points were important; the food was scanty, and the table linen stood much in need of the services of the laundress.

We commented upon the latter fact, and were informed that the napkins were changed at each meal! This we subsequently found to be true; but they were changed after the fashion adopted by Captain Pilmouche, in the old story which everybody knows:

'Sergeant, on Thursday, you will make your men change their shirts!'

'I beg your pardon, Captain, but that is impossible, for they have only one each.'

'There's nothing impossible! The Colonel has given the order.'

'Very well, then; they must change *among themselves!*'

It was thus that our dinner napkins were changed at the Grand International Hotel. Afterwards, when we found how moderate the honest folk who kept the hostelry were in their charges, we felt that we could not deal severely with their little shortcomings; but, just at first, when fresh from the luxurious living of our floating home, we were not disposed to make allowances at the expense of our stomachs, and we set forth in search of nourishment more attractive.

For a moment we thought we had succeeded in finding the object of our search. A large and handsome hotel on the great quay, near the entry of the port, bearing upon its façade, the words 'Hotel of Commerce,' in gigantic letters, was pointed out to us. We entered a lofty and spacious hall, and received a welcome of happy augury. The proprietor, Mynheer Peeters, recognised us, called us by our names, told us that he knew we were on the island, and was happy to see us at his house, and added other complimentary expressions. This was all very well; but when the question of giving us our dinners arose, matters assumed quite another complexion.

'There are so few travellers at this season,' said Mynheer Peeters, 'that I have no table d'hôte!'

'No matter. You can let us have a private room and a dinner all to ourselves.'

'No,' said he with sullen gravity, 'that would upset the house, and I don't want to have everything turned upside down!'

I confess that I looked at this man with stony stupefaction. An innkeeper refusing to let travellers have their dinner! My hands fell helplessly down by my sides. Afterwards, a person to whom I related this anomaly and our amazement, said gravely, 'Peeters is well-to-do; he is rich.' What a country must this be in which wealth serves as an innkeeper's excuse for such an answer!

Under the shock of so extraordinary and unheard-of a refusal, our thoughts turned longingly towards the far distant restaurants of our own Paris, especially towards Bignon, that modern Vatel. But we also felt that the good folk of Flushing have no right to expect our sympathy with them in their state of forlorn forsakenness. Addressing an eloquent remonstrance (imaginary) to the collective inhabitants of this exceptional town, we bade them desist from vain regrets. 'Murmur not,' said we, 'nor make dolorous complaint, on beholding the English, who land at your new port, flee afar from the town, without pausing even for one day within your old walls, without displaying their astonished visages upon your venerable quays. They would be foolish indeed were they to expose themselves to the refusals of Mynheer Peeters, and to the pains of hunger into the bargain, for the sake of contemplating the remains of a place which they have so scientifically bombarded, so skilfully burned, so conscientiously destroyed!'

And now that we are aware of the inhospitable nature of the town, let us admire afresh the engineers who have built the new port, the docks, the basins, and the railway which belongs to them. They have, in fact, executed all these great works at an immense distance from the town itself, and have made difficult, inconvenient, and hopelessly lengthy roads, by which it is to be reached. No doubt this was done as an act of thoughtful foresight, but, notwithstanding that proof of sagacity, these admirable works have remained unused to the present time.

What an astonishing and, still more, what a painful spectacle is presented by that great empty port, with its huge, inactive sluice-gates, its basins without vessels, its docks without bales, and its solitary quays. What do the destinies of a town, what does the fortune of a seaport, depend upon? This problem which troubles the mind, one cannot ignore nor escape from it, but neither can one solve it.

If there ever was in the world a seaport whose situation would seem to ensure its being busy and frequented, Flushing is that seaport. It is placed at the extremity of the Continent, at the mouth of the Scheldt. It is easy of approach, has a commodious harbour, open in all weathers, accessible in all winds, and it is connected with Central Europe by a railway whose branches join the great lines in Holland, Belgium, and Germany. At the present time, as in Guicciardini's day, it may be said that almost all vessels coming out and going from the east, west, and south have to pass by there. And yet, notwithstanding this, the merchant fleets, which sail through its roadstead, pass before its port, and either reascend the Scheldt, or, putting out to sea, proceed to the north-west or the south-west to discharge their rich cargoes.

From the beginning of its history fortune has been unkind to Flushing. Middelburg was already a large town, well known in Europe, doing a brisk trade, and frequented by merchants of all countries, while as yet Flushing was only a rural place, which served as a passage into Flanders. It was not until the middle of the sixteenth century that its seigneur, Adolphus of Burgundy, incited much more strongly by the desire to have a strong place under his control, than by any intention to create a trading port, enclosed it within walls, and erected gates. But the ships continued none the less to double the point of Rammekens, and to navigate the difficult Sloe, in order to make Arnemuiden and approach Middelburg.

In 1581 the Seigneur of Beveren, the last seigneur

of the country, having died insolvent, the two seigneuries of Flushing and Veer were put up to sale. Thus William the Silent was enabled to acquire two marquisates. He paid 140,600 florins for that of Veer, and only 77,000 florins for that of Flushing. We find, therefore, that the latter town was considered at that period to be of just one-half the importance of its northern rival in the island of Walckeren, and yet no one failed in those days to recognise the advantages of its situation. The writers of the period admitted that Flushing was 'accommodated with an excellent port.'

Two centuries and a half previously (in 1315) Count William II. had endowed it with privileges, in the hope of attracting strangers. In 1485 the people of Sluis had seized it, with the intention of fortifying it, and settling in the island. Then, suddenly, after having committed some robberies and a few murders, they fled. The Emperor Maximilian resided there for some time; he liked the place, and issued certain ordinances from thence under the heading, '*Gegeven in ons logiz te Vlissinghe*,' or 'Given from our house at Flushing.' On two occasions Charles V. and Philip II. came thither to embark for Spain, and the old Emperor declared that it was 'a passage of such importance that by good right it might be called the key of the sea of these Low Countries.'[1] He even included among his secret instructions to his son a strong

---

[1] See in the archives of Middelburg, *Register Publicatien en Ordonnantien*, at the date of 1488, No. 597 of the *Inventaris*.

recommendation to 'be careful to guard that place well,' and a map of the period, which may be seen in the great Atlas of the Zealand Society, describes 'Vlissinghen' as 'the best and most commodious port of the Island of Walckeren.' What is the explanation of the curious fact that this loudly proclaimed superiority has been from the first ineffective?

After the death of Charles V. that faithful executor of the paternal will, Philip II., resolved to fortify the town. At the moment of his embarkation, when he was going to take possession of the throne of Spain, a sharp altercation took place between himself and William of Orange, on the very spot where we now stand. Philip reproached the Prince with placing difficulties in the way of his policy, and William endeavoured to exculpate himself by throwing the responsibility upon the States.

'No, no! not the States,' exclaimed the sombre monarch angrily, 'but you, yourself, you!' And then, as if to render his answer more impressive, he turned to the famous Pacheco, and said, 'Remember my commands.'[1]

Those commands were that Flushing should be turned into a fortress of the first class. In the following month the works were begun, in conformity with the orders of Philip. The workmen proceeded,

---

[1] Mr. Motley says of Pacheco: 'He was the chief engineer of Alva, and had accompanied the Duke in his march from Italy. He afterwards secured a world-wide reputation as the architect of the Antwerp citadel.' The latter was, no doubt, the more urgent work (for which the fortification of Flushing was abandoned) alluded to by the author. (Translator.)

under the direction of Pacheco, to make the excavations for the erection of a citadel, but their labours were soon suspended for lack of money, and it became necessary to discharge the men. The learned engineer himself left the town in order to execute other works which were of more urgent necessity, and when he returned, thirteen years afterwards, to resume his interrupted task, he met with an ignominious death on his arrival at Flushing.

During that long interval great events had taken place. Zealand was ready to enter into open revolt against the King of Spain. A few days earlier Brill had fallen into the hands of the 'Beggars of the Sea,' and the people of Flushing had celebrated that severe defeat inflicted on the Duke of Alva with great rejoicings.

Alva, who on learning this irreparable loss, resolved to strengthen himself in the other ports of the North Sea, so as to isolate Brill, and localise the devastations of the 'Beggars,' sent quartermasters to Flushing to prepare quarters for a body of troops. These quartermasters treated the population with their habitual insolence and rudeness, and their exactions were out of all reason. A tumult arose, the quartermasters were seized by the people, and when the troops arrived on the following day, instead of finding all things in readiness, they were welcomed by cannon balls.[1]

---

[1] Mr. Motley, who quotes Roz as his authority, gives a different account of this transaction in his *Rise of the Dutch Republic*. He says,

Stopped by the tide, unable either to advance or to retreat, fast bound under the fire from the fort, the Spaniards sent a flag of truce—its bearer being obliged to swim to the shore—and promised, if the fire was discontinued, to withdraw so soon as the tide should serve, without attempting to disembark. The desired truce was granted, and on the following day the vessels sailed in the direction of Goes, where they hoped to be better received.

The citizens, now masters of the town, fearing a surprise and terrible reprisals, stood well on their guard. The various companies took up a position upon the ramparts, and mounted guard there, with their banners displayed. A few days later Pacheco and his staff of engineers appeared in the offing. They were ignorant of the retreat of the troops, and deceived by the fluttering banners, they thought their soldiers had taken peaceable possession of the quarters that had been assigned to them, and they sailed briskly into the port. No sooner had they landed than they were seized and thrown into prison, where they lay until they were taken out to be hanged.

after describing the Seigneur de Herpt's harangue to the people: 'A half-drunken, half-witted fellow in the crowd valiantly proposed, in consideration of a pot of beer, to ascend the ramparts and to discharge a couple of pieces of artillery at the Spanish ships. The offer was accepted, and the vagabond, merrily mounting the height, discharged the guns. Strange to relate, the shot thus fired by a lunatic's hand put the invading ships to flight. A sudden panic seized the Spaniards, the whole fleet stood away at once in the direction of Middelburg, and were soon out of sight.' (Translator.)

In vain did the chief engineer to the King of Spain offer large sums, not, indeed, that his life might be spared—he knew that was forfeit beyond redemption—but that he might be put to any other death than hanging. He was said to be related to the Duke of Alva: the rumour was enough to seal his doom. 'He had great regret in dying,' says François le Petit, in his 'Grande Chronique de Hollande et de Zélande,' 'but especially in being hanged, and would willingly have given a great sum of money, to have procured that the rope should be changed for the sword. But the citizens and sailors were so incensed against him, that they liked better to see him dangling from the gibbet than his money lying in their purses.'

From that moment there was waged between the people of Flushing and the Spaniards a merciless war, characterised on both sides by sanguinary deeds and terrible reprisals. The Prince of Orange, on learning that the town had risen, despatched troops thither from Brill, and gathered the Protestants from all countries to the centre of resistance. 'They received thus some six hundred soldiers, some English, some Walloons and Flemings come from London, and a French company of close upon five hundred men, with other forty French from Dieppe, to their succour.' Being thus assured of the efficient defence of the town, the people of Flushing could thenceforth give themselves up to all those enterprises which their adventurous spirit might suggest.

They selected for their admiral one Pietersen, a

desperate ruffian, whom Meteren, with true Calvinistic indulgence, depicts in the following fashion: 'This man was otherwise one simple to behold, but who was in authority among his own people, and those of the navy, for that he was a man of courage.' Under Pietersen's command they cruised about the Scheldt, stopping the merchant-ships, at first, limiting themselves to taking their guns and ammunition, but afterwards capturing the merchandise, confiscating the ships, and putting the persons on board them to ransom.

Before long their audacity knew no bounds. The spies whom they employed at Antwerp kept them carefully informed, so that, no sooner was an expedition despatched than they were ready to encounter it with irresistible fury. Thus they dispersed the squadron of the Count de Medina Cœli, and twice prevented the fleet of Sancho Davila from revictualling Middelburg. Immediately on their emancipation, they became the terror of the Spaniards in the Scheldt, and on the high seas. Extraordinary exploits, deeds of daring unheard of until then, became mere matters of course. The chronicles of the time abound in narratives of the memorable exploits of these terrible men. One will suffice us, as an example.

Meteren relates that, on the 14th of January, 1573, 'taking advantage of the high tide and the darkness of the evening, they set out with ten ships, sailed up the Scheldt, passed under the Spanish batteries in full sail, and entered the port of Antwerp, where they captured a number of merchant vessels, in the midst of the enemy's squadron. While the confusion was at its height, the crew of one of the ships landed, rushed into the town, set their admiral, Bouwen Ewortsen, who was imprisoned in the house of the Ecoutête, at liberty, carried off a certain number of the inhabitants, and, at dawn, dragged them into the boats, which profited by the current and the wind, and put off with their prize.'

It was natural that such daring deeds should spread terror everywhere. By those 'Beggars of the Sea' there was no quarter given; they carried on a war without truce or grace, a quite merciless struggle. Meteren tells us that all the Spaniards who were taken on the sea were tied together, two and two, with their hands behind their backs, and flung into the water.' 'All the Spaniards who fell into their hands on the land they hanged immediately, or else they bound them together, two and two, and threw them, living, from the top to the bottom of the rampart.'

Flushing took great pride in the universal terror inspired by its formidable seamen; regarding their sanguinary fame as a fair title of honour, and wearing it as a halo. Poets sang the praises of the fierce sea-warriors. Here are couplets, two centuries and a half old, which a Zealand bard puts into the mouth of the warrior city:—

> ' Partout où le soleil se mire dedans l'onde,
> On a veu triompher mes belliquex vaisseaux ;
> L'orgueil, qui prétendoit à l'empire du monde,
> S'est noyé devant moy dans l'abyme des eaux.
>
> ' Ses navires voguans sur l'humide campagne
> Lèvent toutes leurs voiles au bruit de mon canon,
> Et pour faire trembler le démon de l'Espagne,
> Il ne faut seulement que réciter mon nom.'

The celebrity of Flushing lies in this, above all, that the town was a military port. It was admirably adapted to be one of the advanced posts of European commerce, but it became, by the force of circumstances, a sort of arsenal to the United Provinces, and the only great men to whom it gave birth were illustrious warriors.

After the two terrible admirals before-mentioned, we must enumerate Worst, Hollart, Cornelis, and Jan Evertzen, whose tombs we saw at Middelburg, and, lastly, the most famous of all the Dutch admirals, Michael Adriaens van Ruyter.

These heroes were all born at Flushing, and served their apprenticeship to seamanship there. Van Ruyter began, as we have already said, as a ropemaker, and we saw the wheel in the Museum of the Zealand Society, at which his master set him to work. Afterwards he was a sailor, then a pilot, subsequently a ship's captain, an admiral, and finally Admiral of the United Provinces. He made the voyage to the East Indies eight times, that to Brazil three times; he won three great naval battles; and he died at seventy, of the effects of a wound which he received before Aosta, in Sicily. His was a life full of labour, indeed: Michael van Ruyter well deserved the statue that Flushing has erected to him, and perhaps the resentment which the English feel towards the memory of that great man counted for something in the bombardment which they inflicted, long after, upon his watch tower.

At every period of its history Flushing was a standing menace to maritime Albion. We learn from the annalists that, in 1576, its cruisers carried off 'English ships laden with much precious merchandise.' However well they were manned, they were taken by force and carried into 'Vlissinghen.' It is needless for me to recapitulate the famous feats of Van Ruyter, or to dwell on the terror which was spread over all the North Sea, and felt even in London, when it was known that the Zealand fleet had quitted its moorings.

Daring and bravery, which constituted the glory of the men of Flushing in old times, still characterise them at the present day. And at the epoch of the wars of the Empire, the town of Flushing may claim a large share of the dauntless deeds of that unequal strife in which the continental navy endeavoured to make head against the unrivalled fleet of England.

All readers to whom the history of the sea is familiar know the name of Captain Niklaus Jarry, the commander of the 'Vlissinger.' They also know that of Peter the Turk, the commander of the 'Zeuw,' and I am sure that the memory of the old sailor,

Christian Cornelis, who, with Johan Koens, the cabin boy, distinguished himself in the affair of the ship 'Vriendschap,' is still preserved at Flushing. It is for fame of that kind that Flushing cares above all; the faces of her old tars are those which she prefers. In 1794 the portrait of Cornelis was sold in the streets, and a statue would certainly have been erected to him had it been at that time the custom to bestow statues on all great men.

Every medal has its reverse, and these maritime and warlike triumphs were followed by a terrible reckoning with fate. Flushing was about to pay the penalty of its renown. The sea, jealous of the great feats of the city, rushed into its streets and swallowed up one-half of it, and then the English came and burned down all that remained. In 1808 the first catastrophe, the terrible inundation, took place. On the 15th of January the water rose in the streets to the height of the first floors of the houses, the people went about in boats; the damage done was immense. The following year, just when that disaster was almost repaired, and the city was beginning to look like itself again, the English fleet appeared in the offing, and the bombardment began.

That was a terrible bombardment. Bombshells, Congreve rockets, and red-hot bullets rained upon the unhappy town; in an instant the whole place was on fire. A series of very curious engravings has preserved the memory of the different phases of this bombardment, which was unprecedented in the history of Holland, and I do not know any more sad and grievous spectacle. Hundreds of houses were destroyed by the bombshells, the churches were battered by the bullets, the Congreve rockets set fire to whole quarters of the town, but the most terrible of all these disasters was the complete destruction of the Stadhuis.

This, according to Meteren, who watched the progress of building, was an elegant edifice of grey cut stone. Engravings still in existence prove that it was correctly classed among the finest buildings in the country. It consisted of two storeys, raised upon a basement, with rustic arches. The façade was composed of a projecting building, terminating in a pinnacle, and adorned, according to the taste of the time, with a curious assemblage of syrens, pyramids, and emblematical, mythological, and allegorical devices. The two wings had five projecting windows in each storey, and the apertures were separated by handsome pilasters. The whole bore a resemblance to the Hôtel de Ville at Antwerp, and formed a fine and effective monument.

This handsome Stadhuis had been built during the occupation of the English, when Flushing, together with Brill, were pledged for sums lent by the crown of England, and the cannon which reduced it to ashes were English. Poor Stadhuis! On its site there now stands a private dwelling-house, also ancient, and of a grave and handsome aspect, but not in the least monumental.

The new Stadhuis, with another house which faces it, and is called the 'House of the Statues,' on account of certain gods and goddesses on the top of it, furnishes a noble and interesting specimen of the architecture of Zealand in the eighteenth century. In this sense it merits the attention of the archæologist, but there is nothing remarkable in its interior. On the second storey there is a sort of treasure-room; it contains some curious old articles in silver, some of them historic pieces, and a silver bottle which is precious in every sense. It is to this that the city, it is said, owes its name. The Flemish word for bottle is 'flesch' (pronounced 'fless'), hence Flessingen. This is simple, indeed it is too simple, for I remember to have read in an old manuscript that the town was founded and named by a certain Walchrinus, Prince of the Belgæ, five hundred years B.C., while the bottle in question is considerably more modern, having been brought into the country by St. Willibrod, 1200 years at least after the disappearance of the problematical Walchrinus.

The bottle that is exhibited to the visitor is, most probably, only a silver case enclosing another flask, for I do not suppose such antiquity as that of the seventh century is claimed for this piece of silversmith's handiwork. It is certainly ancient; but its ornamentation with fantastic animals, curious foliage, monkeys playing the guitar, and other strange designs, goes no farther back than the fourteenth or fifteenth century.

After what I have said of the bombardment of Flushing, no one will be surprised to learn that ancient monuments are rare in the city. Only a few remain standing, I mean of such as are worthy of study. The battered churches are not very interesting; two or three handsome houses, and the Exchange, a brightly-tinted, picturesque little building, are nearly all that are worth seeing and remembering.

On the other hand, Flushing abounds in charming points of view. Its streets, which are scrupulously clean, are sufficiently irregular to afford great variety of aspect; and it has nooks and corners, especially beyond the old port, which are not surpassed for warm and bright colouring, and quaint, varying lines, by any other nooks in Holland.

Flushing is a place in which it would be very pleasant to reside for some time, if only one could get better food, and get it more easily, and also if there were a little more animation there. And yet, even in these respects, one may come to an arrangement with heaven—I mean with one's stomach and one's eyes. After a few days, we succeeded in discovering a confectioner, who turned out to be a first-rate cook. The worthy Ouverkerke—let me give him his name—consented, at the price of much money, to furnish us with some delicious little clandestine dinners; and, though the quays are solitary, and the great basins of the port are empty, there is the roadstead to contemplate, while one strolls upon the old bastions; and it, at least, is always animated.

That very animation is a source of vexation rather than gladness to the people of Flushing. They bemoan themselves that, from the heights of those once illustrious ramparts, they are compelled to behold innumerable ships pause for a moment in the offing, take up a pilot, and then sail on towards the north or the east, to discharge the wealth with which they are laden at Antwerp or Rotterdam. With true Batavian tenacity they still cling to the hope of overcoming this disheartening indifference. In vain does the enormous port remain empty, in vain do the vast basins and gigantic docks remain deserted; in vain do the colossal sluice-gates, ever inactive, rest motionless upon their sturdy hinges. Not for such reasons as these are settled plans to be abandoned, or works begun to be suspended. While we were staying at Flushing some millions were being expended on the construction of another sluice-gate, 'so that if one of those that give access to the new port should be out of order, another issue may be provided by which ships can either enter or get out of the Walcheren canal.' In the face of the total absence of any ships whatever, this appeared to us to be a superfluity of foresight. Nevertheless, who can tell what the future has in reserve? For my own part, I hope with all my heart, that the future of Flushing is charged with the realisation of these patriotic previsions.

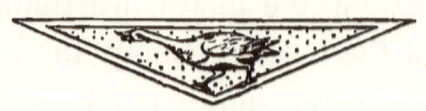

THE EXCHANGE AT FLUSHING.

CHAPTER XVII.

THE RAGE OF THE SCHELDT—BRESKENS—FORT NAPOLEON—GROEDE—THE FLEMISH NOSE—AXEL—SIEGES AND PITCHED BATTLES—'DURA LEX'—HULST—THE VIRTUES OF A PEOPLE—FLEMISH FIDELITY.

HAVE just said that the roadstead of Flushing presents an animated aspect; I ought to add, that the kind of promontory formed by the town, and the dams which flank that promontory on both sides, form one of the most picturesque landscapes in the whole country.

From whatever side we contemplate the city from the dykes, its brown profile, thrown out against a silver sky, is beautiful and impressive. The massive towers, the slender spires, the bright coloured houses, the windmills, with their great sails, the grassy bastions, and the tops of the lofty trees, which rise above the ramparts and the roofs, mingling their irregular lines and combining their brilliant hues, form a whole gallery of pictures, ever varying and always attractive.

Again, when we look towards the roadstead, over that immense opaline basin, bordered on the horizon by a thin, almost imperceptible, grey line, the contrast is so striking that we ask, in a sort of amazement, how those bright patches of verdure, those walls of dark red brick, those masses of black basalt, those tarred piles, in a word—all this amalgam of intense colours, can start up from an iridescent sea of pearl and silver?

This is on fine days, you must remember. Let the weather become bad, and the spectacle changes. Then the tempest lets loose all its fury on the vast estuary. The coasts and the dykes echo afar its mournful lamentations. The Scheldt, waiting to escape, meets the ocean, which bars its way, and all nature seems to join in the equatic strife, of which man, in spite of his ships of iron and of wood, is sometimes the victim, and frequently the toy.

To the kindness of M. Verbrughe, the chief of the Belgian pilot-service, we owed the opportunity of being actually present at one of these dangerous battles. 'I have a sloop to try, to-morrow,' he had said to me the day before. 'It will be a rough business, for the sea will be boisterous. Will you join the party?' We eagerly accepted his invitation.

I must inform you, in the first place, that the sloops belonging to the Belgian pilot-service are small masterpieces of construction, models of maritime cabinet-making, bits of jewellers' work in polished planks and copper bolts; tightness, strength, and elegance are all combined in them. On this occasion, the crew were all picked men, pilots and student pilots, all men of tried courage and experience, familiar with the sea, and who capped physical courage with moral energy.

We set out, a party of ten, in that undecked sloop, and commenced a giddy course upon the turbulent arm of the sea. Our bark seemed to fly upon the summit of the waves, which were not indeed of an extraordinary height, but the violence of the current was such that we were all aware of a terrible latent danger. At one moment we skimmed by a mass of wreckage, in less than a second it was swept away to such a distance that we could hardly discern it.

'If anyone were to fall overboard,' said M. Verbrughe to me at the same instant, 'it would be useless to try to recover him. We should never be able to reach him.'

Then we understood why the chief of the Dutch pilot-service had so strongly urged me to be prudent, and had dissuaded us from undertaking this dangerous crossing in our little *tjalk*. It was not, however, until we were returning that we had a full experience of the violence of the waves and the currents at the mouth of the Houd. At that moment we had everything in our favour—wind, tide, and current. 'Look quickly at your watches,' said our captain, as we were passing alongside a huge buoy, 'we are now eleven kilometers from Flushing.' We looked at our watches; it was ten minutes past one o'clock. At thirty-five minutes past we were inside the stockade on the arrival side. We had done eleven kilometers in twenty-five minutes.[1]

At first, I must confess, we thought this statement was either an error, or a jest at the expense of our credulity, so fantastic did our course seem to have been. But when we afterwards measured it upon the chart, we found that we had not been deceived, and we yielded to evidence. Then Constant and I remembered that at one moment during that bewildering voyage, we had looked steadfastly at the town towards which we were being driven by all the strength of our sails, and all the force of the current, and seen it grow large in an astonishing manner, like those dioramic pictures which seem to spring at the spectators. This impression, coming to the aid of a reckoning which was not to be impeached, convinced us that we had just accomplished the most marvellous voyage that we ever in our lives should have the chance of making.

During our stay at Flushing we made several excursions on the Scheldt, but I must say that not one of them left us such impressive memories. On the other occasion the weather was calmer, and the waves in their ordinary condition. We visited the opposite bank, landing at Breskens, and making an excursion from thence into the Flemish portion of the Zealand provinces.

---

[1] Eight kilometers make five English miles.

The country is interesting, rich, fertile, and carefully cultivated, but it struck us that it has lost that special distinctive character which is so remarkably preserved in Walcheren and North and South Beveland. The highroads have, besides, a totally different aspect; they are wider and straighter, and, although they are shaded here and there by pine trees, they have not that resemblance to the avenues of a vast park which characterizes the other parts of the country. On each side are quickset hedges, forming a natural barrier, but the most striking feature is that the roadway is occasionally below the fields which border upon it. The opposite is the case in the islands, especially in Zuidbeveland, where all the roads are made upon the dykes, and overlook the surrounding country.

The houses also have a different aspect. They are not yet the houses of Flanders, but they are no longer those of Zealand; and, if I were to compare them with the habitations of any other country, I should say that they resemble the small houses and cottages in the country districts of England. As for the inhabitants, we saw so few of them that we should find it difficult to tell what they are like.

The principal curiosity of Breskens is its fort. The position of that village at the extreme point of Flanders, jutting out into the Houd, and forming a pendant to Flushing on the other shore of the Scheldt, clearly indicated that a redoubt ought to be established there. It is evident that the cross-fire from the great Zealand port and the village which faces it would command the passage and forbid the entry into the river. Nevertheless, it was only under Stadholder Frederick Henry that the idea of utilising the exceptionally advantageous situation was entertained, and that a battery was constructed there.

Before long the closing of the Scheldt rendered those works useless, and the bastions which had been constructed were allowed to fall into ruin.

The project was resumed at the end of the last century, during the strife between Napoleon and England, a period which is still called in Zealand 'den Franschen tijd,' or 'the French time.' The Emperor, who wanted to make the Scheldt inaccessible to the English fleets, had a casemated battery constructed at Breskens in all haste, and called by his own name. For ten years it was called 'Fort Napoleon.' In 1835 the Government of the Netherlands, desirous in its turn to have the navigation of the Houd under its control, enlarged and strengthened this fortress, which, after 1815, had laid aside its imperial designation, and assumed the more modest appellation of Fort Breskens.

And now this poor fort is again abandoned and falling once more into ruin. On the top of its casemates vulgar potatoes grow, and its ancient chambers are used by the peasant, who rents the place, as storerooms for his hay and dried peas. *Sic transit gloria!* That of war as well as every other kind, and perhaps more quickly than any. And thus it is that, owing to its novel distinction, Fort Breskens constitutes the counterpart of that sentimental and heroic story, 'Le Soldat-Laboureur.'

The village formerly guarded by Fort Breskens is neither large nor populous, but in respect to cleanliness it belongs absolutely to Zealand. The wide high street is kept with scrupulous care, and some of its curiously built houses, together with the blacksmith's forges set up in the high street, and surmounted by fantastic weathercocks, remind one of a whole series of pictures of the old Dutch school, more especially of 'The Halt' and 'The Forge,' by Wouvermans.

Groede, our next station, is situated at the distance of a full league inland. It is also a village, but larger and more populous, no less clean, no less scrupulously cared for, with tolerably straight streets, sharp-pointed paving stones, brick houses, an old church, in the centre of a square space, and an inn next door to the church.

The whole of this rustic scene presents a peaceful, comfortable, prosperous aspect. One's mind reposes in the midst of such cosy tranquillity, painful thoughts depart, and a gentle serenity takes their place. Perhaps this sense of quietude, so difficult to define, may arise from the apparent impossibility that there can be any poor or distressed persons in such a fair and prosperous place.

We made a brief halt at the inn, or rather in its courtyard, where we sat at a rickety table, and had the fag end of an orchard to look at. We ate fresh bread and drank new milk, and the old hostess scasoned our modest repast with some sprightly talk, which afforded us no little amusement. I shall never forget that scene, nor the warm, bright sunshine which gilded it. The courtyard, with its picturesque disorder, the whitewashed walls, the tall red roof, the old pear-tree, laden with green fruit, the linen spread out to dry on the fence, the little pails of shining metal in a corner, and the old peasant woman, smiling and chattering; all this made up a picture worthy of the palette of Johannes Verineer.

We ate the bread, we drank the milk, we exchanged friendly farewells with our hostess, and then we resumed our way towards Breskens and our boat. Our visit to Groede was, however, marked by one last incident. As we passed before a school, an excellent specimen of building, I assure you it unfortunately occurred to look in at the windows. Then uprose all the pupils, every eye was turned on us, arms were raised, hands were waved, and tongues began to wag. In vain did the venerable 'magister' strive to recall the wandering attention of his pupils; expressive gestures and loud tones equally failed to produce any effect, and we were fain to hide ourselves as quickly as possible from the curiosity of the children, lest they should have to suffer for our unlucky intrusion on their studies.

Our last excursion on the Western Scheldt brought us, with all our belongings, to Ter Neuzen. We had to cross the Channel in order to continue our route from thence. I need not dwell on this arm of the river, as I have already said enough about it. Our passage was made in a sailing boat, very prosperously, in perfectly calm weather, and without accident of any kind; unless indeed we were to count the complete absence of wind as an accident, for it obliged us to pass half the day in the channel, while, with a good wind, we could have crossed easily in two, or at the most three, hours.

As it was quite dark when we landed at Ter Neuzen, we had to seek a lodging at once, postponing our inspection of the town to the following day. It does not take long to see Ter Neuzen, nor is there much to interest the visitor. If I were to be assured that it is destined to become an important place, I should readily believe it, because its position, at the furthermost point of Flanders, and also the canal which connects it with Ghent, promise a prosperous commercial future. But that Ter Neuzen should become a great city seems to me an impossibility. There is nothing in it to constitute the beginnings of a great city; not a monument, not a street, not a square, not an indication that any such lofty destiny awaits the town.

The narrow and small way of life of its population, formed of pilots, purveyors, and seamen, is expressed in the scanty proportions of the houses themselves. Seafaring people, accustomed to live in a ship's cabin, are quite satisfied to have one room for a house when they are on land, hence those tiny dwellings to be found in most seaside towns; and it seems that, with the exception of two or three streets of one-storey houses, the whole of Ter Neuzen is inhabited by sea-going folk.

This dearth of old dwelling-houses and monuments is surprising in a country in which not only the cities, but the villages and hamlets are adorned with archaic buildings. We must not, however, conclude from thence that Ter Neuzen is a modern town. On the contrary, it boasts respectable antiquity. No doubt, like its neighbours, Ter Neuzen commenced its career under the form of a fishing hamlet. Its name is derived, it appears, from its shape—that of a nose. '*Nasi figura namen habet*,' says Blaeu, the geographer, and he is to be believed, for he is a grave personage; yet I must acknowledge that I have examined the map of the town thoroughly and repeatedly, but have never yet succeeded in making out the shape of a nose upon it. It may be suggested that the outline of the town has undergone considerable modification since its name was assigned to it. That is quite possible, but I have referred to the ancient maps, even to that of Blaeu himself, and have been equally unsuccessful. Only one other hypothesis remains; it is that the shape of the Flemish nose itself has undergone a change!

The development of Ter Neuzen seems to have been slow. The town merely vegetated while it was in the possession of the Spaniards, who, although the 'Beggars' occupied its port after 1572, do not appear to have appreciated the importance of its position at any time. When they again became masters of this promontory, which was indispensable to the protection and defence of the Scheldt, they surrounded it with insignificant works, which were easily carried by the troops of the States. The latter were wiser than their dispossessed opponents; they hastened to plant themselves, this time, after a substantial and definitive fashion upon that projecting patch of Flemish soil.

At the same time that they fortified the town, the States granted certain important privileges to Ter Neuzen. Until then it had remained under the jurisdiction of Axel; thenceforward it was free from that jurisdiction. A periodical fair was instituted, and to this the peasants of all the surrounding districts were bound, under penalty of a fine of three Paris livres for each breach of the statute, to carry their butter, milk, eggs, cheese, flax, linseed, etc., etc. Vessels cruising in the Scheldt were thus brought to the port to lay in stores, and the influx soon assumed a certain importance, although, as I have said before, it never exceeded moderate limits.

At a later period the fortifications were enlarged, and combined with the system of the dykes, so that in case of need the surrounding country might be flooded. In Blaeu's time the position of Ter Neuzen was regarded as almost impregnable. 'It is very strong,' he tells us, 'because, although it is situated well inland, the sea, coming into the Scheldt twice a day, covers the fields which surround it, and renders access to it very difficult.'

At the present time Ter Neuzen is protected on two sides by the great river. On the others, bastions, lunettes, and outworks extend their scientific lines to defend it against attacks by land. It boasts, in addition, a small arsenal, or at least magazines of arms and ammunition, a little park of artillery, and casemated bomb-and-shell-proof barracks. I do not think its ambition ever extends to wishing for a conflagration, in order to demonstrate the strength of its defensive works and the heroism of its inhabitants. The views of Ter Neuzen are of a more pacific kind; and it reckons for its development upon the fraternal concord that now exists between two neighbouring nations, upon those closely-knit bonds of mutual sympathy and common interest which unite two friendly peoples.

Axel, the suzerain town of Ter Neuzen until the later years of the sixteenth century, lies inland a few miles below that promontory. It is very ancient, and, like all the small Flemish cities, has had a troubled existence. It now reposes, after its past and gone adventures, in such placid tranquillity that for the greater part of its extent it looks like a large and thriving village. If a public square and two or three streets were suppressed, you would never believe yourself to be standing in the midst of a town with a history of 800 years, a town which was important in the thirteenth century, when it was under the military occupation of Jan of Avesnes.

In the turbulent episodes through which the country of the Flemings passed, in the shocks and the disasters which befel it, we may say, periodically, Axel had its full share in its day. At first only a small village, grouped around an abbey, it speedily becomes, as we learn from Vredius, an agricultural town of some importance. After a time looms were set going at Axel, and from that day forth it shared in the movement that pervaded all Flanders. By turns the ally or the enemy of Ghent, Axel had to suffer doubly from its vicinity to the great capital. In 1350 the town was, in fact, burned by the people of Ghent because it had not associated itself with their insurrection. A century later, having taken part with its proud neighbour, it was soundly chastised by Philip the Good, who surrounded it with walls and ditches, to protect it from the return of the people of Ghent, and placed a small garrison in the town to ensure its future fidelity.

Thanks to these precautions, Axel enjoyed during one entire century absolute tranquillity, which did much for its wealth and development; yet it never rose in the hierarchy of cities above the status of 'a good little town,' assigned to it by Meteren.

In 1579 the assassination of the burgomaster of Axel, which was perpetrated by the order of Imbise of Ghent, roused the dormant spirit of the town. From that moment Axel became entirely devoted to the Prince of Orange; and although it underwent a temporary military reoccupation by the Spaniards in 1583, it remained so firmly attached to the States that it lent all the assistance in its power to the return of their army. That return took place in 1586. 'In that year,' writes an annalist, 'Prince Maurice, and Sidney, being in Flanders, came secretly in the night, on July 16, from Ter Neuzen to Axel, a little town very well situated, which they took by scaling a wall that separated the water from the ditches. This was done without much bloodshed.' From that day forth the fate of Axel was decided; the town remained in the hands of the United Provinces. In vain did the Spaniards make a fresh attempt to recover possession of it in 1593; they signally failed, but, being unable to obtain the mastery over it, they did all in their power to compass its destruction. They raised fortified posts all round it, and garrisoned them with soldiers, who, under pretext of skirmishing, pillaged the country and despoiled the inhabitants. In vain did Prince Maurice send the Count of Solms, with a dashing troop of cavalry, to put an end to this perpetual pillage; when the troops of the States, after a rapid campaign, had to rejoin the main body of the army, the depredations of the enemy recommenced, and it may be said that from that time dates, if not the fall of Axel, at least the decline of its prosperity.

The town, as I have said, has nothing very curious to show. There are no ancient monuments, few streets, and hardly any public squares ; the only one which really merits that name is the space in which the Stadhuis stands. This Stadhuis is an ordinary house, with a diminutive clock-tower imitating a belfry, and a little granite portico, adorned with two lions, of piteous and despondent mien. Add to these two petroleum lamps, a pump in the place of the traditional fountain, an old shed, which in the high and palmy days was the Exchange, and now affords shelter to the town fire-engines, a little inn with its screen of meagre trees, and a few houses of unpretending aspect, painted a pearl-grey colour, and you will have a sufficiently exact idea of the great square of Axel.

At the moment when we were inspecting this village Forum, the square was absolutely solitary, not a soul was visible in it, except ourselves. Presently twelve o'clock struck from the little tower, and a young gentleman, bareheaded, and severe of countenance, appeared at the head of the steps, a long slip of folded paper in his hand. After having ceremoniously saluted the empty square, he proceeded to read the contents of the paper, in a low and hurried voice ; then he bowed once more, turned on his heel, and re-entered the Stadhuis. We were much surprised by this sudden apparition, and the unexpected reading, which was evidently addressed to us, for there was nobody else on the spot ; but after a little reflection, we arrived at the conclusion, that the young gentleman, with the bare head, had just accomplished one of those legal formalities, which, though reasonable enough in their origin, become complete fictions by lapse of time.

The day of the week was Sunday, and at noon of that day, in virtue of certain ancient enactments, publication of marriages and municipal acts has to be made from the threshold of the Stadhuis, in order to invest them with the necessary notoriety. We had been unexpected spectators of this formality, which has fallen into disuse in most of the communes, but which, whether it blows, rains, or thunders, takes place at Axel, after the same fashion, every Sunday at noon. *Dura lex, sed lex.* So wills the law.

Three other peculiarities, which we noticed at Axel, surprised us not a little. The first was the cumulation of certain functions. The tailors are also barbers, *Kleermaker en Barbier* is inscribed on many a signboard, or neatly written on cards, and displayed in windows.

Then the names of clubs or *Societeiten,* as they are called here, are of extraordinary length. The 'Societet,' which we visited, and where we partook of an excellent breakfast, is called, ' *Vriendschap, eendracht, burgers, is een onvreeck' bren band zystemnt—en huis—en have—en stad—en vaderland!* ' all this, being interpreted, means, 'Friendship, union! Citizens, behold here an inviolable bond upon which rest home, goods, the city, and our country.'

I imagine that this title, which was bestowed in 1796 on the newborn society, and which contains excellent precepts, undergoes curtailment in its practical application.

Our third subject of wonder, or rather, of observation, is the costume of the people. The districts around Axel reveal unmistakeably, by their appearance, that they do not belong to Zealand. The rustic architecture also informs us that we have left that country. The thatched roofs, the walls built of tufa, the smears of grey and bluish-white with which the bricks are covered, announce the neighbourhood of Flanders. And, nevertheless, two of the Zealand characteristics still remain : the costumes and the prevalent neatness, that distinctive mark of the Batavian race. This neatness, is, it is true, manifested in a less absolute fashion; by which I mean, that there is a little more irregularity in the lines, a little less primness in arrangement, and that all the houses have not, without exception, that spotless and perfect orderliness which in Zealand makes them all look as if they had just come out of the hands of the workman. Similar remarks apply to the costumes. The young girls, who are of a heavier type, wear a more clumsy style of dress: the waist comes up under the arms, the diameter of the petticoat is greater, colours are more vivid; but we still find the bare arms, the invariable handkerchief covering the neck, the pretty coquettish cap, and the abundance of jewellery so dear to the Zealand women. The men also wear small hats with a narrow brim, buttoned vests, wide trousers, waist-belts, and shoe buckles, and these facts are all the more remarkable, that at the distance of a few kilometers, at Hulst, for example, which is a quarter of an hour by rail from Axel, this costume is no longer worn.

Nevertheless, Axel and Hulst belong not only to the same nation and the same province, but even to the same section of the province, and the same part of the territory, their latitude is the same, and their distance from the Belgian frontier is identical. Never did two small towns present a more marked difference from each other: accent, language, religion, the habits and customs of daily life, costumes, dwellings, in each and all they form a surprising contrast. At Axel we are still in Zealand—at Hulst we are already in Flanders. How is this divergence to be explained?

An ethnical remark gives us the key to it, and that remark is all the more important that it exhibits the immutable fidelity of these populations to their ancient traditions.

When at the end of the Eighty Years' War a sort of calm prevailed in this corner of Flanders, that point of territory which, during more than a century, had served as a battle-field to the combatants, was almost entirely depopulated. The towns, deprived of their inhabitants, were more like entrenched camps than industrious cities, the constantly devastated fields had remained uncultivated, the cottages were falling into ruin, and the villages were deserted. Two currents of immigration then set in: from the north and the south of Zealand, and Flanders, little colonies travelled towards that deserted land, coming to repeople the ruined villages and the solitary towns. The Flemings occupied Hulst, whilst the Zealanders installed themselves at Axel, and since then have remained there. Two centuries and a half have passed since that colonisation from two different points took place, without bringing about any fusion, without producing the smallest alteration in the characteristics proper to each of the two races. Hulst is Catholic; Axel is Protestant. At Hulst the people speak with a Flemish accent; at Axel, with the accent of the United Provinces. The latter derives all its inspiration from Zealand, the costume, the habits and the 'netheid,' of the old Zealanders are preserved like pious traditions. In the former, example is taken by Flanders, and the costumes, like the language, are Belgian rather than Dutch. Is not this contrast extraordinary, is not such persistence a curious fact?

I have just said that the corner of land upon which Hulst is built was almost depopulated at the epoch of the religious wars. This is strictly true. The existence of the little town was as much disturbed by those terrible years as that of its neighbour Axel, and it may indeed be said that the number of trials which it had to endure was greater, because Hulst began to hold a certain rank in its province at an earlier period than did Axel. We find mention of the former in the eleventh century: a charter of the Countess Margaret records that, in 1070, Philip of

Alsace had accorded his protection to the citizens of Hulst, and the gracious Princess, as a reward for the fidelity of these burgesses granted them exemption from *tonlieu* (the tax paid for the right of dispensing goods on the market-place), throughout all the provinces of Flanders. This valuable privilege was due to its brave inhabitants, for as old Blaeu remarks, 'If Hulst was the victim of perilous calamities, it is to the virtue of its citizens, and not to their vices, that it owes the fact.'

Among the virtues attributed to Hulst by the learned geographer, we must cite its fidelity to its legitimate princes. From 1350, when the town was emancipated by Louis de Nevers, and placed in possession of communal liberties, it remained attached to its counts, and that attachment led to its being ten times taken, pillaged, and burnt by its insurrectionary neighbours. The important privilege of which I have just spoken, and which was so graciously conferred upon the town by the Countess Margaret, was indeed only a compensatory advantage for the act of incendiarism perpetrated in 1452 by the people of Ghent, which had entirely destroyed the city, leaving only its church standing.

All these terrible diasters, to which we must add the attacks, surprises, assaults, and other violence, which it had to undergo at the epoch of the Wars of Independence, fade before the great siege of 1597, which Blacu himself does not hesitate to qualify as '*acerrimam obsidionem.*'

The Archduke Albert, who was then at the commencement of his career, held that his military honour was concerned in the reduction of the little fortress; at least his contemporaries give us clearly to understand this. 'The officers constituting the council of war,' Meteren tells us, 'did not consider that the place merited to have so much expended upon it and so much blood spilt, for it was reckoned that the besiegers had lost over 3,000 men and 800 who were wounded and maimed, and it was only the Archduke who showed himself obstinate in this respect.' The Prince would not commence his career of arms by a defeat, hence his tenacity, which would otherwise seem inexplicable. This siege, was, in fact, a continuous battle. From July 10 until August 15 the conflict raged day and night, almost without intermission. A great number of 'seigneurs, captains, and chiefs remained on the field,' and among the number of victims was one illustrious above all others, the commander of the besieging army, one of our compatriots, an old soldier of the League, and formerly lieutenant to the Duke de Mayenne. 'Marshal de Rhosne, received at the beginning of August a blow on the head, and with him there were killed more than 100 captains and men of mark, so that the soldiers would not march unless they saw their captains and chiefs going on before them.'

The little force who had so valiantly borne the rude attack were finally obliged to capitulate, for no succour could reach them. The conditions were honourable; 'the agreement was that which follows,' says an historian of the time. 'His Highness, being desirous of favouring all those who have done their duty well in action of war, permits the Governor of Hulst (Count of Solms) and his officers to retire whither they will, whether by land or by water, having their banners displayed, their drums beating, their fuses alight, and their guns loaded, with all their arms, baggage, chariots, equipages, boats, and sloops.'

Thus the citizens had the power of quitting the city, and they used it largely. More than 200 families belonging to the Reformed religion retreated into the provinces of the north, and the Austrian and Spanish insolence speedily caused a much greater number to follow that grievous example.

We have already indicated what were the consequences of this desertion, and need not return to this subject. That this short narrative may be as complete as possible, I will recapitulate a few other incidents of war, in which the fate of Hulst was at stake.

In 1640 the troops of the States had almost surprised Hulst, but the Count de Fuentes came to the assistance of its garrison, beat the Dutch, and killed their chief, Count Casimir-Henry of Nassau; and it was not until five years later, after a siege of seven weeks, that Prince Frederic-Henry succeeded in getting possession of Hulst. Since then the town has remained united to the Netherlands, to which it was definitely assigned by the treaty of Münster. The

States caused it to be strongly fortified, and conferred numerous privileges upon it.[1]

Hulst became the capital of one of the four 'offices' of Zealand-Flanders, and reckoned twelve villages under its jurisdiction. But notwithstanding these advantages, whose importance it duly appreciated, notwithstanding its fidelity to its seigneurs, the town remained rigidly constant to its religion and its customs, and it even followed throughout all their evolutions the usages of those Flemish populations to whom it owed its repeopling, and to whom it remained indissolubly united by the ties of kin.

---

[1] Never has the name of any town been so often named in the 'Register of Octrois' of the States-General. The student of those valuable records comes constantly upon the name of Hulst, and that of Hulster-Ambacht.

CHAPTER XVIII.

ROSENDAAL, THE VESTIBULE OF ZEALAND—BREDA—ITS CASTLE, WALLS, AND BASTIONS—THE HISTORY OF A PEAT-BOAT—THE MUSEUM OF ARMS—A MARVELLOUS PRINT—THE 'COMPROMISE' AND THE PEACE OF BREDA—TOMBS IN THE CHURCH.

HULST almost touches the Belgian frontier. A few turns of the wheels of the locomotive, and we are in another country. As our intention was to go to Antwerp, that we might be present at the centenary of Rubens, we did not allow ourselves to be stopped this time by that political barrier which in former journeys we had respected.[1]

We pursued our way by St. Nicholas to Malines; and, after we had accomplished our pilgrimage, re-entered the Netherlands, by way of Rosendaal.

Rosendaal, the valley of roses; it is a beautiful name, full of sweet promises, which, alas! are ill fulfilled.

One day, when I was stopped at the Dutch custom-house, I heard the poor little town called by another

[1] See our *Voyage aux Frontières menacées*.

name more prosaic and less gracious. A traveller spoke of it as the 'vestibule of Holland.' Topographically, the expression may be correct, but morally I protest against its significance, for never did vestibule reveal less of the wealth and comfort of the house.

Although it is ancient, and has from all time been united by double bonds to the Netherlands and the House of Orange-Nassau, Rosendaal would hardly be guessed to be a Dutch town; and its railway station, through which all travellers coming from France, England, and Belgium must pass, does not prepossess them in favour of the country they are about to visit. Small, dirty, and inconvenient, devoid of anything to recruit the traveller after the fatigue of his journey, this station, although the most frequented, is assuredly one of the most inconvenient in the whole country. Some day or other it will be found absolutely necessary to remedy this state of things. My complaint is not novel. I am aware that many other travellers have protested before me, but when equity and good sense are on one's side one should never leave off protesting.

Rosendaal as a station does not deserve that any one should stop there, and as a town it is of no great interest. That it is old its houses tell us, and, still more plainly than its houses, history, and the travellers of old times, affirm the fact. Three centuries ago Guicciardini wrote: 'Rosendaal is a very fine village, upon the water, with great navigation.'

Only the first of these qualifications remains to it. The village is always 'fine,' that is to say, well peopled, but its fragile beauty has been effaced by the action of years, and perhaps of man. In the days when our Florentine visited it Rosendaal was what was called a 'good franchise ;' it formed part of the domain of the Prince of Orange, and was a dependency of the Barony of Breda.

As there is nothing to see in the solitary streets of Rosendaal as it now exists, we directed our steps towards Breda, a very curious town, and one of the most important in the country.

The land through which the road from Rosendaal to Breda lies is varied, rich, and well-cultivated ; but it has not the extraordinary fertility, the 'fatness' of the soil of Walcheren and Zuidebeveland. Here and there patches of moorland and bracken mingle their sombre tints with the golden hues of the harvest, and alternate with the wonderful greensward of the vast fields. This land, such as we saw it, with its varieties of soil, which give it a certain picturesque effect, is famous of old. It was held, with its woods and its fields, to be one of the fairest seigneuries in all the Low Countries. It belonged to the 'Kampen,' but to that part of it which was most fertile and suitable for agricultural purposes. The old writers are very emphatic on the subject. 'Prince Maurice,' says Blaeu, 'calls it his Tempé,' and the celebrated geographer enumerates with delight 'its fields, which are throughout all its extent of an admirable fertility, its meadows, which are eternally green, the fair avenues of old trees, which, disposed in right lines or in quincunces, bordered the roads, and led to all the surrounding residences, as well as the forests of oak and of pines, which rear their heads in its neighbourhood.'

A century earlier, Meteren, who was generally little given to description or accessible to the delights of landscape, spoke of Breda in similar detail. 'It is situated in the Kampen,' said he, 'in a flat country, where there are good arable lands, with fair meadows and woody places.' Add to these meadows and to these woods two rivers, which, after having bathed the country and watered the fields and the plantations, come into conjunction under the very walls of the city and give it its name. Breda is derived from *Breed*, which means ' broad,' and from *Aar*, the name of one of these watercourses, which is enlarged at this place by its confluence with the Mark.

The origin of Breda is by no means so clear as the etymology of its name. The old annalists explain it by the intervention of certain ' Danes ' (?), who were the first settlers in these green regions, and who established a *castellum* at the confluence of the two rivers. This castle is mentioned between the years 840 and 850. In 888 the little company, who had come thither to seek shelter and protection beneath the walls of the ' castel ' of Breda, was so considerable that Witger IV., one of the seigneurs of the country, granted to the settlement the title of a town.

In the ensuing ages a continuous strife raged between the possessors of the 'castel' and the Dukes of Brabant. The latter besieged it over and over again; but it was not destroyed until the twelfth century, in 1124, if we may believe a Latin distich, recorded by Meteren, and repeated by his contemporaries:

> 'Anno Milleno Centeno bis Duodeno
> Castrum de Breda, cum turri corruit alta.'

It is, however, not until 1252 that the title of 'Seigneur of Breda' appears in the old charters, and it is then borne by a certain Henry, son of Godefroy of Berg, and it is not until after the cession consented to by Duke John of Brabant in favour of the Seigneur of Polanen, that the records emerge from obscurity. 'In the year 1326, the Monday after St. Valentine's Day, Geraerd of Raffingem, Liedkerke, and Lens, having sold to John of Brabant the seigneurie and the goods of all the country of Breda, with all its appurtenances, the said Duke John sold, with the consent of his son Godevaert and his eldest daughter, Joan, Countess of Holland and Zealand, the said seigneurie of the country of Breda, on April 1, with all its appurtenances, to John of Polanen, the young Seigneur of Leck, by reason of 436 *mailles*,[1] to enjoy the same as his rightful heritage.'

Thus say the old chronicles, and from that day it is easy for us to trace, without the possibility of error, the history of this important fief. We know in fact that John of Polanen died in 1377, leaving one

---

[1] An old French coin.

son, John, who took the title of Seigneur of Leck and Breda, and that this son left a daughter named Joan, who, in 1404, married Engelbrecht of Nassau, and brought him the barony as her dowry.

The history of the glorious house of Nassau is too well known for us to investigate it further. The family heritage of Polanen was one of the chief jewels in the coronet of the Counts, for in addition to Breda and its territory, the barony comprised within its jurisdiction the town of Steenbergen, and seventeen rich and populous villages. It must be said for the new barons that they thoroughly appreciated the importance to them of the possession of such a seigneurie. Also that from the first day to the last hour they laboured unremittingly to make Breda a fortress of the first class. From 1410 onwards, we find Engelbrecht of Nassau, first renewing the original fortifications, then substituting lofty ramparts for them, surrounding the city with a deep moat, and turning the two rivers which crossed it out of their course so as to add a potent natural obstacle to the works which he had erected. In 1535 Henry of Nassau, in order to keep up with the progress of his age, completes his ancestor's work. Forty years later, William the Silent encloses these ramparts in a second bastioned circle, conforming to the exigencies of the science of artillery, and in addition, he flanks them with towers. In 1622, his son Prince Maurice increases the resisting power of this new enclosure by throwing out, upon its weak points, five demilunes, communicating with each other by covered ways. Lastly, in 1682, by order of Prince William III. Menno Coehoorn, the Vauban of Holland, once more transforms its system of defence by covering the advanced posts of the fortress with new works, and combining 'water-lines' with 'counter approaches,' so as to render the place impregnable.

The special favour with which the family of Nassau always regarded their good city of Breda is more satisfactorily proved by the especial care with which they embellished it, than by all these warlike precautions.

Its superb church, which is not only one of the largest, but also one of the most remarkable in the country, was, if not completely built, at least finished, by Engelbrecht of Nassau, who erected the choir.

The palace of the governor—we can still distinguish the arms of Nassau allied with those of Mérode over its gate—was built by Justin, the bastard son of William the Silent, and Governor of Breda, between 1606 and 1625.

The Vleeschhal, or meat market, belongs to the same period. Lastly, the Castle of Breda, which may be regarded as one of the purest, most correct, and most complete monuments produced by the Renaissance in these countries; that Castle which Guicciardini, of classic taste, did not hesitate to call 'one of the most beautiful constructions in all the Low Countries,' is the work of Count Henry of Nassau.

In the sixteenth century, an epoch of great taste,

this elegant structure enjoyed a well-deserved celebrity. 'The Count Henry, who was a brave lord,' says Meteren, 'caused a new palace to be built, with a court, all surrounded with water, with galleries founded upon pillars of freestone, and a gilded frontispiece,' and he adds, 'there were in this place many fair chambers and a long hall raised upon pillars, with a very fine stair, the whole made of freestone, and by very good masters.'

At that epoch, however, the edifice was not so near completion as that it might be judged of as a whole. It was not until 1690, when William III. ascended the throne of England, that the two wings were finished; but that Prince, who was a man of tact and taste, directed Romans, the architect, charged with this supplementary task, to carry it out in exact conformity with the plans of the Italian architect, Bologna, who had conceived the original plan, and commenced its realisation. Thanks to this precaution, the Castle of Breda has preserved its primitive character; and although it has not remained intact down to our day, still it is, at the present time, one of the best preserved specimens of architecture left by the Italian Renaissance.

Its general plan consists of a vast parallelogram, built of brick, and flanked at each angle by octagon towers. The interior of the court is arranged in the Milanese fashion, with arcades resting upon columns, with Tuscan capitals. In the tympanum of each arch is carved a medallion, representing a great personage of ancient history; and this great cloister, elegant in form and noble in style, is built of freestone, as Meteren tells us. The great hall, 'founded upon pillars,' of which the old annalist speaks, still exists, and serves as a refectory; for, after having been a dwelling for princes, after having afforded a retreat to Mary of England, the widow of William II., and sheltered Charles II. of England, in his exile, this historic pile has become a military school.

It was regarded by the French army, in 1795, as the property of the Orange family, and, having been confiscated by the Republic, was converted at first into a barrack, and afterwards into a hospital. Great damage was inflicted upon it, the splendid furniture was almost entirely destroyed, magnificent tapestries in silk and gold, representing the Counts and Countesses of Nassau, the Siegneurs and Dames of Breda, all on horseback, and of life size, were torn down, rolled up, despatched to the Hague, and sold at a very low price. This deplorable change in its destiny lasted, to the great detriment of the edifice, until 1814, at which epoch the palace once more came into the possession of the house of Nassau.

William I. made no effort to restore its pristine splendour to the Castle of Breda. He did not wish to make it a royal residence; by the pleasure of its legitimate master, this sumptuous dwelling became the Dutch Saint-Cyr, and at the present day its galleries, its porticos, and its courts are occupied by cadets of the army of the Netherlands.

If the French troops misconducted themselves at the Castle of Breda, it must be admitted that they were not the only persons who had been guilty of grave offences against that princely habitation. In 1567, the Castle suffered severely from the soldiers quartered within its walls. Confiscated by the Duke of Alva, as the private property of the Prince of Orange, a rebel against the King, it was, together with the town which it commanded, and all the seigneuries dependent upon it, added to the royal estates. 'The country and the town,' says a contemporary, 'have been cast under the government of the Spaniards, and reduced to great misery,' and we may readily believe that the Castle was not better treated.

It was re-occupied in 1577 by the troops of the States; and four years later was again surprised by Claude of Berlaimont, Seigneur of Hautepenne, who took it after a most sanguinary conflict, and abused his victory, as he always did, 'using much cruelty in his triumph, sparing neither women nor children, neither the young nor the old, nor ecclesiastics nor seculars, in the houses or in the streets, sacking and killing all.' Again we may suppose that the Castle fared no better.

It was retaken nine years afterwards, in 1590, by a very singular stratagem. The adventure is well known, and may be found in a number of narratives of the time, for it was a famous event. Our compatriot, Du Maurier, has called it the 'miraculous taking of Breda with a peat-boat,' and I will borrow his account of the event, because, although it has been many times related, I do not think I ought to pass it over in silence on this occasion.

Du Maurier says: 'A boatman, named Adrian, of Bergues, who furnished peat to the garrison of Breda, being discontented with the Spaniards, proposed to Prince Maurice to surprise the place by putting soldiers into the hold of his boat; which the Prince having found possible, he gave the conduct of this great design to Charles of Herauguière, a Walloon gentleman, native of Cambray, captain of infantry in his troops, held to be a man of strong head and strong hand, who, when he had this order, made choice of seventy soldiers of different companies, and of certain ages, of approved valour. These soldiers he put in the hold of the boat, where they were very ill at their ease, not being able to be otherwise than lying down or bending, the rest of the boat being laden to a great height with peat. It was then extremely cold, and, besides, they had water up to their knees, which came in by a slit, but this was happily plugged. This excessive cold made them all cough much, but especially Matthew Helt, lieutenant (whose name merits to be placed here for the courage which he displayed on this occasion), for not being able to prevent himself from coughing as they were approaching the Castle, he drew his poniard and adjured his comrades to kill him, so that the enterprise might not fail, and that he might not be the cause of their destruction. But the boatmen prevented his cough being heard by working the pump frequently, as if the boat were taking in water.

'The garrison, composed of Italians, lacking fuel, the soldiers, on account of the ice, helped to draw the boat through a sluice-gate into the enclosure of the Castle, even as the Trojans introduced the wooden horse into their city, which gave occasion to a poet of the time to compare the taking of Breda with that of Troy.[1]

During this time Prince Maurice, who had spread a report that he was about to descend on Gertrudenberg, had really directed his course towards Breda, with a numerous body of troops. Herauguière, who knew him to be in the neighbourhood, came out of his hiding-place in the middle of the night, killed forty men of the guard, and opened the gates to the Prince, who penetrated into the Castle with the Counts of Hohenlohe and Solms, Francis Vere, the general of the English troops, Famas, who commanded the artillery, and Admiral Julian of Nassau.[2]

Herauguière, the fortunate chief of this adventurous enterprise, was recompensed for his boldness and bravery by the government of the town which he had so ably restored to its legitimate lord.[3] All

---

[1] Du Maurier, *Mémoires pour servir à l'Histoire de Hollande*.

[2] In memory of this great deed a medal was struck; on one side was engraved these words: *Breda a servitute Hispana vindicata ductu principis Mauricii a Nassau* 4, *Martij* 1590, and on the other was represented the boat, with the device: *Parate vincere aut mori*.

[3] The Prince and the States continued to testify their gratitude to the

his soldiers were largely rewarded, and the boatman, Adrian of Bergues, received a liberal pension. Lastly, even the peat-boat participated in the triumph; from that day it was preserved in the armoury of the Castle as a glorious memento of this daring deed.

This armoury was formerly extremely rich in valuable trophies. There were to be seen the culverins, cannons, and bombards which the Kings of Hungary presented to the family of Nassau, in remembrance of its heroic services 'against the Turk.' Besides these, there were fifty-two pieces, of all calibres, given by the Emperor Ferdinand to the Seigneurs of Breda. But when the Duke of Alva, came to the city as Governor of the country, he regarded this arsenal of honour as a fair prize, and had the guns melted down. Fifty years later, Spinola, when master of the city and its castle, took a similar view of Herauguière's boat. He had it burned.

Let us say, as some defence for this act on the part of the Spanish general, that the resistance of the town and the exceptional siege he had just made it undergo, were calculated to exasperate him in no small degree. For eleven long months he had employed every resource of his science and his genius for the reduction of Breda. He had exhausted his army in daily conflicts without gaining a decisive victory,

---

widow of the brave Herauguière. We have found on the *Register of Octrois and Pensions* the grant of a pension of 1,000 livres to Marie of Groenveld, widow of Herauguière. This deed is dated October 12, 1602.

for it was famine, and not the sword, that vanquished the inhabitants, and delivered over the town to him.

Never, it may safely be affirmed, were Breda and the surrounding districts more full of animation than during that epic siege. Blaeu has recorded the plan of it in one of those marvellous maps which have won so high a reputation for him. But we have other testimony, much more complete and vivid than his, to this great feat of war. I allude to the fine engraving by Jacques Callot, published, in Paris, by Israel Sylvestre, and composed of six plates which, when joined together, form a continuous picture. We could not desire a page of history more full and complete than is that extraordinary work of art, one of the finest, most delicate, most exact, truest, and most amusing in its details that has ever been given to the world.[1]

There are thousands of figures in this drawing which shows us the entire city, with its public buildings, its houses, streets, squares, and canals. The details of the fortifications of the town are all given, the works of both the besiegers and the besieged, the surrounding country, with all its features, its villages, woods, marshes, fields, farms, flocks, and herds, stretching away for an immense distance. The camp of the Spaniards is represented, with its external wall, its gabions, siege batteries, tents, waggons, huts,

---

[1] This marvellous work has recently been reprinted. The War Office at the Hague possesses a very fine impression of it.

artillery, stores, soldiers, and all that crowd of parasites who in those days followed armies in the field —quacks, bone setters, fortune-tellers, Jews pursuing every kind of trade, abandoned women, and debauched vagabonds. Among this innumerable multitude of microscopic personages we see marauders carrying off cattle, soldiers, intent on pillage, putting the peasants to ransom, drunken cavaliers in pursuit of a plump and recalcitrant country girl. And all this time, in other parts of the scene, guns are thundering, muskets are going off, drums are beating, trumpets are sounding, colours are flying, and horsemen and foot soldiers, full of warlike ardour, are rushing upon each other with truly wonderful fury and life-likeness.

Although this admirable drawing, a masterpiece of humour and observation, is certainly the finest and most important picture ever inspired by the history of Breda, it is by no means the only one. In the first place, the adventure of the peat-boat was commemorated by an engraving by J. Luken; and afterwards, a series of plates by R. von Hooghe celebrated the Peace of Breda. For that city is not renowned for its warlike exploits only; it is also famous for its pacific conventions, and the treaties which were signed there are numerous. After the 'compromise' of 1556, which was the first act of resistance directed against the Spaniards, the Plenipotentiaries of the Western nations assembled at Breda no less than three times. In 1575, 1667, and 1746, the town was chosen as the scene of the deliberations of ambassadors delegated by the most powerful Sovereigns of Europe.

It was the treaty of 1667, the famous 'Peace of Breda,' that Romain von Hooghe represented in his engravings. He makes us spectators of the public rejoicings which accompanied and followed that great act of international policy; of the salutes of artillery, the procession of state coaches, and the display of fireworks. He shows us the improvised fountains,— among others, a perambulating elephant discharging wine from its proboscis—devices of questionable taste, it is true, but then, everybody was so glad that peace was concluded!

With von Hooghe for our guide, we might visit every quarter of the town, and recognise each; also, all its principal buildings, and the streets, which have not undergone much change since that old time. But to do so would be to make an unnecessary delay. The capital of the ancient barony is a handsome, airy, cosy, well-built town, but the artist and the archæologist find little in it to reward their researches. The visitor may rest awhile with pleasure under the shade of the fine trees in its superb public garden, stroll about its clean bright streets, and observe the features of its market-place. But it has no buildings, except the Church, to attract his attention, for the Stadhuis, built in 1534, was completely rebuilt at the end of the last century, and there is nothing remarkable in the interior of it, with the exception of some portraits by Mijtens, Baan, and Honthorst. It is true that the archives of Breda are among the most precious and interesting in the kingdom, but they have fallen into such a state of neglect and dilapidation that we avoided them. We should really have been sorry to see the garret in which they are left to rot uncared for.

Let us return to the Church. Its proportions are fine; its style, although belonging to the tertiary ogival period, is not too florid. The steeple is celebrated for its height, and still better deserves to be celebrated for its exquisite form and finished elegance. The proportions of the interior are equally fine; and this church would be one of the most complete and remarkable buildings of its kind, had it never been meddled with by the Protestants and the French. The Protestants seized upon the sanctuary, despoiled it of its ornaments, destroyed its altars, and disfigured it with the benches, pulpits, and galleries which are necessary accessories of their form of worship; and our compatriots (we ought to blush for them), devastated its tombs.

These tombs, it is true, were those of the family of Orange; and it must be borne in mind that at the revolutionary period, not only the troops of Dumouriez, but also the Batavian patriots were actuated by a sort of fury against that princely house. I recall these facts to explain, not to excuse, such deeds. The iconoclasts, who laid destructive hands upon these funereal monuments, were all the more culpable in that they mutilated works of art of inestimable value.

The most celebrated of these tombs is that of Engelbrecht II. of Nassau. So proud and grand is its aspect, that tradition has not hesitated to attribute its statues to Michael Angelo. The great Florentine had, however, no hand in this work; which, though indisputably very fine, is of a later period than that of Michael Angelo, and seems to be German, and not Italian at all. The design of this noble place of burial is so exceptional, that I must linger a moment to describe it. On a slab, very slightly raised above the ground, repose the Count and his wife, Maria of Limburg, Princess of Baden, side by side, upon a matting of marble, each figure wrapped in a winding-sheet, the eyelids closed, the faces calm and thoughtful. At the four corners, four heroes of antiquity, Cæsar, Regulus, Hannibal, and Philip (personifying the four characteristic qualities of the deceased warrior), each resting one knee upon the ground, and clad in admirably wrought armour, raise upon their shoulders a large slab of marble, on which are placed the cuirass and arms of the Prince.

I wish I could depict for you the proud bearing of the four heroes, show you in detail the ornamentation of their cuirasses, which is extraordinarily fine and delicate, and point out to you the hands and feet of the two recumbent figures, exquisitely modelled and marvellously supple. But it would take a volume to describe the tombs of Breda adequately, and it is better to say no more than to arouse an interest which I should be unable to gratify.

There are at least ten tombs of great beauty and artistic merit, besides that matchless monument. Among them I ought, in justice, to mention that of Engelbrecht I., that of Jan of Nassau, and that of the Seigneur of Polanen, and after those, the tombs of the Seigneurs of Borgnival, and Renesse, of Nicolas Vierling, Joannes Hultinins, etc., which are all marvellous specimens of the architecture of the best days of the Renaissance.

The names of the artists who executed these masterpieces of mortuary sculpture have not been handed down to us. Perhaps, indeed most probably, the archives of the town contain information respecting them; but in their present state it would be impossible to examine those documents.

CHAPTER XIX.

TILBURG—THE MONUMENT TO WILLIAM II.—A CAPITAL—HERTOGENBOSCH'S—THE DUCAL FOREST—THE BUDDING OF A TOWN—TWO MEMORABLE SIEGES—INDUSTRY AND COURAGE—AN ARCHITECTURAL PEARL—THE STADHUIS AND ITS TREASURE—'ADIEU, BASKETS! THE GRAPES ARE ALL GATHERED.'

N leaving Breda our route lay clear before us. We had still to visit Bois-le-Duc, after which our excursion would be near its close. The railway carried us towards the former capital of the Duchy of Brabant, but on the way thither we wished to have a look at Tilburg. This town, which is quite modern, little known, and in no wise celebrated, would not occupy any place at all among the notable localities of the Low Countries, but for the melancholy recollection which attaches to its name; I allude to the death of William II.

It does not take more than an hour to see Tilburg throughout all its length and breadth. To say this is to imply that it is a small place; and, indeed, Tilburg looks less like a town than a big village with wide streets, low houses, gardens jammed in between the houses, and honest folk standing in the doorways looking curiously at the rare passers-by who disturb the tranquil scene. It possesses no historical, interesting, or curious buildings. Only the tower of its church is ancient, and even that has quite a modern spire. The interior has been recently restored, the walls have been scraped and pointed, the windows enlarged and rounded, the columns adorned with portentous capitals, the confessionals and pulpits are far from elegant. The town boasts another sacred edifice, which is only just built; it is, indeed, quite fresh from the hands of the masons, and is in much better taste, but the examination of contemporary architecture is not within the scope of this work; I shall, therefore, say no more of the indisputable merits of the new church.

The Stadhuis, which stands close to the most ancient of these sanctuaries, is commonplace, modern, and unmeaning. In all the town there are but two points of interest: the monument erected to William II., and the Castle in which that prince resided.

The monument is simple, but elegant. It consists of a pyramid of blue granite, placed upon a well-proportioned pedestal, and bearing upon its surface, about half-way up, a medallion portrait of the deceased King. The Castle, which is in the background, is also very simple; but it is very far from being in equally good taste, and we cannot help wondering how a monarch, whose civil list included several sumptuous residences, and especially Loo, and the House in the Wood, could have been so fond of this queer fortress.

The royal residence of Tilburg belongs to that pseudo-style, in every sense deplorable, and full of architectural contradictions, which is called Gothic-English. Certain buildings at the Hague, the stables of the Prince of Orange, for instance, are terrible examples of the absurdities into which builders, bitten with these extravagant ideas, may be led. I need not expatiate upon them.

King William III., on giving up the royal Castle in which he had no inclination to reside, wished to have it converted into a school. This was a very good idea.

If Tilburg be like a village, Bois-le-Duc is like a large town. I have just said that it was formerly one of the four capital cities of the Duchy of Brabant, and never, to my knowledge, had a town of twenty-five thousand inhabitants more of the air and aspect of a capital. Its streets are long and wide, its houses are large and handsome, its public squares are spacious, airy, well-paved, and very clean. Its old buildings, appearing here and there, testify to an existence of several centuries, and indeed we know that the importance of Bois-le-Duc is a fact of ancient date, though the place is not of exceptional antiquity.

In the twelfth century, the territory which it

occupies, and the country that surrounds it, were completely covered with forests. As the Dukes of Brabant came thither regularly to hunt, the great wood became known as *Silva Ducis*—'the forest of the Duke.' But the people of Guelders came there also, and turned its dark recesses into dens of robbers and cut-purses, making excursions from thence into the surrounding country, and returning to the recesses of the forest with entire impunity. It was to put an end to the depredations of these dangerous marauders that, in 1184, Duke Godfrey had a portion of the ducal forest cleared, and that, in 1196, his son, Duke Henry, had a castle built, in order to keep a watch on and to overawe his troublesome neighbours. Dwellings accumulated around the castle, and the budding city took the name of the forest in which its first foundations were laid. Such was the origin of that 'city which held the fourth place among the four capital towns of Brabant,' and which is called in Dutch Hertogenbosch's, in Latin, *Silva Ducis*, and in French Bois-le-Duc—appellations differing in form, but all bearing the same signification.

Never did a town increase and acquire importance of the first order more rapidly. The prince had laid the foundations of this quick-growing greatness; he had given the impulse; the inhabitants did the rest. In less than a century the castle was surrounded by a town which seemed to have sprung from the earth; and soon transformed itself into an opulent city. The part which it played in the politics of the country became defined; by its rapid advance it won the title and the prerogatives of a capital, and in 1453, it had almost attained its utmost development.

Bearing in mind what were the difficulties of all kinds that beset the existence and the growth of cities at that epoch, to what hardships and harassing they were subjected by the suspicion of their suzerains, and the jealousy of their rivals, we may well be astonished that such fortune and importance were so rapidly achieved. It should also be borne in mind that by a special privilege of nature that portion of Brabant had been from all time peopled by an energetic, obstinate, and above all extremely industrious race, on whom all the old writers of different periods have lavished praise and admiration. Let us hear what Guicciardini has to say of them: 'The people of this city are warlike and valiant,' he tells us, 'retaining more of the former fierceness and stubborn nature of the Belgæ than any other of the neighbouring people; and yet they are greatly civilised, the town being mercantile, and well supplied with good masters and artisans in all kinds of trades. Among other things, they make much cloth there, and a great quantity of linen, which reaches every year to the number of twenty thousand pieces, which may be worth about two hundred thousand crowns. An incalculable number of knives, of a very good temper, are also made there, and an incredible quantity of fine pins of all kinds, and of the one and the other many are sent out to all parts of the world.'

Is it not curious to find this double fabric of cloth and linen in the country so early as the sixteenth century, spreading prosperity around, creating wealth, and still to see Bois-le-Duc, and the neighbouring towns, Endhoven and Tilburg, owing their chief resources, and their well-being, in this our own day, to their looms?

The union of those two great qualities, industry and valour, is sufficiently rare to entitle a city which possesses it, and turns it to advantage, to high honour and credit. The people of Guelders were taught how great is the strength which those virtues confer. In 1582, having come into the vicinity of Bois-le-Duc (into what was called its 'Mayoralty,' or the territory under its jurisdiction), for purposes of devastation and pillage, they were met by the militia of the town, and severely chastised. 'They were almost all killed or taken prisoners,' writes an old Chronicle, ' and it may be said, that there returned none of them to the town.' From that time they kept themselves quiet. It was especially at the period of the Wars of Independence, that the valour and constancy of the inhabitants of Bois-le-Duc were displayed to the full. Like all the Brabant people, they were firmly attached to the Catholic faith, and refused to come into the Union of Utrecht; and they even took advantage of some disturbances which arose, to expel the Protestants who had risen against their 'Magistrat.' On the other hand, however, they refused to grant access to their city to the troops of the Duke of Parma, asserting their intention of taking care of themselves. 'Never, an historian tells us, 'did they consent to receive any garrison from the King. Raising recruits upon their own territory, they had them drilled under the command of officers belonging to the town, and with them manned their ramparts, and even made expeditions in the open. They always refused any assistance that was offered to them; suffered only a few officers to enter the fortress; and although several overtures were made to them, on both one side and the other, they never departed from their resolution.

They had ample reason, in fact, to rely upon their own strength, and in doing so, they did not presume too far upon their valour. Events justified them fully. The little army of citizens won glorious renown in 1601; when the city, besieged by Prince Maurice, and also reduced to its own forces, not only resisted that victorious general, the greatest warrior of his time, but also obliged him, by prodigies of zeal and bravery, to raise the siege, after twenty-seven days of incessant attack.

Meteren relates this brilliant feat of arms in detail. The old annalist devotes several pages, which are well worth reading, to the obstinate defence of their city by its brave citizens, and the heroism displayed by the women and even the children. From his narrative we learn what the population of Bois-le-Duc is capable of in difficult circumstances. It is also interesting to learn how deeply the young Stadtholder felt the humiliation of being obliged to withdraw from his proudly assumed position, and relinquish an enterprise which he had hoped to bring easily to a successful termination.

The fortune of war is a fickle fortune. In 1629, Frederick-Henry took Hertogenbosch's, after a siege which will remain for ever celebrated among sieges, and at which the King and Queen of Bohemia and the Dukes of Wittemberg and Holstein were present. The capitulation was signed on the 14th of December; and, two days afterwards, Count Grobbendonk, governor of the city, vacated it with the whole of his garrison, the Catholic authorities, the Bishop and clergy, the occupants of the convents, and a number of citizens who were too seriously compromised, or who refused to submit to the new rulers.

Bois-le-Duc was thenceforth placed under the authority of the States; its territory was annexed to the United Provinces, and its churches were handed over to the Calvinists.

But, although the population had been subdued, it remained unsubmissive, and above all, unconverted. The city was immutably faithful to its faith and its traditions. Bois-le-Duc and its 'Mayoralty' were still fervently Catholic; and a visitor who travelled through the Low Countries in the last century,[1] when referring to the Proclamations of 1725 and 1730, against the Roman Catholic clergy and the religious order, writes, that 'Notwithstanding the persecution, the number of Catholics is still so considerable, that

---

[1] See *Les Délices des Pays Bas.*

in many villages, except the minister, his clerk, and the officials of the State, there is not one to be found of the Reformed Religion.'

As it was then, so it is now; through all its vicissitudes Bois-le-Duc has preserved its faith intact. When Calvinistic exclusiveness was replaced in those centuries by religious liberty, the population was found to be as much 'Roman' as in 1629, indeed perhaps more completely so. The modern Catholics set themselves to the observance of their newly enfranchised faith with a zealous and self-asserting fervour, not uncommon to the enjoyment of a benefit of which one has long been deprived. Then, as always happens, politics entered speedily into the matter. Calvinism was regarded as a former oppressor, endeavouring to resume its lost ground and its vanished domination. And the clergy, without reflecting that the emancipation of Catholicism was the work of the Revolution, regarded Calvinism and Liberation as a common adversary, against which they must direct all their energies, and incite all their disciples.

I have sufficiently discussed the subject of Clericalism in the Belgian territory of Flanders, and the Dutch territory of Brabant, in my books, entitled respectively, 'Voyage aux Frontières menacées,' and 'Het Land van der Gengen,' and I shall now leave that subject.

The great church of Bois-le-Duc is certainly the finest Gothic building in all the Netherlands. It belongs to the ogival period, bordering on the flamboyant. Its decoration is of extraordinary richness, but yet it does not fall into the exaggeration which injures the purity of line and spoils the beauty of so many buildings in our country, by what I may call lapidary vegetation! In the Northern countries examples of the really flamboyant style are rare; architecture was so much behindhand there, that the Renaissance had manifested itself before Gothic efflorescence had reached its apogee. This explains how it happened that the Church of St. John, although belonging to the fifteenth century, was saved from the over-profusion of ornament with which it was threatened.

The vaulted roof of the nave rises to a superb height, supported by thirty-two elegant pillars. A remarkable triforium, pierced and trilobed, rises above the arcades, and augments the grace of this magnificent 'ship.' The choir is majestic in the extreme. In addition to these artistic beauties, there is a justly celebrated baptistery in gilded bronze, and a pulpit and other wood carvings in very good style, although much more modern. Altogether, the church of Bois-le-Duc is worthy in every respect of its great reputation.

Unfortunately there is a reverse to the medal. This church, so elegant of form and so rich in ornament, is built of bad materials. So faulty is the stone used in its construction that it crumbles under the action of rain, and is blown away in dust by that of wind. At the present day the old building, after long suffering from those inevitable ills, would no longer present the form of a monument, had not pious hands repaired it, tending its wounds with admiring love of which it is well worthy. Nor has the State, on its side, been grudging of its grants for the same worthy purpose. It is to be hoped that nothing will interfere to arrest the progress of this restoration, and that it may prove successful.

Judging by the old streets of the city, Gothic buildings must have been very numerous in the ancient 'Silva Ducis.' At present they are rare, and the Church of St. John is so vastly superior to the others which still remain, that it is almost unbecoming to mention them. I prefer to conduct you immediately to the Stadhuis; built in 1620—not, indeed, that its architecture is attractive, for the building is of grey stone, and is massive and heavy—but because the interior contains certain precious objects well deserving of attention.

In the first place there are the archives, very full, complete, well-arranged, and containing, in addition to a great number of valuable maps, catalogued registers and daybooks from A.D. 1300, down. Then there is a collection of seals coming down from 1295 to the present time, and comprising four hundred and ninety-seven specimens, which pass from the Roman to the Gothic, and from that to the contemporary style. To these succeed the drinking-cups of the Guilds, the insignia of the public functionaries, and ancient arms. Among the latter is a small culverin, which belonged to Count Egmont. At a little distance from this assortment we find a number of instruments of punishment and torture—one is a sort of wooden sentry-box, all covered with carvings representing lizards, toads, and serpents, in which women of infamous character were shut up. The collection of collars, knives, pincers, vices, hatchets, and branding-irons is very complete; in fact, it extends from the rack to the guillotine. One cannot deny progress in the presence of these objects.

There is also a small collection of pictures, allegories by Van Thulden, portraits of the family of Orange, a view of the Stadhuis, by Beerstraaten; the only statue that was saved, when, in 1566, the Iconoclasts sacked the Church of St. John; and, lastly, a room hung with the famous old green tapestries of Flanders.

This public collection is not the only one at Bois-le-Duc; hard by there is another, no less well-arranged, with a large and select library, medals, prehistoric vases, Roman lamps, mediæval pottery, glass and earthenware, Indian arms, banners of the Confraternities, the badges of the Guilds, and a few pictures relating to the history of Bois-le-Duc. In this collection we find a 'plaque' in old Delft ware, representing the famous combat of Bréauté and Lekkerbeek, a legendary battle, or heroic duel, in which twenty-one Frenchmen fought twenty-one Flemings. A stratagem secured the victory to the latter; they cut the bridles of their adversaries' horses, and the

Frenchmen being unable to manage their steeds, were defeated.

It was in 1600, and on the heath of Vucht, not far from Bois-le-Duc, that this famous encounter took place. I might take you to Vucht, a pretty village, about a league from the great Brabant city, with the purpose of showing you, not the celebrated field of battle, but an infinitely more pleasing picture; a bouquet of living flowers, a group of young beauties, composing the most amiable and cheery family you could ever wish to see. I might also take you to one of the neighbouring Castles, and show you an entire museum of curiosities, with which the feudal dwelling is furnished from top to bottom, filling the rooms, blocking up the corridors, encumbering the staircases, invading even the outer walls. Again, without quitting Bois-le-Duc, I might introduce you into the sanctuary of the most venerable Confraternity in all the province, the *Illustre lieve Vrouwe Brœderschap*, or 'Illustrious Confraternity of Our Lady,' let you see its old house, admirably restored in the antique style, and its registers, which are, so to speak, the 'Libro d'Oro,' of the ancient 'Silva Ducis.' But this cannot be, the clock has struck the hour for retiring. We must resume our homeward way; as our French saying has it, 'Adieu, paniers! les vendanges sont faites.' The train is alongside the platform, and waits for nobody. Let us take a last look at the city, a last glance into the distance, at the vast polders that surround it, and which, as they could be flooded at will, formerly rendered Bois-le-Duc impregnable. Let us salute Zalt Bommel, with its fine church and its Gothic steeple, as we pass; let us cross the Waal and the Rijn. Afar, a great tower comes in sight, its lofty pierced spire shows clear against the sky. This is Utrecht, and we have reached our journey's end.

APPENDIX.

Note 1.

(The Spanish Expedition to Duiveland and Schonwen in 1575), page 47.

In Mr. Motley's work, 'The Rise of the Dutch Republic, he describes the celebrated passage of the Spanish troops with great force and animation. His version differs from that of M. Havard in several particulars. The latter assigns the conduct of the daring expedition to Mondragon; but Mr. Motley says that its leader was 'Don Osorio d'Ulloa, an officer distinguished for his experience and bravery,' and describes Mondragon, the 'grand commander,' as standing on the shore at Philipsland, 'to watch the setting forth of the little army.' M. Havard, in relating the attack made upon the wading column from the Zealand ships, says: 'It was impossible for the Spaniards to defend themselves, or to retaliate.' Mr. Motley says: 'At times they halted for breath, or to engage in fierce skirmishes with their nearest assailants. Standing breast-high in the waves, and surrounded at intervals by total darkness, they were able to pour an occasional well-directed volley into the hostile ranks.' M. Havard says that on the day after the landing of the Spanish troops, they took Viassen; but Mr. Motley states that the town first seized by the successful adventurers was Brouwershaven.

Note 2.

'*Le droit de communier*,' page 75.

'WHEN, in 1285, Floris V. granted to the inhabitants the "right of community," which conferred municipal existence on their city,' &c.

This obsolete phrase is explained as follows by M. Littré: '*Communier*: Terme d'ancienne législation. Nom donné à ceux qui étaient de la communauté d'une ville, d'une commune.'

Note 3.

The Poet Cats, page 207.

M. HAVARD wishes to correct an error in his description of Brouwershaven. A statue—which is, however, but a poor work of art—has been erected to the memory of the poet Cats, in the city of his birth.

www.ingramcontent.com/pod-product-compliance
Lightning Source LLC
Chambersburg PA
CBHW022117290426
44112CB00008B/707